CONTENTS

PREFACE

Schools have a mission of great importance to our nation; they are responsible for keeping our children safe while educating them and helping prepare them to be responsible and productive citizens. The December 14, 2012, shooting at Sandy Hook Elementary School in Newtown, CT, that claimed the lives of 20 children and 6 adults, has heightened congressional interest in school security. Policymakers have begun debating whether school security can be further enhanced, and if so, how best to accomplish that goal. A wide variety of proposals have been offered at the federal level, such as funding for expanded mental health services for students, funding for training on mental health awareness for school staff, funding to assist schools in improving school climate, funding for more school counselors, and funding for more school resource officers (SROs) or other armed security personnel. Wayne LaPierre, Executive Vice President and CEO of the National Rifle Association, has proposed putting an armed police officer in every school in the country as a way to prevent mass shootings. President Obama has proposed creating incentives for Community Oriented Policing Services (COPS) grants to be used to hire more SROs in the current year. In addition, he has requested $150 million in funding for a new Comprehensive School Safety Program. This new grant program would provide school districts and law enforcement agencies with funding to hire new SROs and school psychologists, among other things. This book focuses on one of these proposals, the renewed focus on providing federal funding for more SROs as a means to preventing school shootings. It examines the distribution of and current number of SROs, the potential sustainability of any increase in the number of SROs, and the effect that SROs may have on students and the academic setting. It also examines what available research studies suggest about the extent to which SROs may reduce school violence. These are issues Congress may consider while contemplating an expansion of SRO programs.

Chapter 1 - Some policymakers have expressed renewed interest in school resource officers (SROs) as a result of the December 2012 mass shooting that occurred at Sandy Hook Elementary School in Newtown, CT. SROs are sworn law enforcement officers who are assigned to work in schools.

For FY2014, the Administration requested $150 million in funding for a Comprehensive Schools Safety Program under the Community Oriented Policing Services (COPS) program. The proposed program would provide funding for hiring school safety personnel, including SROs, civilian public safety personnel, school psychologists, social workers, and counselors. Funding would also be available for purchasing school safety equipment, developing and updating public safety plans, conducting threat assessments, and training crisis intervention teams.

Data from the Bureau of Justice Statistics show that the number of full-time law enforcement officers employed by local police departments or sheriff's offices who were assigned to work as SROs increased between 1997 and 2003 before decreasing slightly in 2007 (the most recent year for which data are available). Data show that a greater proportion of high schools, schools in cities, and schools with enrollments of 1,000 or more report having SROs.

Two federal grant programs promoted SRO programs: the COPS in Schools (CIS) program, which was funded until FY2005, and State Formula Grants under the Safe and Drug Free Schools and Communities Act (SDFSCA), which was funded until FY2009. The CIS program provided grants for hiring new, additional school resource officers to conduct community policing services in and around primary and secondary schools. Local educational agencies could use funds they received under the SDFSCA State Formula Grant program for, among other things, hiring and training school security personnel.

The body of research on the effectiveness of SRO programs is limited, both in terms of the number of studies published and the methodological rigor of the studies conducted. The research that is available draws conflicting conclusions about whether SRO programs are effective at reducing school violence. Also, the research does not address whether SRO programs deter school shootings, one of the key reasons for renewed congressional interest in these programs.

There are several questions Congress might consider in the context of grant funding specifically for SRO programs.

- **Does the current level of school violence warrant congressional efforts to expand the number of SROs in schools across the country?** Data suggest that schools are, generally speaking, safe places for children. During the 2010-2011 school year there were 11 reported homicides of children at school. The number of youth homicides that occurred at school remained less than 2% of the total number of homicides of school aged children for each school year going back to the 1992-1993 school year. In 2010, fewer children reported being the victim of a serious violent crime or a simple assault while at school compared to 1994. However, data also show that some schools—namely middle schools, city schools, and schools with a higher proportion of low-income students—have higher rates of reported violent incidents, and schools with a higher proportion of low-income students had higher rates of reported serious violent incidents.

- **Is funding for a wide-scale expansion of SRO programs financially sustainable?** If Congress expanded the number of SROs through additional federal funding, it is likely that many of those officers would go to law enforcement agencies serving jurisdictions of fewer than 25,000 people (data show that nearly 88% of police departments and almost half of sheriff's offices serve jurisdictions of fewer than 25,000 people). Traditionally, COPS grants have provided "seed" money for local law enforcement agencies to hire new officers, but it is the responsibility of the recipient agency to retain the officer(s) after the grant expires. Since smaller law enforcement agencies tend to have smaller operating budgets and smaller sworn forces, retaining even one or two additional officers after a grant expired might pose a significant financial burden.

- **Would additional SROs result in more children being placed in the criminal justice system?** Research in this area is limited to a small number of studies, but these suggest that children in schools with SROs might be more likely to be arrested for low-level offenses. On the other hand, some studies indicate that SROs can deter students from committing assaults on campus as well as bringing weapons to school. Schools with SROs may also be more likely to report non-serious violent crimes (i.e., physical attack or fights without a weapon and threat of physical attack without a weapon) to the police than schools lacking SROs.

Chapter 2 - There has been a growing interest in placing sworn police officers in schools as SROs to improve school safety. However, when this project began in May 2000, little was known about SRO programs. The purpose of the National Assessment was to identify what program "models" have been implemented, how programs have been implemented, and what the programs' possible effects may be. To obtain this information, *Abt Associates conducted a nationwide survey of established and relatively new SRO programs and collected implementation data by telephone and on site from 19 SRO programs.*

Three subcontractors assisted in collecting, analyzing, and reporting the data:

- The Center for Criminal Justice Policy Research at Northeastern University,
- The Justice and Safety Center, College of Justice and Safety, at Eastern Kentucky University, and
- the Center for the Prevention of School Violence in North Carolina.

Two consultants assisted Northeastern University in collecting and analyzing the data:

- Timothy Bynum, School of Criminal Justice at Michigan State University, and
- Scott Decker, Department of Criminology and Criminal Justice at the University of Missouri-St. Louis.

This report describes the activities the project team conducted for the National Assessment and summarizes the study findings. The report has five sections, which follow the chronology of the project:

- **Mail Survey**—a summary of the methodology and findings of the first significant project task.
- **Selection of Study Sites**—a review of the site selection criteria and the sites selected.
- **The Site Visits**—a description of the preparation for, goals, and conduct of the site visits.
- **Modifications to the Research Methodology**—a description of the change from an outcome study to a process evaluation for the large new sites and the reasons for the change.

- **Data Analysis and Findings**—a summary of the methodology and findings of the five other reports prepared under the project.

In addition to this Final Project Report, the study produced five other reports:

1. The *National Survey of SRO Programs and Affiliated Schools* summarizes the results of 322 responses to a mail survey of law enforcement agencies with SRO programs and 108 responses from affiliated schools.

2. An *Interim Report: Fear and Trust* summarizes preliminary impressionistic observations concerning (a) perceptions of fear about campus safety among school administrators, faculty, and students among 15 of the 19 sites and (b) trust in the police among these groups in the 15 sites.

3. *Case Studies of 19 School Resource Officer (SRO) Programs* provides in-depth descriptions of each program's history, SROs, program activities, and program monitoring and evaluation.

4. *Results of a Survey of Students in Three Large New SRO Programs* presents the results of a survey of nearly 1,000 students designed to identify the relationship between perceptions of safety and the SRO program.

5. *Comparison of Program Activities and Lessons Learned among 19 School Resource Officer (SRO) Programs* compares the 19 programs in terms of seven key dimensions, with a focus on lessons learned: choosing a program model; defining specific SRO roles and responsibilities; recruiting SROs; training and supervising SROs; collaborating with school administrators and teachers; working with students and parents; and evaluating SRO programs.

Chapter 3 - The purpose of the National Assessment was to identify what program "models" have been implemented, how programs have been implemented, and what lessons selected programs may have for other programs. To obtain this information, *Abt Associates and its subcontractors collected implementation data by telephone and on site from 19 SRO programs.*

This cross-site report discusses commonalities and differences among the 19 sites with a particular focus on lessons learned—information based on the experience of the sites that can benefit other jurisdictions in setting up or improving an SRO program.

The report focuses on seven issues:

1. Choosing a Program Model
2. Defining Specific SRO Roles and Responsibilities
3. Recruiting SROs
4. Training and Supervising SROs
5. Collaborating with School Administrators and Teachers
6. Working with Students and Parents
7. Evaluating SRO Programs

Chapter 4 - In the United States, more than 75 million students are enrolled in elementary and secondary schools and institutions of higher education (IHEs). Safeguarding their security while they pursue an education is a paramount concern of federal, state, and local governments, as well as the school districts, schools, and institutions that enroll these students. The December 14, 2012, shooting deaths of 20 children and 6 adults at Sandy Hook Elementary School in Newtown, CT, have heightened congressional concerns about school security.

Both the Elementary and Secondary Education Act of 1965 (ESEA), as amended by the No Child Left Behind Act of 2001 (NCLBA; P.L. 107-110), and the Higher Education Act of 1965 (HEA) contain requirements regarding crime and student safety. The ESEA also includes specific grant programs that support efforts to prevent school violence.

The ESEA authorizes the federal government's major programs to assist disadvantaged students, address teacher quality issues, provide support to limited English proficient and immigrant students, prevent school violence and drug abuse, and provide support for public school choice in elementary and secondary schools. While the prevention of school violence is not the primary focus of the ESEA, several ESEA programs could potentially contribute to this effort, most notably ESEA Title IV, Part A, the Safe and Drug-Free Schools and Communities Act (SDFSCA). In addition, the ESEA contains specific provisions related to students attending unsafe schools— the Unsafe School Choice Option.

The HEA authorizes the federal government's major student aid programs that support postsecondary education attendance, as well as other significant programs such as those providing aid to special groups of IHEs and support services to enable disadvantaged students to complete secondary school and enter and complete college. While the HEA does not authorize specific programs to address campus crime and security issues, Section 485(f) of Title IV of the HEA contains statutory requirements related to campus crime and security, known collectively as the Jeanne Clery Disclosure of Campus Security Policy and Campus Crime Statistics Act (the Clery Act). Institutions must comply with these requirements to participate in the federal student aid programs and other programs authorized by Title IV (e.g., Pell Grants).

This report discusses these provisions and programs as they apply to elementary and secondary schools and IHEs. It begins with a description of programs and requirements included in the ESEA, which is followed by a discussion of relevant requirements included in the HEA.

In: School Resource Officers
Editor: Andrew O'Murphy

Chapter 1

SCHOOL RESOURCE OFFICERS: LAW ENFORCEMENT OFFICERS IN SCHOOLS[*]

Nathan James and Gail McCallion

SUMMARY

Some policymakers have expressed renewed interest in school resource officers (SROs) as a result of the December 2012 mass shooting that occurred at Sandy Hook Elementary School in Newtown, CT. SROs are sworn law enforcement officers who are assigned to work in schools.

For FY2014, the Administration requested $150 million in funding for a Comprehensive Schools Safety Program under the Community Oriented Policing Services (COPS) program. The proposed program would provide funding for hiring school safety personnel, including SROs, civilian public safety personnel, school psychologists, social workers, and counselors. Funding would also be available for purchasing school safety equipment, developing and updating public safety plans, conducting threat assessments, and training crisis intervention teams.

Data from the Bureau of Justice Statistics show that the number of full-time law enforcement officers employed by local police departments or sheriff's offices who were assigned to work as SROs increased between 1997 and 2003 before decreasing slightly in 2007 (the most recent year for which data are available). Data show that a greater proportion of high schools, schools in cities, and schools with enrollments of 1,000 or more report having SROs.

Two federal grant programs promoted SRO programs: the COPS in Schools (CIS) program, which was funded until FY2005, and State Formula Grants under the Safe and Drug Free Schools and Communities Act (SDFSCA), which was funded until FY2009. The CIS program provided grants for hiring new, additional school resource officers to conduct community policing services in and around primary and secondary schools. Local educational agencies could use funds they received under the SDFSCA State Formula Grant program for, among other things, hiring and training school security personnel.

---

[*] This is an edited, reformatted and augmented version of the Congressional Research Service Publication, CRS Report for Congress R43126, dated June 26, 2013.

The body of research on the effectiveness of SRO programs is limited, both in terms of the number of studies published and the methodological rigor of the studies conducted. The research that is available draws conflicting conclusions about whether SRO programs are effective at reducing school violence. Also, the research does not address whether SRO programs deter school shootings, one of the key reasons for renewed congressional interest in these programs.

There are several questions Congress might consider in the context of grant funding specifically for SRO programs.

- **Does the current level of school violence warrant congressional efforts to expand the number of SROs in schools across the country?** Data suggest that schools are, generally speaking, safe places for children. During the 2010-2011 school year there were 11 reported homicides of children at school. The number of youth homicides that occurred at school remained less than 2% of the total number of homicides of school aged children for each school year going back to the 1992-1993 school year. In 2010, fewer children reported being the victim of a serious violent crime or a simple assault while at school compared to 1994. However, data also show that some schools—namely middle schools, city schools, and schools with a higher proportion of low-income students—have higher rates of reported violent incidents, and schools with a higher proportion of low-income students had higher rates of reported serious violent incidents.

- **Is funding for a wide-scale expansion of SRO programs financially sustainable?** If Congress expanded the number of SROs through additional federal funding, it is likely that many of those officers would go to law enforcement agencies serving jurisdictions of fewer than 25,000 people (data show that nearly 88% of police departments and almost half of sheriff's offices serve jurisdictions of fewer than 25,000 people). Traditionally, COPS grants have provided "seed" money for local law enforcement agencies to hire new officers, but it is the responsibility of the recipient agency to retain the officer(s) after the grant expires. Since smaller law enforcement agencies tend to have smaller operating budgets and smaller sworn forces, retaining even one or two additional officers after a grant expired might pose a significant financial burden.

- **Would additional SROs result in more children being placed in the criminal justice system?** Research in this area is limited to a small number of studies, but these suggest that children in schools with SROs might be more likely to be arrested for low-level offenses. On the other hand, some studies indicate that SROs can deter students from committing assaults on campus as well as bringing weapons to school. Schools with SROs may also be more likely to report non- serious violent crimes (i.e., physical attack or fights without a weapon and threat of physical attack without a weapon) to the police than schools lacking SROs.

INTRODUCTION

Schools have a mission of great importance to our nation—they are responsible for keeping our children safe while educating them and helping prepare them to be responsible and productive citizens. The December 14, 2012, shooting at Sandy Hook Elementary School in Newtown, CT, that claimed the lives of 20 children and 6 adults, has heightened congressional interest in school security. Policymakers have begun debating whether school security can be further enhanced, and if so, how best to accomplish that goal. A wide variety of proposals have been offered at the federal level, such as funding for expanded mental health services for students, funding for training on mental health awareness for school staff, funding to assist schools in improving school climate, funding for more school counselors, and funding for more school resource officers (SROs) or other armed security personnel.

Wayne LaPierre, Executive Vice President and CEO of the National Rifle Association, has proposed putting an armed police officer in every school in the country as a way to prevent mass shootings.[1] President Obama has proposed creating incentives for Community Oriented Policing Services (COPS) grants to be used to hire more SROs in the current year.[2] In addition, he has requested $150 million in funding for a new Comprehensive School Safety Program. This new grant program would provide school districts and law enforcement agencies with funding to hire new SROs and school psychologists, among other things.

This report focuses on one of these proposals—the renewed focus on providing federal funding for more SROs as a means to preventing school shootings. It examines the distribution of and current number of SROs, the potential sustainability of any increase in the number of SROs, and the effect that SROs may have on students and the academic setting. It also examines what available research studies suggest about the extent to which SROs may reduce school violence. These are issues Congress may consider while contemplating an expansion of SRO programs.

BACKGROUND ON SCHOOL RESOURCE OFFICERS

Many people probably have a basic understanding of what an SRO is: a law enforcement officer who works in a school. However, some policymakers, before considering legislation to increase the number of SROs in schools across the country, are likely to have questions beyond "what are SROs?" Some of these questions might include the following:

- What role do SROs play in the school environment?
- Why have schools and law enforcement agencies started SRO programs?
- How many SROs are there around the country?

Each of these questions is addressed in this section of the report. Subsequent sections discuss: the federal role in promoting SROs; research on the effectiveness of SROs; the Administration's proposals; and select issues for Congress.

The Role of School Resource Officers

Police agencies have traditionally provided services to schools, but it has only been over the past 20 years where the practice of assigning police officers to schools on a full-time basis has become more wide-spread.[3] Criminal justice and education officials sought to expand school safety efforts—which included assigning law enforcement officers to patrol schools— in the wake of a series of high-profile school shootings in the 1990s.[4] Expanding the presence of SROs in schools was also partly a response to rising juvenile crime rates during the 1980s and early 1990s.[5]

It has been argued that SROs are a new type of public servant; a hybrid educational, correctional, and law enforcement officer.[6] While the duties of SROs can vary from one community to another, which makes it difficult to develop a single list of SRO responsibilities, their activities can be placed into three general categories: (1) safety expert and law enforcer, (2) problem solver and liaison to community resources, and (3) educator.[7] SROs can act as safety experts and law enforcers by, assuming primary responsibility for handling calls for service from the school, making arrests, issuing citations on campus, taking actions against unauthorized persons on school property, and responding to off-campus criminal activities that involve students.[8] SROs also serve as first responders in the event of critical incidents at the school. SROs can help to solve problems that are not necessarily crimes (e.g., bullying or disorderly behavior) but that can contribute to criminal incidents.[9] Problem-solving activities conducted by SROs can include developing and expanding crime prevention efforts and community justice initiatives for students. SROs can also present courses on topics related to policing or responsible citizenship for students, faculty, and parents.[10]

There are two definitions of "school resource officer" in federal law and both definitions include some of the responsibilities outlined in the previous paragraph. Under the authorizing legislation for the Community Oriented Policing Services (COPS) program (42 U.S.C. §3796dd-8), a "school resource officer" is defined as

> a career law enforcement officer, with sworn authority, deployed in community-oriented policing, and assigned by the employing police department or agency to work in collaboration with schools and community-based organizations—(A) to address crime and disorder problems, gangs, and drug activities affecting or occurring in or around an elementary or secondary school; (B) to develop or expand crime prevention efforts for students; (C) to educate likely school-age victims in crime prevention and safety; (D) to develop or expand community justice initiatives for students; (E) to train students in conflict resolution, restorative justice, and crime awareness; (F) to assist in the identification of physical changes in the environment that may reduce crime in or around the school; and (G) to assist in developing school policy that addresses crime and to recommend procedural changes.

Under the Safe and Drug Free Schools and Communities Act (20 U.S.C. §7161), a "school resource officer" is defined as

> a career law enforcement officer, with sworn authority, deployed in community oriented policing, and assigned by the employing police department to a local educational agency to work in collaboration with schools and community based organizations to— (A) educate students in crime and illegal drug use prevention and safety; (B) develop or expand community justice initiatives for students; and (C) train students in conflict resolution, restorative justice, and crime and illegal drug use awareness.

The two definitions of an SRO share some similarities. Both define SROs as law enforcement officers who engage in community-oriented policing activities and who are assigned to work in collaboration with schools and community-based organizations. Both definitions also focus on developing community justice initiatives for students and training students in conflict resolution, restorative justice, and crime awareness. The definition of an SRO under the Safe and Drug Free Schools and Communities Act includes a focus on educating students in crime and illegal drug use prevention and safety, which is consistent with the purposes of the act. The definition of an SRO under the authorizing legislation for the COPS program focuses more on how SROs could address a school's crime problems through a more traditional law enforcement/security approach. As such, SROs under the COPS definition concentrate on addressing crime and disorder problems, gangs, and drug activities occurring in and around the school; assist in the identification of changes to the physical structure of the school or the area around the school that could help reduce crime; and assist in developing school policy that addresses crime.

Reasons for Establishing SRO Programs

A national survey of schools, and the law enforcement agencies that provided services to the schools that responded to the survey, found that school principals and law enforcement officials have different views about why schools do or do not have SROs. The results of the survey indicate that in very few cases was the level of violence in the school the key reason for starting an SRO program (approximately 4% of both school and law enforcement agencies cited this as the reason for starting the SRO program).[11] About one-quarter of schools reported that national media attention about school violence was the primary reason for starting the SRO program, while about one-quarter of law enforcement agencies cited school disorder problems (e.g., rowdiness or vandalism) as the primary reason an SRO was assigned to a school.[12] However, the most common response for both groups was "other." Respondents who marked "other" as their answer were asked to describe the reason why they started an SRO program. There were a variety of responses from both groups, including "received a grant to start the program," "part of community policing efforts," "part of a drug awareness program," or "improve school safety."[13]

Approximately 22% of schools reported that the primary reason they *did not* have an SRO was because they did not have adequate funds, while 43% of law enforcement agencies reported that inadequate funding was the primary reason why the schools they served did not have an SRO.[14] On the other hand, two-thirds of schools reported that the primary reason they did not have an SRO was because there was no need for one.[15] In comparison, 28% of law enforcement agencies reported that schools did not have an SRO because there was not a need for one.[16] There was also disagreement over whether the school would benefit from having an SRO. A majority of schools (55%) reported that they did not think the school would benefit from having an SRO, while 71% of law enforcement agencies reported that schools would benefit from having an SRO.[17]

The survey data show a divide between educators and law enforcement officers regarding the potential benefits of SRO programs. The results of the survey might reflect the different philosophies of educators and law enforcement officers. Schools focus on educating children, and teachers and education administrators might be opposed to an SRO program if they believe that the presence of an SRO will disrupt the learning environment, portray the school as being unsafe, or upset students. On the other hand, law enforcement personnel are philosophically oriented towards public safety. Their initial response to a crime problem in schools might focus on increasing law enforcement's presence at the school as a means of deterring criminal behavior.

How Many School Resource Officers Are There Nationwide?

Police have traditionally provided services to schools, but it has only been in the past 20 years that assigning officers to work in schools full-time has become widespread.[18] Data available from the Bureau of Justice Statistics (BJS) and the National Center for Education Statistic (NCES) provide some insight into the total number of SROs and the type of schools that they serve, but the data are not collected and reported regularly. The BJS's Law Enforcement Management and Administrative Statistics (LEMAS) survey is conducted periodically every three or four years. The survey collects data on the number of SROs employed by various law enforcement agencies, but it does not collect data on the type of schools SROs serve. The most recent LEMAS data available are from the 2007 survey. The NCES's School Survey on Crime and Safety (SSCS) collects data on the locale, enrollment size, and level of schools that have SROs. The SSCS is administered every other school year, but the most recent SSCS data available on the distribution of SROs are from the 2007-2008 school year survey.

LEMAS survey data show that the number of full-time law enforcement officers employed by local police departments or sheriff's offices who were assigned to work as SROs increased between 1997 (the first year data were collected) and 2003 before decreasing slightly in 2007.[19] As shown in **Figure 1**, there were approximately 6,700 more police officers or sheriff's deputies assigned to work as SROs in 2007 compared to 1997, but there were approximately 800 fewer SROs in 2007 compared to the peak in 2003. The data show that the number of sheriff's deputies assigned to work as SROs increased between 1997 and 2007, while the number of police officers working as SROs decreased between 2003 and 2007 after increasing in 2000 and 2003.

Data from the LEMAS survey also show that the overall proportion of police departments and sheriff's offices that reported assigning officers or deputies to work as SROs decreased between 2000 and 2007, but trends in police departments' and sheriff's offices' use of SROs went in different directions. In 2007, as shown in **Figure 2**, 38% of local law enforcement agencies reported using SROs, which was down from the peak of 44% in 2000. However, the proportion of sheriff's offices that reported using SROs was slightly higher in 2007 compared to 2000 (50% of sheriff's offices reported using SROs in 2007 compared to 48% in 2000).

Data from the SSCS for the 2007-2008 school year show that a greater proportion of high schools, schools in cities, and schools with enrollments of 1,000 or more report the presence of SROs. NCES reports that 37% of high schools *did not* have an SRO present at least once a week during the 2007-2008 school year, compared to 45% of middle schools and 76% of elementary schools.[20] Also, 59% of city schools *did not* have an SRO present at least once a week, compared to 65% of suburban schools, 57% of town schools, and 72% of rural schools.[21] Finally, 26% of schools with enrollments of 1,000 or more students *did not* have an SRO present at least one day a week while 57% of schools with enrollments of 999-500 students, 73% of schools with enrollments of 499-300 students, and 84% of schools with enrollments of less than 300 students did not have an SRO present at least once a week.[22] One limitation of the data is that they might not account for schools that had a less-frequent SRO presence. The SSCS principal questionnaire for the 2007-2008 school year asked "[d]uring the 2007–08 school year, did you have any security guards, security personnel, or sworn law enforcement officers present at your school *at least once a week*? [emphasis original]"[23] Therefore, if the SRO was at the school every-other- week, that officer's presence would not be captured by the data.

FEDERAL FUNDING FOR SCHOOL RESOURCE OFFICERS

SRO programs have been encouraged by the federal government through grants provided to local jurisdictions.[24] Two federal grant programs provided funding for the hiring and placement of law enforcement officers in schools across the country: the COPS in Schools (CIS) program and the State Formula Grants program through the Safe and Drug Free Schools and Communities Act. Funding for these programs ended, respectively, in FY2005 and FY2009.

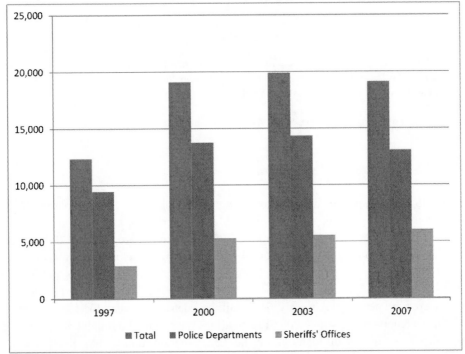

Source: CRS presentation of data from the U.S. Department of Justice, Office of Justice Programs, Bureau of Justice Statistics, *Local Police Departments* for 1997, 2000, 2003, and 2007 and *Sheriff's Offices* for 1997, 2000, 2003, and 2007.

Figure 1. Full-Time School Resource Officers Employed by Local Law Enforcement Agencies.

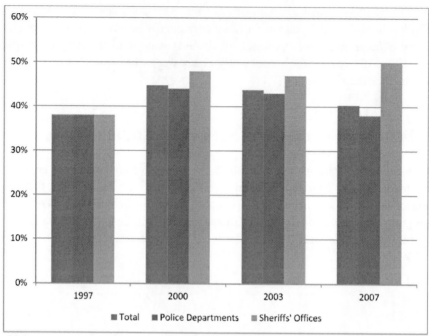

Source: CRS presentation of data from the U.S. Department of Justice, Office of Justice Programs, Bureau of Justice Statistics, *Local Police Departments* for 1997, 2000, 2003, and 2007 and *Sheriff's Offices* for 1997, 2000, 2003, and 2007.

Figure 2. Percent of Local Law Enforcement Agencies Using School Resource Officers.

The COPS in Schools (CIS) Program

The CIS program provided grants for hiring new, additional school resource officers to conduct community policing services in and around primary and secondary schools.[25] Congress first provided funding for the COPS in Schools program in 1999 after the Columbine school shooting.[26] Funding for the CIS program was set aside from appropriations for the COPS Hiring Program (CHP). Congress provided funding for this program from FY1999-FY2005.[27] Appropriations for CIS peaked between FY2000 and FY2002, when Congress appropriated approximately $180 million each fiscal year for the program. The COPS Office reports that nearly 7,200 SRO positions were funded through CIS grants.[28] Even though there has not been funding for the CIS program for several fiscal years, law enforcement agencies can use grants they receive under the CHP to hire SROs.[29]

Safe and Drug Free Schools and Communities Act (SDFSCA)

The SDFSCA is the federal government's major initiative to prevent drug abuse and violence in and around elementary and secondary schools.[30] The SDFSCA was initially enacted in 1994 (P.L. 103-382) in response to concerns about increased school violence and drug use among school- aged youth.[31] The SDFSCA was most recently reauthorized as part of the Elementary and Secondary Education Act (ESEA) in P.L. 107-110, the No Child Left Behind Act of 2001. The SDFSCA program as authorized supports two major grant programs—one for State Formula Grants and one for National Programs.[32]

However, FY2009 was the last year that funding was provided for the State Formula Grant Program. Since FY2010, funding has only been provided for National Programs. The State Formula Grant Program distributed formula grants to states, and from states to all local educational agencies (LEAs), as required by law. LEAs could use their grants for a wide variety of authorized activities, including for the hiring and training of school resource officers.[33]

RESEARCH ON THE EFFECTIVENESS OF SCHOOL RESOURCE OFFICERS

SROs engage in many activities that could contribute to school safety. A national survey of schools found that schools with SROs had significantly greater levels of law enforcement involvement compared to schools without assigned officers.[34] Schools with SROs were more likely to report that

- school facilities and grounds were patrolled,
- safety and security inspections were conducted,
- student leads about crimes were investigated,
- arrests were made, and
- there were responses to crime reports from staff and students.[35]

In addition, schools with SROs were more likely to work with law enforcement to create an emergency plan agreement; develop a written plan to deal with shootings, large scale fights, hostages, and bomb threats; and conduct risk assessments of the security of school buildings or grounds.[36] Schools with SROs were also more likely to have police officers involved in mentoring students and advising school staff.[37] However, while the results of the survey show that SROs are undertaking actions that might contribute to safer schools, they do not indicate whether these actions reduce school violence.

Despite the popularity of SRO programs, there are few available studies that have reliably evaluated their effectiveness.[38] A more specific critique of the literature on SRO programs notes that to properly assess the effect of SRO programs it is necessary to collect data on reliable and objective outcome measures during a treatment period (i.e., a period in which SROs worked in schools) and a control period (i.e., a period in which no SROs were present).[39] Data on the control period could be collected from comparable schools without SROs or from the same school before the SRO was assigned to the school.[40] Data from both the treatment and control conditions should be collected over a long enough period of time that they generate a stable estimate of the outcome measures, and the outcome measure should not be influenced by the placement of the SRO in the school (e.g., using the SRO's incident reports).[41] At the time this review of the literature was published (2011), no evaluations of SRO programs met this standard.[42]

One summary of the body of literature on the effectiveness of SRO programs notes that

[s]tudies of SRO effectiveness that have measured actual safety outcomes have mixed results, some show an improvement in safety and a reduction in crime;[43] others show no change.[44] Typically, studies that report positive results from SRO programs rely on participants' perceptions of the effectiveness of the program rather than on objective evidence. Other studies fail to isolate incidents of crime and violence, so it is impossible to know whether the positive results stem from the presence of SROs or are the results of other factors.[45]

A study of 19 SRO programs sponsored by the National Institute of Justice did not draw any conclusions about their effectiveness because very few of the programs included in their study "conducted useful and valid assessments of their programs."[46]

More recent research has attempted to address some of the shortcomings of previous studies on the topic by using broader datasets and statistical techniques that control for possible confounding variables, but they still suffer from some limitations. For example, a study by Tillyer, Fisher, and Wilcox found that students in schools where police were present and/or involved in the school's daily decision making were no less likely than students in schools where the police were not present and/or involved in decision making to report that they were the victims of a serious violent offense, believe they were at risk for being victimized, or were afraid of being victimized.[47] However, this study used data collected mostly from children in rural schools in Kentucky, which could raise questions about whether the results are generalizable to other locales. Another study by Jennings et al. found that the number of SROs in a school had a statistically significant negative effect on the number of reported serious violent crimes, but not on the number of reported violent crimes.[48] Nonetheless, this study only used one year of data, which means that it is not possible to determine if reported crimes in high schools decreased after the school started an SRO program.

A third study by Na and Gottfredson used a dataset that allowed the researchers to evaluate whether the reported number of offenses decreased after schools started SRO programs.[49] The results of the analysis show that schools that added SROs did not have a lower number of reported serious violent,[50] non-serious violent,[51] or property crimes.[52] However, schools that added SROs had a higher number of reported weapon and drug offenses.[53] There are some limitations to this study, namely (1) the reported number of crimes might be influenced by the presence of an SRO; (2) the sample of schools included in the study is not representative of all schools in the United States (it over-represents secondary schools, large schools, and non-rural schools); and (3) the effects of adding SROs may be confounded with the installation of other security devices (e.g., metal detectors) or other security-related policies.

The body of research on the effectiveness of SRO programs is noticeably limited, both in terms of the number of studies published and the methodological rigor of the studies conducted. The research that is available draws conflicting conclusions about whether SRO programs are effective at reducing school violence. In addition, the research does not address whether SRO programs deter school shootings, one of the key reasons for renewed congressional interest in these programs. There are logical reasons to believe that SROs might help prevent school shootings; to wit, that someone might not attack a school if he or she knows that there is an officer on-site, or SROs developing a relationship with the student body might facilitate reporting of threats made by other students. In addition, placing an officer in a school might facilitate a quicker response time by law enforcement if a school shooting occurs. However, none of the research on the effectiveness of SRO programs addresses this issue.

Promising Practices for Successful SRO Programs

A report published by the COPS Office notes that there is a lack of research on SRO programs, so it is not possible to identify a "one-size-fits-all" series of recommendations for implementing a maximally successful SRO program.[54] The report, however, identifies several promising practices for a successful SRO program. First, it emphasizes that all schools should develop a comprehensive school safety plan based on a thorough analysis of the problem(s) the school is facing and resources should be deployed accordingly. The report also notes that while SROs might be an important component of an overall safety plan, they should not be the only component. In some instances, school safety plans might not require the deployment of an SRO. If the school decides to use an SRO, there should be clear goals for the program, SROs should engage in activities that directly relate to school safety goals and address identified needs, and data should be collected to determine whether the program is achieving its goals. Finally, the report notes that effective SROs engage in problem-solving policing rather than simply responding to incidents as they occur.[55]

The report notes that there are operational obstacles that can threaten the success of an SRO program, including a lack of resources for the officer such as time constraints or lack of training, or turnover and reassignment.[56] These challenges can be addressed with a proper framework, but it can require in-depth discussion and negotiations between school administrators and the law enforcement agency.

The report also stresses that schools and law enforcement agencies should be aware of any pitfalls before agreeing to establish an SRO program.[57] There may be philosophical differences between school administrators and law enforcement agencies about the role of the SRO. Law enforcement agencies focus on public safety while schools focus on educating students. Establishing an operating protocol or memorandum of understanding (MOU), according to the report, is a critical element of an effective school-police partnership.[58] The MOU should clearly state the roles and responsibilities of the actors involved in the program.[59] Researchers who conducted an evaluation of 19 SRO programs note that "[w]hen SRO programs fail to define the SROs' roles and responsibilities in detail before—or even after—the officers take up the posts in the schools, problems are often rampant—and may last for months and even years."[60]

According to the report, selecting officers who are likely to succeed in a school environment— such as officers who can effectively work with students, parents, and school administrators, have an understanding of child development and psychology, and who have public speaking and teaching skills—and properly training those officers are identified as two important components of a successful SRO program.[61] While it is possible to recruit officers with some of the skills necessary to be an effective SRO, it is nonetheless important to provide training so officers can hone skills they already have or develop new skills that can make them more effective SROs.[62] It might also be important for SROs to receive training before or shortly after starting their assignment. The study of 19 SRO programs mentioned previously concluded that *"any delay in training can be a serious problem* [emphasis original] because SROs then have to learn their jobs by 'sinking or swimming.'"[63]

THE ADMINISTRATION'S PROPOSED COMPREHENSIVE SCHOOL SAFETY PROGRAM

The Administration requested $150 million in funding for a Comprehensive Schools Safety Program as a part of its FY2014 budget request for the COPS program. The COPS Office would work with the Department of Education to administer the program. The proposed program would provide funding for hiring school safety personnel, including SROs, civilian public safety positions, school psychologists, social workers, and counselors. Funding would also be available for purchasing school safety equipment; developing and updating public safety plans; conducting threat assessments; and training crisis intervention teams. The stated purpose of the program is to "bring the law enforcement, mental health, and education disciplines together to provide a comprehensive approach to school safety."[64] The Administration reports that the program would require law enforcement and school districts, in consultation with school mental health professionals, to apply for funding together and use the grant to fills the gaps in their own school safety and security efforts. The Administration emphasizes that "[f]unding may also be used to support training for any personnel hired to ensure that their presence in the schools does not lead to unnecessarily harsh discipline and arrests for youth misbehaving, and that they will support other school personnel in implementing evidence-based positive behavior strategies."[65]

The Administration's proposed program would provide grants for hiring SROs like the CIS program, but unlike the CIS program, grants under the proposed program could also be used for hiring non-sworn personnel such as civilian public safety officers (i.e., security guards), school psychologists, social workers, and school counselors. The program has a focus on the mental health and counseling aspect of school safety, an element that was present in the State Formula Grants under the SDFSCA. Under the Administration's proposal, grants could be used to "improve school and community safety by expanding school-based mental health programs through the hiring of qualified mental health professionals."[66] Further, "qualified mental health professionals can improve safety by providing a broad spectrum of assessment, prevention, crisis response, counseling, consultation, and referral activities and services to students and the school community."[67]

Under the Administration's proposal, grants could be used for purchasing school safety equipment, developing and updating safety plans, and conducting threat assessments. This is similar to the purposes of the Matching Grant Program for School Security,[68] which was last funded by Congress in FY2011. Under that program, grants could be used for (1) the placement and use of metal detectors, locks, lighting, and other deterrent measures; (2) security assessments; (3) security training of personnel and students; (4) coordination with local law enforcement; and (5) any other measure that, in the determination of the Director of the COPS Office, may provide a significant improvement in security.[69] State formula grants under the SDFSCA could also be used for purchasing metal detectors or related devices and developing and implementing comprehensive schools security plans.

The Administration's proposal appears to be an attempt to bring multiple stakeholders together to develop a comprehensive approach to school security measures. It acknowledges that while SROs and physical security measures might be a part of a comprehensive school security plan, there are other elements that need to be addressed, such as the mental health of troubled students. It also would allow local governments to apply for funding for a school safety plan that does not include SROs. The proposed program could benefit applicants because it would allow them to submit one application for a grant that could be used for a variety of purposes instead of having to apply for funding under several different programs. It might also eliminate the possibility that funds from different grant programs are used for the same or similar purposes. The proposed program is intended to facilitate a more collaborative and comprehensive approach to school safety measures by requiring representatives of school districts, law enforcement, and mental health services to develop a school safety plan in order to apply for funding. However, since grants under the proposed program would be for comprehensive school security programs, it is possible that individual grant awards would be larger than they would be if grants were simply awarded for SROs or physical security infrastructure, meaning there could be fewer awards overall. Also, if there are barriers to stakeholders collaborating on a school safety plan, the requirements of the program might prohibit some communities from receiving funding.

SELECT ISSUES FOR CONGRESS

There are several issues Congress could consider should policymakers choose to debate whether to provide funding for SRO programs. Some of these issues might include the following:

- Do current trends in school violence warrant congressional efforts to expand SRO programs?
- Is it possible to sustain a significant expansion in SRO programs?
- What effect might an expansion of SRO programs have on the educational setting?

Trends in School Violence

An overarching issue is whether the current level of school violence warrants congressional efforts to expand the number of SROs in schools across the country. The recent shooting in Newtown, CT, has heightened the nation's focus on school shootings, but it has been reported that schools are generally safe places for both students and staff.[70] Twelve out of a total of 78 public mass shootings between 1983 and 2012 that have been identified by CRS occurred in academic settings. Eight of these happened at primary or secondary education facilities.[71] Four of the 12 public mass shootings in education settings involved high school or middle school students as assailants.[72]

Data show that homicides of children while at school, in general, are rare events. For the 2010-2011 school year, the most recent school year for which data are available, there were 31 school-associated violent deaths,[73] of which 11 were homicides of children ages 5-18 while at school (see **Figure 3**).[74] The number of school-associated violent deaths and homicides of children ages 5-18 while at school for the 2010-2011 school year was below the average number of school-associated violent deaths (45) and homicides of children at school (23) since the 1992-1993 school year. To put the number of reported at-school youth homicides in context, the number of youth homicides that occurred at school remained less than 2% of the total number of homicides of school aged children for each school year going back to the 1992-1993 school year.[75] For example, there were a total of 1,595 homicides of children ages 5-18 during the 2008-2009 school year; of those, 17 (1.1%) occurred while the child was at school.[76]

School violence, however, goes beyond just school shootings. School violence can include sexual assaults, robberies, assaults, and threats of violence against children while they are at school. In a December 2012 report on violent crime against youth, the BJS reported that the rate of serious violent crime[77] against youth ages 12 to 17 on school grounds decreased 62% between 1994 (17.4 per 1,000) and 2010 (6.6 per 1,000).[78] Trends in simple assault victimizations for children ages 12-17 were similar to victimizations for serious violent crimes. Reported victimizations for simple assaults on school grounds decreased 81% between 1994 (70.3 per 1,000) and 2010 (13.2 per 1,000).

Data published in the *Indicators of School Crime and Safety* report, show that schools are generally safe, but there are some schools with higher levels of violence and disorder than others. Approximately 74% of public schools reported one or more violent incidents and 16% reported one or more serious violent incidents during the 2009-2010 school year (see **Table 1**). It is estimated that there were 1.2 million violent incidents and 52,500 serious violent incidents during that school year. The rate of violent incidents was 25.0 per 1,000 students while the rate of serious violent incidents was 1.1 per 1,000 students. However, data also show that some schools— namely middle schools, city schools, and schools with a higher proportion of low-income students (defined as the proportion of students who are eligible for free or reduced-price lunch)— have higher rates of reported violent and serious violent incidents.

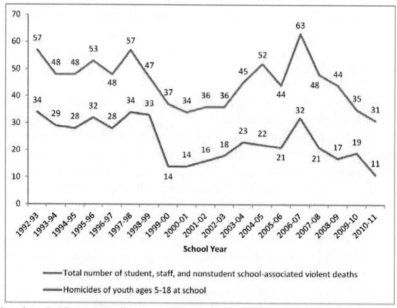

Source: Taken from Table 1.1 in Indicators of School Crime and Safety, 2012.
Notes: Data from the 1999-2000 school year onward are subject to change as additional information about confirmed cases is received and assessed.

Figure 3. Number of School-Associated Violent Deaths and Homicides of Youth Ages 5-18 at School.

Table 1. Percentage of Public Schools Recording Violent and Serious Violent Incidents at School, Number of Incidents, and the Rate of Crimes Per 1,000 Students, by School Characteristics, School Year 2009-2010

School Characteristic	Total Number of Schools	Violent Incidents[a]			Serious Violent Incidents[b]		
		Percent of Schools	Number of Incidents	Rate per 1,000 Students	Percent of Schools	Number of Incidents	Rate per 1,000 Students
Total	82,800	73.8%	1,183,700	25.0	16.4%	52,500	1.1
School Level[c]							
Primary	48,900	64.4%	482,100	21.3	13.0%	21,900	1.0
Middle	15,300	90.5%	375,200	40.0	18.9%	13,600	1.5
High School	12,200	90.9%	264,400	21.4	27.6%	13,500	1.1
Combined	6,400	73.7%	62,000	20.8	15.5%	—d	—d
Enrollment size							
Less than 300	18,900	62.8%	111,300	27.2	10.4%	6,100e	1.5e
300-499	25,200	71.3%	274,400	26.5	15.7%	14,200	1.4
500-999	29,800	76.4%	487,900	25.0	15.9%	16,400	0.8
1,000 or more	8,900	95.4%	310,100	23.2	32.8%	15,700	1.2
Locale							
City	21,500	74.9%	396,300	28.8	21.7%	17,400	1.3
Suburban	23,800	73.5%	371,000	22.4	15.5%	16,200	1.0
Town	12,100	80.3%	166,300	28.2	15.6%	6,300	1.1
Rural	25,300	70.2%	250,100	22.5	13.2%	12,600	1.1
Percent of students eligible for free or reduced-price lunch							
0-25%	17,100	62.6%	141,700	11.9	10.5%	6,700	0.6
26-50%	22,700	76.0%	290,500	22.1	16.2%	12,500	1.0
51-75%	23,800	73.8%	334,400	27.3	15.8%	13,100	1.1
76-100%	19,100	81.4%	417,200	41.3	22.9%	20,100	2.0

Source: Taken from Table 6.2, Indicators of School Crime and Safety: 2012.

a. "Violent incidents" include rape, sexual battery other than rape, physical attack or fight with or without a weapon, threat of physical attack with or without a weapon, and robbery with or without a weapon.

b. "Serious violent incidents" include rape, sexual battery other than rape, physical attack or fight with a weapon, threat of physical attack with a weapon, and robbery with or without a weapon.

c. Primary schools are defined as schools in which the lowest grade is not higher than grade 3 and the highest grade is not higher than grade 8. Middle schools are defined as schools in which the lowest grade is not lower than grade 4 and the highest grade is not higher than grade 9. High schools are defined as schools in which the lowest grade is not lower than grade 9 and the highest grade is not higher than grade 12. Combined schools include all other combinations of grades, including K-12 schools.

d. Reporting standards not met.

e. Interpret data with caution because the margin of error for the estimated statistic is relatively large.

The above data suggest a key question: have SROs contributed to the reduction in school violence? The National Association of School Resource Officers (NASRO) draws a link between decreasing school violence and the presence of SROs:

> Over the past two decades, America's public schools have become safer and safer. All indicators of school crime continue on the downward trend first reported when data collection began around 1992. In 2011, incidences of school-associated deaths, violence, nonfatal victimizations, and theft all continued their downward trend. This trend mirrors that of juvenile arrests in general, which fell nearly 50% between 1994 and 2009—17% between 2000 and 2009 alone. This period of time coincides with the expansion of School Resource Officer programs as part of a comprehensive, community-oriented strategy to address the range of real and perceived challenges to campus safety.[79]

Data suggest that the decline in violent victimizations experienced by children at school might, in part, be the result of an overall decline in crime against juveniles and not the result of more SROs working in schools. Data from the BJS show that between 1994 and 2010 there was a 77% decrease in the number of serious violent victimizations and an 83% decrease in simple assaults against youth ages 12 to 17 (see **Figure 4**).

Data from the Office of Juvenile Justice and Delinquency Prevention (OJJDP) also show that the number of juvenile homicides is lower than the previous nadir in 1984.[80] There were a reported 1,448 homicides of juveniles in 2010, down from the peak of 2,841 juvenile homicides in 1993 (see **Figure 5**).

Sustainability of a School Resource Officer Expansion

As previously noted, there have been proposals to increase the number of SROs as a way of preventing school shootings. Some policymakers might view a program that provides grants for hiring SROs, like the CIS program, as a way to expand the number of police officers assigned to schools across the country. Federal funding provided through the CIS program has been cited as contributing to the expansion of SRO programs.[81] As previously discussed, in 2003 there were approximately 19,900 reported SROs, up from approximately 12,300 SROs in 1997. Between FY1999 and FY2002, the COPS Office, through the CIS program, had funded nearly 6,300 SRO positions. The LEMAS data do not indicate how each SRO position is funded, but a survey conducted by the National Association of School Resource Officers (NASRO) of attendees at their 2004 national conference found that 45% of respondents indicated that their SRO positions were currently or formerly supported by a CIS grant.[82] The NASRO survey does not represent an unbiased national sample of SRO programs, and any results should therefore be interpreted with caution, but it is one of the few indicators of how many SRO positions were funded by CIS grants. The available data suggest that CIS funding probably supported a significant expansion of SRO programs across the country. The data also suggest that local law enforcement agencies have funded a majority of SRO positions, and they have continued to do so even after grants through the CIS program expired.

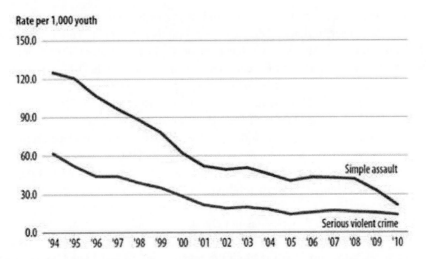

Source: U.S. Department of Justice, Office of Justice Programs, Bureau of Justice Statistics, *Violent Crime Against Youth, 1994-2010.*
Notes: Data based on two-year rolling averages beginning in 1993.

Figure 4. Serious Violent Crime and Simple Assault against Youth Ages 12 to 17 1994-2010.

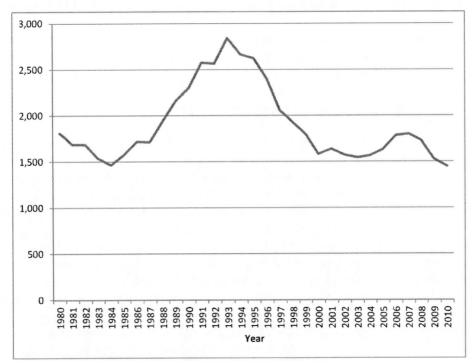

Source: U.S. Department of Justice, Office of Justice Programs, Office of Juvenile Justice and Delinquency Prevention, *OJJDP Statistical Briefing Book.*

Figure 5. Reported Number of Juvenile Homicides, 1980-2010.

Even a conservative estimate of the cost of placing an SRO in each school in the country shows that it could cost billions of dollars to accomplish that goal. This estimate is partly founded on assumptions based on 2007 data (the most recent available). Data from the NCES show that in the 2009-2010 school year there were 98,817 public schools in the United States.[83] Data from the BJS show that there were a total of 19,088 SROs in 2007 (see **Table A-1**and **Table A-2**). If it is assumed that the number of SROs did not decrease in subsequent years and it is further assumed that each SRO is assigned to work in only one school, it would mean that there would need to be an additional 79,729 SROs hired to place an SRO in each school in the United States. Data from the BJS show that in 2007 the average minimum salary for an entry-level police officer was $32,900[84] and for an entry-level sheriff's deputy it was $31,100,[85] and the weighted average minimum salary for an entry-level law enforcement officer in 2007 was $32,412.[86] Assuming that the average minimum salary for entry-level police officers and sheriff's deputies has not changed, it would cost about $2.6 billion to hire the additional 79,729 SROs needed to place an SRO in each school. However, this cost could be higher because, as previously discussed, the number of SROs declined between 2003 and 2007. In recent years, many law enforcement agencies faced significant budget constraints due to the recent recession, so it is possible that the number of SROs continued to decline as they were reassigned or laid-off. Also, it is possible that the salaries for entry-level police officers and sheriff's deputies have increased since 2007. On the other hand, the estimated cost could be lower if SROs were assigned to patrol more than one school in some school districts.

If Congress acted to expand the number of SROs, it is likely that many of those officers would go to law enforcement agencies serving jurisdictions of fewer than 25,000 people. Data from the BJS show that nearly 88% of police departments and almost half of sheriff's offices serve jurisdictions of fewer than 25,000 people.[87] However, a smaller proportion of police departments and sheriff's offices that serve populations of less than 25,000 reported using SROs in 2007 (see **Table A-3** and **Table A-4**).

Not surprisingly, data from the LEMAS show that law enforcement agencies serving smaller jurisdictions have smaller operating budgets. Concomitantly, smaller law enforcement agencies have, on average, fewer sworn officers. Policymakers might consider whether it would be financially sensible to provide federal funding to place an SRO in every school across the country, or to even substantially expand the number of SROs. Traditionally, COPS grants have provided "seed" money for local law enforcement agencies to hire new officers, but it is the responsibility of the recipient agency to retain the officer(s) after the grant expires. Since smaller law enforcement agencies tend to have smaller operating budgets and smaller sworn forces, retaining even one or two additional officers after a grant expires might pose a significant financial burden. If the law enforcement agency cannot retain the new SROs after the grant period ends, then the federal government has only supported a temporary expansion of SRO programs. The COPS Office has required law enforcement agencies that receive hiring grants to retain any officers hired with federal funds for at least one year after the grant period ends. While this might help promote the retention of federally-funded law enforcement officers, this requirement, if applied to any potential funding Congress might provide for hiring SROs, might limit who decides to apply for grants.

The Effect of School Resource Officers on the Educational Setting

An August 21, 201, story in the *Washington Post* highlighted several incidents of students in public schools in Texas being ticketed and required to appear in court for behavior that was traditionally dealt with by teachers and principals.[88] This and similar stories[89] might raise some concern among policymakers that a wide-scale expansion of SRO programs could contribute to what has been referred to as the "school-to-prison pipeline." One review of the literature on SROs asserts that the increased use of police officers in schools facilitates the formal processing of minor offenses and harsh responses to minor disciplinary situations.[90]

On December 12, 2012, the Senate Judiciary Subcommittee on the Constitution, Civil Rights and Human Rights, held a hearing titled "Ending the School-to-Prison Pipeline." In his opening statement Chairman Richard Durbin stated that

> For many young people, our schools are increasingly a gateway to the criminal justice system. This phenomenon is a consequence of a culture of zero tolerance that is widespread in our schools and is depriving many children of their fundamental right to an education.[91]

While recent interest in SROs programs has stemmed from proposals to use SROs as a way to prevent school shootings, it should be noted that SROs are more than armed sentries whose sole purpose is to stand guard and wait for an attack. SROs are sworn law enforcement officers who, among other things, patrol the school, investigate criminal complaints, and handle law violators. Therefore, while assigning an SRO to a school might serve as a deterrent to a potential school shooter, or provide a quicker law enforcement response in cases where a school shooting occurs, it will also establish a regular law enforcement presence in the school. There might be some concern that any potential deterrent effect generated by placing SROs in schools could be offset by either the monetary cost associated with a wide-scale expansion of SRO programs or the social costs that might arise by potentially having more children enter the criminal justice system for relatively minor offenses.

Research on SROs and School Arrests

A study conducted by Theriot used data from a school district in the southeastern United States to test the criminalization of student misconduct theory.[92] Theriot's analysis produced mixed results. Middle and high schools with SROs had more arrests per 100 students than schools without SROs, but this relationship was no longer significant when the analysis controlled for school- level poverty. The results of the study indicated that students in schools with SROs were more likely than students in schools without SROs to be arrested for disorderly conduct, which lends credence to the idea that student misbehavior is being criminalized. The researcher also found that schools with SROs had lower arrest rates for assault and possessing a weapon on school grounds. The researcher opined that this suggests that SROs might serve as a deterrent. For example, students might be less likely to bring a weapon to school if an SRO is present because they fear they might be caught. Students might also be less likely to fight if they believe they will be arrested for assault. A critique of Theriot's study notes that the analysis did not collect data for a long enough period before

SROs were assigned to some schools and the control group (i.e., the non-SRO schools) still had some contact with law enforcement.[93]

The study conducted by Na and Gottfredson, discussed previously, also included an analysis of whether schools that added SROs had a greater percentage of crimes reported to law enforcement and whether a greater proportion of students were subject to "harsh discipline" (i.e., the student was removed, transferred, or suspended for five or more days).[94] The researchers found that schools that added SROs were more likely to report non-serious violent crimes (i.e., physical attack or fights without a weapon and threat of physical attack without a weapon) to the police than schools that did not add SROs. The reporting of other crime types and the reporting of crime overall, were not affected by the addition of SROs. The results of Na and Gottfredson's analysis mirror the finding of Theriot's study. Na and Gottfredson conclude that their findings are "consistent with our prediction that increased use of SROs facilitates the formal processing of minor offenses."[95] However, their analysis also found that students at schools that added SROs were not any more likely than students at schools that did not add SROs to be subject to harsh discipline for committing any offense that was reported to the police.

School Security Measures and School Disciplinary Policies

The use of SROs in schools occurred in the context of increasing concern about security in schools and the concomitant adoption of more security measures in schools and the strengthening of school discipline policies. Although research on the efficacy of security measures in reducing school violence is limited, schools have been adopting more security measures over time. Between school year 1999-2000 and 2009-2010 there was an increase in the percentage of schools adopting the following security measures: restricting access to buildings during school hours (from 75% to 92%); using one or more security cameras to monitor the school (from 19% to 61%); and requiring faculty to wear badges or picture IDs (from 25% to 63%).[96] During the same time period the percentage of students reporting the presence of security guards and/or assigned police officers at school increased from 54% to 68%.[97]

Following the adoption of the Gun Free Schools Act (GFSA) in 1994,[98] some schools expanded on the GFSA's prohibition against guns in schools by adopting school-wide policies with strict disciplinary consequences for other rule violations. These so called "zero tolerance" policies vary from school to school, but are generally characterized by the application of specified, mandatory discipline procedures in response to rule violations. Like the hiring of SROs, these policies were intended to improve school security. The theory behind zero tolerance policies is that certain, severe punishments would deter violent behavior by students. However, data on the rising number of out-of-school suspensions that disproportionately impact minority students, as well as data indicating the potential negative effects of suspensions on students, have increased attention on these policies.

Disparities in School Discipline

The most recent U.S. Department of Education biennial Civil Rights Data Collection survey (CRDC) includes data indicating that some school disciplinary measures disproportionately affect minority students and students with disabilities.[99] The CRDC data indicate that African American students were over 3½ times more likely to be suspended or expelled than white students.

Additionally, students with disabilities were more than twice as likely as non-disabled students to receive one or more suspensions.[100]

Although African American students represented 18% of the students in the CRDC survey, 46% of these students were suspended more than once. In zero tolerance school districts that reported expulsions under that policy, Hispanic and African Americans comprised 56% of those expelled, although they comprised 45% of the total student population in these schools. Furthermore, the CRDC survey found that over 70% of students arrested at school or referred to law enforcement were African American or Hispanic.[101]

Efficacy of School Disciplinary Measures

One of the main purposes of zero tolerance discipline policies was to serve as a deterrent to further school violence; however, existing empirical research has been too limited to validate the effectiveness of these disciplinary measures. A task force convened by the American Psychological Association to examine the evidence on the effectiveness of zero tolerance in schools found that

> it is problematic that despite 20 years of school implementation of zero tolerance policies, and nearly 15 years as federal policy, the research base on zero tolerance is in no way sufficient to evaluate the impact of zero tolerance policy and practices on student behavior or school climate.[102]

Concern about the effectiveness of school suspensions and their impact on students has led to a growing body of research on potentially more effective alternatives, particularly efforts to improve school climate.[103] The Centers for Disease Control (CDC) defines a positive school climate as one that is "characterized by caring and supportive interpersonal relationships; opportunities to participate in school activities and decision-making; and shared positive norms, goals, and values."[104] Available research suggests that one of the most important elements in a positive school climate is for students to have a feeling of school connectedness. School connectedness is defined as "the belief by students that adults and peers in the school care about their learning as well as about them as individuals."[105]

The National School Climate Center (the Center) has published numerous reports on school climate.[106] A 2012 report from the Center cites research indicating that a positive school climate influences student motivation to learn, mitigates the effect of socioeconomic factors on academic success, and contributes to less aggression and violence, among other positive outcomes.[107] Both social emotional learning[108] and positive behavior management strategies have been identified by researchers as positive approaches to improving school climate.[109] A program to improve school climate called *School-wide Positive Behavioral Interventions and Supports* (SWPBIS) is currently supported by the U.S. Department of Education through capacity-building information and technical assistance to schools, districts, and states who are implementing SWPBIS. SWPBIS is a three-tiered prevention-based approach to improving schoolwide disciplinary practices. According to the Center, SWPBIS is used in more than 9,000 schools across 40 states.[110] SWPBIS has been linked to reductions in student suspensions and office discipline referrals.[111]

In addition, an interagency initiative titled "Safe Schools/Healthy Students" (SS/HS) focuses on a comprehensive approach to school violence.[112] SS/HS is funded jointly by ED and the U.S. Department of Health and Human Services (HHS), Substance Abuse and Mental

Health Services Administration (SAMHSA). The program is administered by ED, SAMHSA, and the U.S. Department of Justice (DOJ). The SS/HS initiative is a discretionary grant program that provides schools and communities with federal funding, via LEAs, to implement an enhanced, coordinated, comprehensive plan of activities, programs, and services that focus on healthy childhood development and the prevention of violence and alcohol and drug abuse. Grantees are required to establish partnerships with local law enforcement, public mental health, and juvenile justice agencies/entities.

CONCLUSION

The practice of placing SROs in schools has become more popular over the past two decades. As of 2007, there were more SROs working in schools across the country than there were in 1997, though the number of SROs was down from its peak in 2003. Data show that police departments and sheriff's offices have, by-and-large, sustained their SRO programs over the years, even as federal grants for hiring SROs have waned.

The expansion of SRO programs coincided with a decrease in reported serious violent victimizations of students while at school and generally lower numbers of violent deaths and homicides at schools. The extent to which SRO programs contributed to the decrease is not known. Indeed, trends in at-school violence mirror a downward trend in overall violence against children and juvenile homicides. Yet schools are not free of violence and crime, and some schools—such as city schools, middle schools, and schools with a higher proportion of low income students—have higher rates of violent incidents.

Policymakers might contemplate increasing the number of SRO programs across the country as a way to address the threat of mass shootings at or violence in schools. However, the body of research on the effectiveness of SRO programs is noticeably limited, and the research that is available draws conflicting conclusions about whether SRO programs are effective at reducing school violence. In addition, the body of research on the effectiveness of SROs does not address whether their presence in schools has deterred mass shootings.

While a law enforcement presence at a school might facilitate actions, such as security planning or threat assessments, that might promote school safety, and the presence of an SRO might serve as a deterrent to a potential school shooter or provide for a quick response if a shooting occurs, some might be concerned that a regular law enforcement presence might have some unintended consequences for students. Research suggests that the presence of SROs might result in more children being involved in the criminal justice system for relatively minor offenses, and this, in turn, can result in other negative consequences, such as higher rates of suspension or a greater likelihood of dropping-out of school.

The school shooting in Newtown, CT, might lead some policymakers to consider ways to provide funding to law enforcement agencies or school districts to establish or expand SRO programs. However, even a conservative estimate of the cost of placing an SRO in every school across the country shows that this proposal might be too expensive to be feasible. Also, these grants typically have been meant to provide "seed" money for the recipient agencies, and at some point local governments would be required to absorb the cost of a wide-scale expansion of SRO programs.

The analysis presented in this report raises several even more specific issues policymakers might contemplate should Congress consider measures to promote placing more SROs in schools.

- Should the federal government provide grants for school safety that can only be used for hiring SROs, like the CIS program, or should grants be for a more comprehensive approach to school safety, like the Administration's proposed Comprehensive School Safety Program?
- Should the federal government collect annual data on the number of SROs, the type of schools they serve, and their roles in schools?
- If funding is available for hiring SROs, should there be a requirement that the officer(s) attend SRO training before being assigned to a school? Also, should applicants for potential SRO grants be required to submit a signed memorandum of understanding that outlines the responsibilities of the SRO?
- If there are concerns about the presence of SROs resulting in more children being arrested for minor offenses, should there be a limitation on what SROs can do while working at a school? If limitations are placed on the role of SROs, would placing an officer at a school represent the most effective use of the officer's time?
- Should funding for school safety programs be awarded to schools that have higher rates of reported violent incidents or should funding be distributed to law enforcement agencies or LEAs based upon a formula?
- If Congress adopts the Administration's proposal and provides funding for the Comprehensive School Safety Program, would requiring local jurisdictions to submit a comprehensive school safety plan prove to be too onerous a task for some jurisdictions, thereby limiting who would be able to apply for funding? On the other hand, might it provide an indication of which jurisdictions are the best suited for implementing comprehensive school safety programs?
- Should applicants for any potential funding for school safety programs be required to submit a plan for how they will continue funding the program after federal funding ends? Should priority be given to applicants who can continue to operate programs after the grant expires?
- If grants are awarded for hiring SROs, should grant recipients be required to submit data that could be used to analyze the effectiveness of SRO programs and their effect on the educational environment? For example, should grant recipients be required to submit data on reported crimes and arrests of students both before and after an SRO is assigned to the school? If so, what if the school district already has a working relationship with the local law enforcement agency and wants to use a grant to permanently assign an officer or officers to one or more schools? Would such a school district be prohibited from receiving a grant for hiring an SRO since it could not provide unbiased baseline data? Would school districts that could not provide baseline data be prohibited from applying for grants?

APPENDIX. DATA ON POLICE DEPARTMENTS AND SHERIFF'S OFFICES REFERENCED IN THE REPORT

This appendix provides tables for some of the data referenced in the body of the report. **Table A-1** and **Table A-2** provide data on the percent of police departments and sheriff's offices using SROs, the total number of officers and deputies who were assigned to work as SROs, and the average number of SROs by the size of the jurisdiction served.

Table A-1. School Resources Officers Employed by Police Departments

	Percent of Agencies Using				Total Number of Officers				Average Number of Officers			
	1997	2000	2003	2007	1997	2000	2003	2007	1997	2000	2003	2007
All sizes	38%	44%	43%	38%	9,446	13,760	14,337	13,056	3	2	3	3
1 million or more	75%	73%	69%	77%	874	942	855	913	93	85	75	87
500,000-999,999	67%	67%	73%	71%	306	603	760	788	40	26	27	34
250,000-499,999	65%	85%	93%	89%	462	497	715	664	49	15	18	15
100,000-249,999	80%	85%	87%	85%	807	1,193	1,468	1,480	17	8	10	9
50,000-99,999	77%	86%	83%	88%	901	1,380	1,893	1,678	8	4	5	4
25,000-49,999	70%	82%	84%	88%	1,060	1,757	1,734	1,950	5	3	3	3
10,000-24,999	62%	66%	70%	68%	1,493	2,127	2,441	1,992	2	2	2	2
2,500-9,999	42%	45%	44%	34%	2,009	3,095	2,861	2,142	1	2	2	2
Under 2,500	21%	25%	20%	16%	1,533	2,167	1,611	1,447	1	2	2	2

Source: CRS presentation of data from the U.S. Department of Justice, Office of Justice Programs, Bureau of Justice Statistics, *Local Police Departments* for 1997, 2000, 2003, and 2007.

Notes: Average number of officers excludes agencies that did not employ any full-time SROs.

Table A-2. School Resource Officers Employed by Sheriff's Offices

	Percent of Agencies Using				Total Number of Deputies				Average Number of Deputies			
	1997	2000	2003	2007	1997	2000	2003	2007	1997	2000	2003	2007
All sizes	38%	48%	47%	50%	2,897	5,311	5,554	6,032	2	4	4	4
1 million or more	64%	59%	89%	85%	223	872	351	589	11	44	14	23
500,000-999,999	46%	66%	71%	71%	195	418	488	429	7	9	10	10
250,000-499,999	54%	70%	67%	69%	304	607	748	873	5	8	9	10
100,000-249,999	60%	63%	66%	73%	689	951	1,306	1,231	4	5	6	5
50,000-99,999	44%	62%	54%	60%	360	712	749	1,137	2	3	4	4
25,000-49,999	46%	52%	51%	56%	538	805	898	672	2	2	3	2
10,000-24,999	35%	40%	45%	43%	419	603	694	700	1	2	2	2
2,500-9,999	16%	33%	26%	27%	169	344	320	402	1	2	2	2
Under 2,500	21%	25%	20%	16%	1,533	2,167	1,611	1,447	1	2	2	2

Source: CRS presentation of data from the U.S. Department of Justice, Office of Justice Programs, Bureau of Justice Statistics, *Sheriff's Offices* for 1997, 2000, 2003, and 2007.

Notes: Average number of deputies excludes offices that did not employ any full-time SROs.

Table A-3. Per Department Operating Budget and Average Number of Sworn Officers, Police Departments, 2007

	Per Department Operating Budget	Average Number of Sworn Officers
1 million or more	$848,799,000	6,790
500,000-999,999	211,991,000	1,575
250,000-499,999	93,414,000	713
100,000-249,999	38,844,000	289
50,000-99,999	16,068,000	122
25,000-49,999	7,474,000	63
10,000-24,999	3,260,000	31
2,500-9,999	1,127,000	12
Under 2,500	263,000	3

Source: CRS presentation of data from the U.S. Department of Justice, Office of Justice Programs, Bureau of Justice Statistics, *Local Police Departments, 2007.*

Table A-4. Per Department Operating Budget and Average Number of Sworn Deputies, Sheriff's Offices, 2007

	Per Department Operating Budget	Average Number of Sworn Officers
1 million or more	$336,753,000	1,396
500,000-999,999	68,447,000	331
250,000-499,999	34,897,000	194
100,000-249,999	15,139,000	102
50,000-99,999	7,095,000	52
25,000-49,999	3,194,000	28
10,000-24,999	1,659,000	14
Under 10,000	657,000	6

Source: CRS presentation of data from the U.S. Department of Justice, Office of Justice Programs, Bureau of Justice Statistics, *Sheriff's Offices, 2007.*

End Notes

[1] David Nakamura and Tom Hamburger, "Put Armed Police in Every School, NRA Urges," *Washington Post,* December 21, 2012, http://articles.washingtonpost.com/2012-12-21/politics/35950179_1_gun-regulation-national-school-shield-program-gun-violence/2.

[2] The COPS Office announced that applicants for hiring grants under the COPS Hiring Program (CHP) who request funding for hiring and deploying SROs will receive additional consideration for FY2013 CHP funding. U.S. Department of Justice, Community Oriented Policing Services Office, *2013 COPS Hiring Program,* Fact Sheet, p. 2, http://www.cops.usdoj.gov/pdf/2013AwardDocs/CHP/2013_CHP-Preaward-FactSheet.pdf.

[3] Barbara Raymond, *Assigning Police Officers to Schools,* U.S. Department of Justice, Community Oriented Policing Services Office, Problem-oriented Guides for Police Response Guides Series No. 10, Washington, DC, April 2010, p. 1, http://www.cops.usdoj.gov/Publications/e041028272-assign-officers-to-schools.pdf, hereinafter *"Assigning Police Officers to Schools."*

[4] Ben Brown, "Understanding and Assessing School Police Officers: A Conceptual and Methodological Comment," *Journal of Criminal Justice,* vol. 34, no. 6 (November-December 2006), p. 591, hereinafter "Understanding and Assessing School Police Officers."

[5] Chongmin Na and Denise C. Gottfredson, "Police Officers in Schools: Effects on School Crime and the Processing of Offender Behaviors," *Justice Quarterly,* online publication, 2011, p. 3, hereinafter "Police Officers in Schools: Effects on School Crime and the Processing of Offender Behaviors."

[6] Understanding and Assessing School Police Officers, p. 593.

[7] *Assigning Police Officers to Schools,* p. 2.

[8] Ibid.

[9] Ibid., p. 4.

[10] Ibid., p. 5.

[11] Lawrence F. Travis III and Julie K. Coon, *The Role of Law Enforcement in Public School Safety: A National Survey*, July 10, 2005, p. 85, https://www.ncjrs.gov/pdffiles1/nij/grants/211676.pdf, hereinafter "*The Role of Law Enforcement in Public School Safety*."

[12] Ibid.

[13] Ibid., p. 84.

[14] Ibid, p. 86.

[15] Ibid.

[16] Ibid.

[17] Ibid.

[18] *Assigning Police Officers to Schools*, p. 1.

[19] The LEMAS survey collects data from over 3,000 state and local law enforcement agencies, including all those that employ 100 or more sworn officers and a nationally representative sample of smaller agencies. Data are obtained on the organization and administration of police and sheriff's departments, including agency responsibilities, operating expenditures, job functions of sworn and civilian employees, officer salaries and special pay, demographic characteristics of officers, weapons and armor policies, education and training requirements, computers and information systems, vehicles, special units, and community policing activities.

[20] U.S. Department of Education, National Center for Education Statistics, *2007-08 School Survey on Crime and Safety (SSOCS)*, Table 34, http://nces.ed.gov/surveys/ssocs/tables/all_2008_tab_34.asp?referrer=css.

[21] Ibid.

[22] Ibid.

[23] U.S. Department of Education, National Center for Education Statistics, *School Survey on Crime and Safety, Principal Questionnaire, 2007-08 School Year*, p. 8, http://nces.ed.gov/surveys/ssocs/pdf/SSOCS_2008_Questionnaire.pdf.

[24] *Assigning Police Officers to Schools*, p. 1.

[25] U.S. Department of Justice, Community Oriented Policing Services Office, *COPS in Schools (CIS)*, http://www.cops.usdoj.gov/default.asp?Item=54.

[26] Police Officers in Schools: Effects on School Crime and the Processing of Offender Behaviors, pp. 2-3.

[27] Annual appropriations for the CIS program are as follows: $167.5 million (FY1999), $180.0 million (FY2000), $179.6 million (FY2001), $180.0 million (FY2002), $39.7 million (FY2003), $59.4 million (FY2004), $4.9 million (FY2005).

[28] Email correspondence with the U.S. Department of Justice, Community Oriented Policing Services Office, March 11, 2013.

[29] Starting in FY2011, the COPS Office asked law enforcement agencies applying for grants under the CHP to identify a public safety problem area that their grants funds would be used to address. According to the COPS Office, 11.5% of the FY2011 applicants and 22.9% of the FY2012 applicants identified "school based policing" as their problem area. In addition, 10.4% of funded applications for the FY2011 CHP and 22.3% of applications for FY2012 CHP were for school based policing. Email correspondence with the U.S. Department of Justice, Community Oriented Policing Services Office, April 1, 2013.

[30] As part of its proposal to reauthorize the ESEA, which is under consideration in the 113th Congress, the Obama Administration has proposed significant changes to the SDFSCA. The reauthorization proposal would consolidate several smaller programs into a new broader program titled "Successful, Safe, and Healthy Students." For more information on the SDFSCA see CRS Report RL33980, *School and Campus Safety Programs and Requirements in the Elementary and Secondary Education Act and Higher Education Act*, by Gail McCallion and Rebecca R. Skinner.

[31] On October 20, 1994, President William J. Clinton signed into law the Improving America's School Act (P.L. 103-382), which reauthorized the ESEA, and created the SDFSCA as Title IV. The 1994 legislation extended, amended, and renamed the Drug-Free Schools and Communities Act of 1988 (DFSCA; P.L. 100-297). Violence prevention was added to DFSCA's original drug abuse-prevention purpose by incorporating the Safe Schools Act. The Safe Schools Act was originally created by Title VII of the Goals 2000: Educate America Act of 1994 (P.L. 103-227).

[32] Although funding is no longer provided for SDFSCA State Formula Grants, funding continues to be provided for several National Programs. The authorization of appropriations for the SDFSCA expired at the end of FY2008; funding has continued to be provided for National Programs through appropriations legislation.

[33] The SDFSCA includes an extensive list of activities that are allowable uses of funds by LEAs, including the activities that that are part of the President's proposed Comprehensive School Safety Plan, discussed later in this report.

[34] *The Role of Law Enforcement in Public School Safety*, p. 47.

[35] Ibid., pp. 48-49.

[36] Ibid., p. 53.

[37] Ibid., pp. 49-50.

[38] *Assigning Police Officers to Schools*, p. 7.

[39] Police Officers in Schools: Effects on School Crime and the Processing of Offender Behaviors, p. 5.

[40] Ibid., p. 6.

[41] Ibid.

[42] Ibid.

[43] See for example Ida M. Johnson, "School Violence: The Effectiveness of a School Resource Officer Program in a Southern City," *Journal of Criminal Justice*, vol. 27, no. 2 (1999), pp. 173-192.

[44] See for example Arrick Jackson, "Police-school Resource Officers' and Students' Perception of the Police and Offending," *Policing: An International Journal of Police Strategies and Management*, vol. 25, no. 3 (2002), pp. 631- 650.

[45] *Assigning Police Officers to Schools*, p. 8.

[46] Peter Finn and Jack McDevitt, *National Assessment of School Resource Officer Programs: Final Project Report*, Washington, DC, February 28, 2005, p. 47, https://www.ncjrs.gov/pdffiles1/nij/grants/209273.pdf, hereinafter "*National Assessment of School Resource Officer Programs*."

[47] Marie Skubak Tillyer, Bonnie S. Fisher, and Pamela Wilcox, "The Effects of School Crime Prevention on Students' Violent Victimization, Risk Perception, and Fear of Crime: A Multilevel Opportunity Perspective," *Justice Quarterly*, vol. 28, no. 2 (April 2011), pp. 249-277.

[48] Wesley G. Jennings, David N. Khey, and Jon Maskaly, et al., "Evaluating the Relationship Between Law Enforcement and School Security Measures and Violent Crime in Schools," *Journal of Police Crisis Negotiations*, vol. 11, no. 2 (2011), pp. 109-124.

[49] Police Officers in Schools: Effects on School Crime and the Processing of Offender Behaviors.

[50] "Serious violent" crimes included rape, sexual battery other than rape, robbery with or without a weapon, physical attack or fight with a weapon, and threat of physical attach with a weapon.

[51] "Non-serious violent" crimes included physical attack or fight without a weapon and threat of physical attack without a weapon.

[52] "Property" crimes included theft and vandalism.

[53] "Weapons and drug" offenses included possession of a firearm or explosive device; possession of a knife or sharp object; and distribution, possession, or use of illegal drugs or alcohol.

[54] *Assigning Police Officers to Schools*, p. 22.

[55] Problem-solving policing involves changing the conditions that give rise to recurring crime problems. Ibid., p. 24.

[56] Ibid., p. 22.

[57] Ibid.

[58] Ibid., p. 30.

[59] Ibid.

[60] *National Assessment of School Resource Officer Programs*, p. 43.

[61] *Assigning Police Officers to Schools*, p. 23.

[62] Ibid., p. 24.

[63] *National Assessment of School Resource Officer Programs*, p. 44.

[64] U.S. Department of Justice, Community Oriented Policing Services Office, *FY2014 Performance Budget, Office of Community Oriented Policing Services*, March 2013, p. 26, http://www.justice.gov/jmd/2014 justification/pdf/cops-justification.pdf, hereinafter "COPS FY2014 budget justifications."

[65] Ibid., p. 27.

[66] Ibid.

[67] Ibid.

[68] 42 U.S.C. §3797a et seq.

[69] 42 U.S.C. §3797a(b).

[70] *Assigning Police Officers to Schools*, p. 15.

[71] Public mass shootings, as defined by CRS, are "incidents occurring in relatively public places, involving four or more deaths—not including the shooter(s)—and gunmen who select victims somewhat indiscriminately. The violence in these cases is not a means to an end such as robbery or terrorism." CRS Report R43004, *Public Mass Shootings in the United States: Selected Implications for Federal Public Health and Safety Policy*, coordinated by Jerome P. Bjelopera.

[72] Of the eight remaining shootings: a) three involved non-students targeting elementary schools, b) one involved a gunman targeting people at the high school he formerly attended, c) four occurred on college campuses and involved either active or former students. CRS did not identify a public mass shooting involving a student attending elementary school who acted as an assailant in an incident at his or her own school. Ibid.

[73] A "school-associated violent death" is defined as a homicide, suicide, or legal intervention (involving a law enforcement officer), in which the fatal injury occurred on the campus of a functioning elementary or secondary school in the United States. Victims of school-associated violent deaths include not only students and staff, but also others who are not students or staff, such as parents. School-associated violent deaths include those that occurred while the victim was attending or traveling to or from an official school-sponsored

event. U.S. Department of Education, Institute of Education Sciences, National Center for Education Statistics, *Indicators of School Crime and Safety:2012*, Table 1.1, http://nces.ed.gov/programs/crimeindicators/ crimeindicators2012/index.asp, hereinafter *"Indicators of School Crime and Safety."*

[74] Ibid.

[75] Ibid.

[76] Ibid.

[77] "Serious violent crime" includes rape or sexual assault, robbery, or aggravated assault.

[78] Nicole White and Janet L. Lauritsen, *Violent Crime Against Youth, 1994-2010*, U.S. Department of Justice, Office of Justice Programs, Bureau of Justice Statistics, NCJ 240106, Washington, DC, December 2012, p. 9, http://www.bjs.gov/content/pub/pdf/vcay9410.pdf, hereinafter *"Violent Crime Against Youth."*

[79] National Association of School Resource Officers, *To Protect and Educate: The School Resource Officer and the Prevention of Violence in Schools*, October 2012, p. 9, http://www.nasro.org/sites/default/files/pdf_files/ NASRO_Protect_and_Educate.pdf.

[80] U.S. Department of Justice, Office of Justice Programs, Office of Juvenile Justice and Delinquency Prevention, *OJJDP Statistical Briefing Book, Juvenile Homicide Victims, 1980-2010*, Online, released July 31, 2012, http://www.ojjdp.gov/ojstatbb/victims/qa02304.asp?qaDate=2010.

[81] *Assigning Police Officers to Schools*, p. 1; Police Officers in Schools: Effects on School Crime and the Processing of Offender Behaviors, p. 2

[82] National Association of School Resource Officers, *School Safety Left Behind? School Safety Threat Grows as Preparedness Stalls & Funding Decreases*, Final Report on the 4th Annual National Survey of School-based Police Officers, February 2005, p. 20, http://www.schoolsecurity.org/resources/2004%20NASRO% 20Survey%20Final%20Report%20NSSSS.pdf.

[83] U.S. Department of Education, National Center for Education Statistics, *Digest of Education Statistics, 2011*, Table 5, http://nces.ed.gov/programs/digest/d11/tables/dt11_005.asp.

[84] Brian A. Reaves, *Local Police Departments, 2007*, U.S. Department of Justice, Office of Justice Programs, Bureau of Justice Statistics, NCJ 231174, Washington, DC, December 2010, p. 12, http://www.bjs.gov/ content/ pub/pdf/lpd07.pdf, hereinafter *"Local Police Departments, 2007."*

[85] Andrea M. Burch, *Sheriff's Offices, 2007—Statistical Tables*, U.S. Department of Justice, Office of Justice Programs, Bureau of Justice Statistics, NCJ 238558, Washington, DC, December 2012, p. 7, http:// www.bjs.gov/content/pub/pdf/ lpd07.pdf, hereinafter *"Sheriff's Offices, 2007."*

[86] There were a reported 463,147 sworn police officers and 172,241 sheriff's deputies in 2007 for a total of 635,388 sworn law enforcement officers. Therefore the weighted average salary for law enforcement officers was calculated as (($32,900 * 463,147) + ($31,100 * 172,241)) / 635,388.

[87] *Local Police Departments, 2007*, p. 9; *Sheriff's Offices, 2007*, p. 6.

[88] Donna St. George, "Texas Students Sent From Classroom to Courtroom," *The Washington Post*, August 21, 2011.

[89] Leslie Postal and Lauren Roth, "Thousands of Student Arrests Alarm Florida Justice Leaders," *The Orlando Sentinel*, February 10, 2013 Greg Toppo, "Students, Civil Rights Groups Say 'No' to School Cops," *USA Today*, April 6, 2013; Donna Lieberman, "Schoolhouse to Courthouse," *The New York Times*, December 8, 2012.

[90] Police Officers in Schools: Effects on School Crime and the Processing of Offender Behaviors, p. 4.

[91] Office of Senator Richard Durbin, "Durbin Holds Hearing on Ending the School-to-Prison Pipeline," press release, December 12, 2012, http://www.durbin.senate.cfm/pressreleases?ID=7dcaee2b-b40e-4199-bf20- 557b4b1bc650.

[92] The analysis compared arrests at middle and high schools with SROs (SRO schools) to middle and high schools without SROs (non-SRO schools). The researcher took advantage of a natural experiment in the school district whereby the metropolitan city's police department placed an SRO in each middle and high school in the city while middle and high schools in the district that were outside the city limits did not have a SRO assigned to them. SROs were assigned based only on geography, not on a school's need, history of violence, or demographics. Schools outside of the city were patrolled by sheriff's deputies, who focused solely on law enforcement activities, were assigned to patrol more than one school, and received less training in school-based training than their SRO counterparts in the city. Matthew T. Theriot, "School Resource Officers and the Criminalization of Student Behavior," *Journal of Criminal Justice*, vol. 37, no. 3 (May-June 2009), pp. 280-287.

[93] Police Officers in Schools: Effects on School Crime and the Processing of Offender Behaviors, p. 7.

[94] Police Officers in Schools: Effects on School Crime and the Processing of Offender Behaviors.

[95] Ibid., p. 22.

[96] These data are based on responses from the school principal or the person most knowledgeable about crime and safety issues at the school. The three examples included here experienced the greatest percentage increase; for a complete list see Roberts, S., Zhang, J., and Truman, J. (2012). *Indicators of School Crime and Safety: 2011* (NCES 2012-002/NCJ 236021). National Center for Education Statistics, U.S. Department of Education, and Bureau of Justice Statistics, Office of Justice Programs, U.S. Department of Justice. Washington, DC.

[97] This information is based on the percentage of students ages 12-18 who reported selected security measures at school. Roberts, S., Zhang, J., and Truman, J. (2012). *Indicators of School Crime and Safety: 2011* (NCES 2012- 002/NCJ 236021). National Center for Education Statistics, U.S. Department of Education, and Bureau of Justice Statistics, Office of Justice Programs, U.S. Department of Justice. Washington, DC.

[98] The Gun Free Schools Act (GFSA) was included in the 1994 (P.L. 103-382) reauthorization of the Elementary and Secondary Education Act (ESEA). GFSA requires states to enact a law that obligates schools to impose a one year expulsion on any student who brings a weapon to school. However, the law permits the chief administering officer of a local educational agency (LEA) to modify the expulsion requirement on a case-by-case basis.

[99] These data are based on a sample of 7,000 school districts and 72,000 students. Data on suspensions are broken down by race, sex and disability. The Office for Civil Rights indicates that 85% of the nation's public school students are covered by this survey, however it is not intended to be viewed as an estimation of national data. See http://www2.ed.gov/about/offices/list/ocr/docs/crdc-2012-data-summary.pdf.

[100] The survey defines students with a disability as those served under the Individuals with Disabilities Education Act.

[101] http://www2.ed.gov/about/offices/list/ocr/docs/crdc-2012-data-summary.pdf.

[102] American Psychological Association Zero Tolerance Task Force, "Are Zero Tolerance Policies Effective in the Schools? An Evidentiary Review and Recommendations," *American Psychologist*, vol. 63, no. 9 (December 2008), pp. 852-862.

[103] The Department of Education's Office of Special Education Programs funds a Technical Assistance Center on Positive Behavioral Interventions and Supports. The Center provides capacity-building information and technical assistance to schools, districts, and states who are implementing a school climate protocol called *School-wide Positive Behavioral Interventions and Supports* (SWPBIS). SWPBIS is a three-tiered prevention-based approach to improving schoolwide disciplinary practices. According to the Center, SWPBIS is used in more than 9,000 schools across 40 states.

[104] Centers for Disease Control and Prevention, School Connectedness: *Strategies for Increasing Protection Factors Among Youth*, Atlanta, GA, Department of Health and Human Services, 2009, p.7.

[105] See http://www.cdc.gov/healthyyouth/adolescenthealth/pdf/connectedness.pdf.

[106] The National School Climate Center and the Education Commission of the States have developed a definition of school climate: "School climate refers to the quality and character of school life. School climate is based on patterns of students', parents' and school personnel's experience of school life and reflects norms, goals, values, interpersonal relationships, teaching and learning practices, and organizational structures. A sustainable, positive school climate fosters youth development and learning necessary for a productive, contributing and satisfying life in a democratic society. This climate includes (1) Norms, values and expectations that support people feeling socially, emotionally and physically safe. (2) People are engaged and respected. (3) Students, families and educators work together to develop, live and contribute to a shared school vision. (4) Educators model and nurture attitudes that emphasize the benefits and satisfaction gained from learning. (5) Each person contributes to the operations of the school and the care of the physical environment. See http://www.schoolclimate.org/climate.

[107] Available at http://www.schoolclimate.org/climate/documents/policy/sc-brief-v3.pdf.

[108] The Collaborative for Academic, Social, and Emotional Learning (CASEL) defines social emotional learning as: "... the processes through which adults and children develop social and emotional competencies in five areas:" self- awareness, self-management, social awareness, relationship skills, and responsible decision making. Collaborative for Academic, Social, and Emotional Learning, *The Missing Piece: A National Teacher Survey on How Social and Emotional Learning Can Empower Children and Transform Schools*, May 2013, p. 4, http://casel.org/wp-content/uploads/casel-themissingpiece-report.pdf.

[109] Catherine Bradshaw, et al., "Examining the Effects of Schoolwide Positive Behavioral Interventions and Supports on Student Outcomes," *Journal of Positive Behavior Interventions*, vol. 12, no. 3 (July 2010).

[110] Assistance is provided through a U.S. Department of Education funded Technical Assistance Center on Positive Behavioral Interventions and Supports.

[111] Catherine Bradshaw, et al., "Examining the Effects of Schoolwide Positive Behavioral Interventions and Supports on Student Outcomes," *Journal of Positive Behavior Interventions*, vol. 12, no. 3 (July 2010).

[112] For more information on this program see http://www.sshs.samhsa.gov/.

In: School Resource Officers
Editor: Andrew O'Murphy

ISBN: 978-1-62808-850-2
© 2013 Nova Science Publishers, Inc.

Chapter 2

NATIONAL ASSESSMENT OF SCHOOL RESOURCE OFFICER PROGRAMS: FINAL PROJECT REPORT[*]

Peter Finn and Jack McDevitt

FINAL PROJECT REPORT

With support from the Office of Community Oriented Policing Services (the COPS Office), through a cooperative agreement with the National Institute of Justice (NIJ), Abt Associates conducted a National Assessment of School Resource Officer (SRO) programs.

INTRODUCTION

There has been a growing interest in placing sworn police officers in schools as SROs to improve school safety. However, when this project began in May 2000, little was known about SRO programs. The purpose of the National Assessment was to identify what program "models" have been implemented, how programs have been implemented, and what the programs' possible effects may be. To obtain this information, *Abt Associates conducted a nationwide survey of established and relatively new SRO programs and collected implementation data by telephone and on site from 19 SRO programs.*

Three subcontractors assisted in collecting, analyzing, and reporting the data:

- The Center for Criminal Justice Policy Research at Northeastern University,
- The Justice and Safety Center, College of Justice and Safety, at Eastern Kentucky University, and
- the Center for the Prevention of School Violence in North Carolina.

---

[*] This is an edited, reformatted and augmented version of the National Institute of Justice, dated February 28, 2005.

Two consultants assisted Northeastern University in collecting and analyzing the data:

- Timothy Bynum, School of Criminal Justice at Michigan State University, and
- Scott Decker, Department of Criminology and Criminal Justice at the University of Missouri-St. Louis.

This report describes the activities the project team conducted for the National Assessment and summarizes the study findings. The report has five sections, which follow the chronology of the project:

- **Mail Survey**—a summary of the methodology and findings of the first significant project task.
- **Selection of Study Sites**—a review of the site selection criteria and the sites selected.
- **The Site Visits**—a description of the preparation for, goals, and conduct of the site visits.
- **Modifications to the Research Methodology**—a description of the change from an outcome study to a process evaluation for the large new sites and the reasons for the change.
- **Data Analysis and Findings**—a summary of the methodology and findings of the five other reports prepared under the project.

In addition to this Final Project Report, the study produced five other reports:

1. The *National Survey of SRO Programs and Affiliated Schools* summarizes the results of 322 responses to a mail survey of law enforcement agencies with SRO programs and 108 responses from affiliated schools.
2. An *Interim Report: Fear and Trust* summarizes preliminary impressionistic observations concerning (a) perceptions of fear about campus safety among school administrators, faculty, and students among 15 of the 19 sites and (b) trust in the police among these groups in the 15 sites.
3. *Case Studies of 19 School Resource Officer (SRO) Programs* provides in-depth descriptions of each program's history, SROs, program activities, and program monitoring and evaluation.
4. *Results of a Survey of Students in Three Large New SRO Programs* presents the results of a survey of nearly 1,000 students designed to identify the relationship between perceptions of safety and the SRO program.
5. *Comparison of Program Activities and Lessons Learned among 19 School Resource Officer (SRO) Programs* compares the 19 programs in terms of seven key dimensions, with a focus on lessons learned: choosing a program model; defining specific SRO roles and responsibilities; recruiting SROs; training and supervising SROs; collaborating with school administrators and teachers; working with students and parents; and evaluating SRO programs.

MAIL SURVEY

The first significant project task involved conducting a mail survey of SRO programs and affiliated schools, primarily to document the nature of existing SRO programs and to help guide site selection for the site visits. A separate report submitted in May 2001 to NIJ, "Report on the National Survey of SRO Programs and Affiliated Schools," provides a detailed account of the survey methodology and results of the survey. A brief summary of the methodology and findings follows.

Mail Survey Methodology

Using the 1999 Law Enforcement Management and Administrative Statistics (LEMAS) database and the list of COPS Office 1999 grantees, during the summer of 2000 we sent a survey to a random sample of 454 law enforcement agencies with SRO programs, stratified by department size and age. Efforts to increase the response rate included sending postcards to 226 programs that had not returned their surveys after a month and then telephoning programs that did not return their surveys in response to the postcards. Surveys were eventually returned by 322 agencies (71 percent).

The survey instrument's 29 questions addressed five principal areas:

(1) administrative information (e.g., who funds the program);
(2) nature of school safety problems at the participating schools (e.g., bullying);
(3) activities of SROs (e.g., teaching crime awareness classes);
(4) community policing (e.g., groups involved in the collaboration); and
(5) evaluation (e.g., types of data routinely collected).

In September 2000, we mailed a second survey, similar in content to the law enforcement survey, to 295 schools that the responding law enforcement agencies identified in their survey responses. During the week of October 30, 2000, we telephoned 214 schools and faxed every school that had not returned its survey asking it to do so. A total of 108 schools eventually returned the school surveys (37 percent).

Summary of Results of the SRO Survey

The results of the mail survey indicated that *there is tremendous diversity in structure and activities* among the responding programs (e.g., number of full-time SROs, number of schools served). At the same time, *in some respects there is considerable similarity* among responding programs (e.g., law enforcement oversight of the program, provision of specialized training for SROs). Other noteworthy findings included the following.

- Most programs receive funding from more than one source, with the local law enforcement agency by far the most common single source of funding (70 percent of programs).

- The average program serves five schools. Eighty-five percent of programs serve high schools, 65 percent middle schools (grades 6-8), 47 serve elementary schools (K-5 or K-6), and 35 percent junior high schools (grades 7-9).
- In general, most SROs engage in several—often many—distinct and very different activities. For example:
  - SROs in over three-quarters of the programs engage in up to 10 different kinds of law enforcement activities, from patrolling school facilities to issuing citations.
  - SROs in over half the programs advise school staff, students, or families.
  - SROs in at least half the programs focus on teaching students about drugs, legal issues, safety education, crime awareness, and conflict resolution.
- SROs programs spend an average of 20 hours per week on law enforcement activities, 10 on advising or mentoring, 5 on teaching, and 6 to 7 on other activities combined. However, SROs from different programs spend very different percentages of time on law enforcement versus advising versus teaching.

The survey results also showed that *the vast majority of responding schools expressed considerable satisfaction with their programs*. The following observations based on the survey results were also noteworthy.

- While it might be thought that elementary schools are least in need of SRO programs, nearly half the programs surveyed serve elementary schools.
- Many programs are currently addressing many more school safety problems than they were originally established to address.
- It appears that many SROs engage in activities for which they have not been trained, including mentoring and teaching.
- Most programs fail to collect important process and outcome evaluation data.

Several of these observations pointed to areas to explore further during the site visits. The survey also helped us to identify sites to visit as part of the study.

Selection of Study Sites

The second principal project task was selecting 20 programs to study in depth through on-site visits and, as needed, telephone callbacks. We planned to include five of each of the following types of programs in the study:

- large established programs;
- large new programs;
- small established programs; and
- small new programs.

We defined "large" SRO programs as those operated by law enforcement agencies with 100 or more sworn officers and "small" programs as those operated by agencies with less than 100 officers (the Bureau of Justice Statistics' definitions for large and small agencies). As these definitions indicate, "large" and "small" do not, as might be expected, refer to the law enforcement agency's number of SROs but rather the size of the agency. This was because the LEMAS database did not provide information about the number of SROs in each agency. As a result, we used agency size as a "proxy" for SRO program size because we anticipated (correctly) that by selecting agencies with a range of sworn officers we would end up with programs with a range in the number of SROs because larger law enforcement agencies serve jurisdictions with larger numbers of schools and therefore could be expected to have more SROs than smaller agencies.

We defined "established" programs as those that had been in existence at least since 1995—the median length of time for all large established programs that returned the survey (53 percent were established before 1996). The definition of "new" that we used was that the site had not reported the placement of SROs in schools in the past on the 1999 Bureau of Justice Statistics' LEMAS survey and the site was the recipient of a 1999 COPS Office Cops in Schools grant.

Site Selection Process

We used different methods for selecting each of the four different categories of programs.

Large Established Programs
As part of the mail survey of SRO programs (see above), we mailed the survey questionnaire to 119 large law enforcement agencies (100 or more full-time sworn officers) that the LEMAS database indicated had active SROs. With one exception (see below), the 81 agencies that returned the survey represented the pool of candidate sites for inclusion in the study.

Based on our review of the survey responses, we eliminated from consideration:

- agencies with only a verbal agreement with the participating schools, since these programs were not as likely as programs with written contracts or memorandums of agreement to have an effective program, and
- agencies established since 1995, since these programs failed to meet the median length of existence among the large established programs that returned the survey.

We applied the following criteria to the remaining programs.

- *Regional balance.* We selected agencies that were located in different regions of the country, including the Far West, Mid-West, Southwest, and South. We did not find any eligible agencies in the East (most either had only a verbal agreement with the school system or were recently established). Regional diversity was important for ensuring that agencies that wished to replicate a program could find one described in our study reports which they felt was similar to their own. Geographic diversity would also help take into account local peculiarities that might facilitate or hamper the success of an SRO program.

- *Type of agency.* We wanted to include at least one sheriff's department so that other sheriff's departments would feel represented in the study. In addition, police departments and sheriff's departments might have different implementation and operational problems that it would be important for us to identify.

- *Agency size.* Again, for purposes of representativeness, we selected agencies that had different numbers of sworn officers, ranging from 114 to 1,285. In addition, law enforcement agencies with different sworn strength might have different implementation and operational problems that it would be important for us to identify.

- *Type of problem(s) targeted.* We chose agencies that reported they were addressing different types of discipline and crime problems, ranging from gangs to truancy to drug use. Selecting agencies that were addressing the same problem might have limited the generalizability of the study findings to that one problem. With one exception (see below), we also selected programs that reported that their SROs divided their time among law enforcement, teaching, and mentoring.

- *Other considerations.* Several agencies provided us with particularly promising data, suggesting that they were well administered and monitored, and suggesting that the programs could provide the type of information we would need for our report.

We recommended one program for inclusion in the study that had not returned a survey but with which we were already familiar. We included the program because it had a large number of SROs and was a good example of largely law enforcement model (SROs did relatively little teaching and mentoring, and they were not stationed in the schools— they responded to dispatcher requests to go to a school in their assigned clusters).

Large New Programs

In 1999, the COPS Office awarded Cops in Schools grants to 40 large law enforcement agencies (100 or more full-time sworn officers). We used these grantees as the initial pool for selecting sites to include in the study. To guide our recommendations for sites to include in the study, we reviewed the 35 applications that the COPS Office forwarded to us that the agencies had submitted for SRO funding. Even though the programs received their grant award notices in 1999, the COPS Office had found that it generally takes up to a year for an SRO to be deployed under its hiring grants. As a result, we expected to be able to collect baseline data at any of these programs.

Based on our review, we eliminated nine programs that wanted to use COPS Office funding to *add* SROs to an existing SRO program. We eliminated another program that proposed to use COPS Office funding to *maintain* existing SROs. We reasoned that these sites would not be able to provide us with "lessons learned" about setting up an SRO program. They could, of course, provide information retrospectively about the implementation process, but we would already be visiting 10 established programs that would be able to provide that information.

We applied most of the same criteria to the 25 large new programs that we applied to the large established programs except that we added the following three criteria:

- *Responded to the mail survey.* We sent our SRO mail survey to 10 large, new COPS Office grantees. Six agencies returned the survey. Other considerations being equal, we gave greater preference to agencies that returned our SRO survey under the assumption that these agencies were motivated to cooperate with the data collection that the study would require.
- *Strength of community policing.* We examined the proposals to ensure that the agencies were proposing activities for SROs that would go beyond routine law enforcement duties to include the type of educational and mentoring activities, and problem solving strategies, that are more likely to make them effective as well as conform to the COPS Office mission.
- *Previous relationship with the schools.* We gave increased weight to agencies that reported in their COPS in Schools proposals they already had a close and productive relationship with the schools. These relationships might indicate that the agencies took their responsibilities for working with the schools seriously, which would augur well for the success of their SRO programs.

Small Established Programs

Our initial pool for these sites consisted of programs representing law enforcement agencies with fewer than 100 officers that had reported in the LEMAS survey that they had an established SRO program. We intentionally selected the candidate sites only from North Carolina because the State was one of the first to experiment with SRO programs. In addition, there was an organization in the State that was interested in partnering with us on the study (the Center for the Prevention of School Violence) and could make available local researchers who could effectively collect data from departments and schools in rural areas and small towns better than we might have been able to given the center's credibility throughout the State (e.g., extensive experience working with local schools) and its knowledge of the State's SRO programs.

The Center for the Prevention of School Violence identified the sites and alternative sites (that we recommended to NIJ) based on criteria similar to those we used to select large established programs, such as regional balance, type of agency, agency size, and types of problems addressed.

Small New Programs

Our initial pool for small new sites consisted of programs that had not reported having an SRO program previously and that were recent recipients of Cops in Schools grants. We chose all the small new program candidates from Kentucky because the State had recently made a concerted effort to implement SRO programs statewide, and a sizable number of small rural departments in the State had received COPS Office grants in comparison with rural departments in other states. In addition, as in North Carolina, there was an organization (the Justice and Safety Center, College of Justice and Safety at Eastern Kentucky University) in the State that was interested in partnering with us on the study and could make available credible and experienced local researchers.

The College for Law Enforcement at Eastern Kentucky University selected the programs based on criteria similar to those we used to identify large new programs, including the regional location of the site, the nature of the intervention, the relationship between the school and the police department, and the size and type of the agency. A timely COPS in Schools training conference provided an opportunity for the college to bring together all potential sites for the purpose of explaining the project, soliciting participant comment, and assessing their interest in participating in the study.

Site Selection Recommendations

Based on the application of our criteria, we provided our recommended 20 programs to NIJ in April 2001. We also provided a list of alternative programs in case NIJ rejected one or more of our recommended sites or in the event that initial calls we placed to the preferred sites led us to believe that one or more of these agencies was not, in fact, suitable for inclusion in the study or was reluctant or unwilling to host a site visit.

Indeed, one site in Kentucky did refuse to participate, and we were able to replace the site with the next choice on our list of recommended sites. In addition, because one of the large new sites rejected its COPS Office grant, we had to exclude it, too, from the study.

However, by the time this site had turned down the grant, it was too late to substitute another site. As a result, we included only four large new sites in the study, for a total of 19 SRO programs (5 large established, 4 large new, 5 small established, and 5 small new).

In order to preserve the sites' anonymity, we have not identified the sites by name in this report. However, the matrix on the following page identifies selected characteristics of the 19 programs. As shown, 1 agency is located in the Northeast, 2 are in the Midwest, 12 are in the South, 1 is in the South Central, 2 are in the Southwest, and 1 is in the Far West. There was a disproportionate number of programs in the South because all 5 of the small established programs came from South Carolina and all 5 of the small new programs came from Kentucky.

As the matrix shows, 10 agencies were police departments and 9 were sheriff's departments. The number of sworn officers in the 19 law enforcement agencies ranged from 4 to about 1,000. Four agencies had between 4 and 20 officers; five agencies had between 21 and 50 officers; six agencies had between 51 and 150 officers; and four agencies had more than 150 officers—two had between 151-250 and two had between 900 and 1,000. The number of full-time SROs in each program ranged from 1 to 37, with 8 programs employing 1 to 3 SROs; 7 programs employing 4 to 6 SROs; and 4 programs employing 9 or more SROs. There was considerable variation in the grade levels each program served; however, 2 programs stationed SROs only in junior and senior high schools, and 3 programs served just high schools. SROs in 6 programs served elementary schools (spending most of their time, however, with the middle and high schools "fed" by these elementary schools).

Selected Characteristics of the 19 Programs

Type of Program	Region	Type of Police Agency	Number of Sworn Officers	Number of SROs	Number and Grade Levels of Schools Served	Year Began
Large Established	South	Police	51-150	4	3 junior	1995
Large Established	Midwest	Police	51-150	5	5 junior	1995
Large Established	South	Sheriff	151-250	9	4 high 2 junior 8 middle	1995
Large Established	Southwest	Police	900-1,000	21	21 middle 65 elementary	1962
Large Established	Far West	Police	150-250	15	70 schools[a]	1993
Large New	South Central	Sheriff	51-150	6	2 high 2 middle 3 elementary	2001[b]
Large New	Northeast	Police	51-150	3	1 high 2 middle	2001[b]
Large New	Southwest	Police	900-1,000	37	18 high 20 middle	2001[b]
Large New	Midwest	Sheriff	51-150	5	5 high 6 middle 18 elementary	2001[b]
Small Established	South	Police	21-50	1	1 high	1996
Small Established	South	Police	21-50	3	1 high 2 middle	1993
Small Established	South	Sheriff	21-50	4	2 high 3 middle	1994
Small Established	South	Sheriff	21-50	4	2 high 2 middle	1993
Small Established	South	Sheriff	21-50	4	2 high 2 middle	1994
Small New	South	Police	75-150	2	1 high 2 middle 2 elementary	1999
Small New	South	Police	1-20	2	1 high 1 middle 11 elementary	1999
Small New	South	Sheriff	1-20	1	1 high	2000
Small New	South	Sheriff	1-20	1	1 high	2000
Small New	South	Sheriff	1-20	1	2 high 1 middle	1999

[a] SROs are assigned to clusters of K-12 schools, not to a single school.

[b] However, these programs had had officers posted part time in the schools for many years—see the discussion in the text under "Modifications to the Research Methodology."

VISITING THE SITES

Below, we describe the goals of the site visits, preparation for going on site, and the visits themselves.

Goals of the Site Visits

Abt Associates project staff, along with staff from our three subcontractors—Northeastern University, Eastern Kentucky University, and the Center for the Prevention of School Violence—visited each program at least twice. The three primary goals of the site visits were to:

1. document SRO program planning, implementation, and current activities;
2. assess the level of community policing woven into SRO programs and any lessons learned; and
3. identify perceptions of SRO program effectiveness and, where possible, secure local process and outcome data for analysis.

To achieve these goals, site staff:

- conducted an initial "focus group" with all the significant program participants primarily to achieve a consensus on the program's origins and history;
- interviewed program participants and key stakeholders formally and, when possible, informally (e.g., over lunch, riding in the SROs' cruisers, while shadowing the SROs), including School Resource Officers, local law enforcement administrators, nonsworn school security staff, school district superintendents, school board members, principals and assistant principals, teachers, and local government officials (e.g., mayors, city council members);
- met in every site (except for the large established sites due to a miscommunication) with small groups of teachers in the faculty lounge or over lunch, and with students in one or two classrooms, to ask about the SRO program and their perceptions of its effects (these were convenience samples, of course, designed to give only a qualitative snapshot of some of the perceptions of these two groups about the SRO programs and their effects);
- administered surveys to students at the large new programs;
- collected hard copy and electronic data, such as SRO progress reports and program public relations materials; and
- observed SROs' daily activities for at least one full day by shadowing at least one SRO around the campus (and off campus, as needed—for example, when the SRO took a student to the jail for fighting).

In programs that served multiple schools, we either singled out one school for intensive investigation or examined in detail a few schools the program served, choosing schools that were considered by program administrators to have implemented the program most comprehensively and effectively.

Site Visit Planning

We developed a site visit preparation and activities protocol to guide site visit staff in planning and conducting their visits. The planning instructions covered three areas: setting up visits with the sites, planning the visits, and scheduling site activities.

We also developed site interview guides that addressed eight areas:

1. program planning,
2. program implementation,
3. the current program,
4. meetings with groups of students and teachers,
5. an observation checklist for shadowing the SROs,
6. changes in policies and procedures that might influence outcomes,
7. implementation process and outcome data, and
8. site demographic information.

Site Visits

The matrix on the following page indicates when each site was visited, the number of project staff who went on each visit, how may days each site visit lasted, and the total number of days and person days staff spent at each site. As shown, we spent a total of 198 person days on site (between two and three project staff went on most of the visits), or the equivalent of almost 40 work weeks.

There were no difficulties with the site visits except delays on the part of some agencies in scheduling the visits and the need for us to schedule them when school was in session. Every site was accommodating in hosting the program staff and facilitating the interviews with and observations of the SROs.

MODIFICATION TO THE RESEARCH METHODOLOGY

The original study design called for a pre/post impact evaluation of the four large new programs selected for examination. However, as explained below, for reasons beyond anyone's control, the impact evaluation could not be implemented.

First, as noted above, in selecting new sites for inclusion in the study, we used a definition of "new" that required that (1) the site had not reported the placement of SROs in schools in the past on the Bureau of Justice Statistics' LEMAS survey and (2) the site was the recipient of a 1999 Cops in Schools grant. Since these sites were new, we planned to implement pre/post surveys of school students to measure potential changes in perceptions about the SRO program.

As noted above, even though the programs received their grant award notices in 1999, the COPS Office had found that it generally takes up to a year after award for a law enforcement agency to deploy its officers as SRO. As a result, we expected to be able to collect baseline data from all of these programs.

Selected Information about the Site Visits

Site	When Visited	Number of Site Visit Staff per Visit	Duration of Each Site Visit	Total Number of Days On Site	Total Person Days on Site
Large Established	Oct. 15-17, 2001 May 1-2, 2002	1 1	3 days 2 days	5 days	5 days
Large Established	Sept. 26-28, 2001 May 21-22, 2002	1 1	3 days 2 days	5 days	5 days
Large Established	Aug. 28-30, 2001 May 14-15, 2002	1	3 days 2 days	5 days	5 days
Large Established	Oct. 24-26, 2001 April 16-18, 2002	1	3 days 2 days	5 days	5 days
Large Established	June 4,6,7, 2001 May 2002	1 1	3 days 2 days	5 days	5 days
Large New	Mar. 28-29, 2002 Nov. 18-19, 2002	3 2	2 days 2 days	4 days	10 days
Large New	Nov. 5-9, 2001 Dec. 13-14, 2001 Mar. 20-21, 2002 Nov. 4-5, 2002	1 3 3 2	5 days 2 days 2 days 2 days	11 days	21 days
Large New	Sept. 6-7, 2001 Mar. 6-8, 2002 Dec. 2-4, 2002 Jan. 21-23, 2003	2 5 3 2	2 days 3 days 3 days 3 days	11 days	34 days
Large New	Jan. 30-31, 2002 Oct. 21-25, 2002	3 2	2 days 5 days	7 days	16 days
Small Established	Nov. 30, 2001 Nov. 8, 2002	2 2	1 day 1 day	2 days	4 days
Small Established	Oct. 15-16, 2001 Nov. 4-5, 2002	3 2	2 days 2 days	4 days	10 days
Small Established	Nov. 5-6, 2001 Oct.30-Nov.1,2002	3 2	2 days 2 days	4 days	10 days
Small Established	Oct. 29-30, 2001 Oct. 29-30, 2002	3 3	2 days 2 days	4 days	12 days
Small Established	Nov. 7-8, 2001 Nov. 12, 2002	2 2	2 days 1 day	3 days	6 days
Small New	Nov. 26-27, 2001 May 6-7, 2002	2 2	2 days 2 days	4 days	8 days
Small New	May 7-8, 2001 Dec. 3-4, 2001 May 1-2, 2002	2 2 2	2 days 2 days 2 days	6 days	12 days

Site	When Visited	Number of Site Visit Staff per Visit	Duration of Each Site Visit	Total Number of Days On Site	Total Person Days on Site
Small New	May 9-10, 2001 Dec. 5-6, 2002 May 13-14, 2002	2 2 2	2 days 2 days 2 days	6 days	12 days
Small New	May 2001 Dec. 5-6, 2001 May 13-14, 2002	2 2 2	2 days 2 days 2 days	6 days	12 days
Small New	May 2001 Feb. 21-22, 2002 May 16-17, 2002	2 1 1	1 day 2 days 2 days	5 days	6 days
TOTAL	6/4/01 – 1/ 31/04	2-4 visits	1-5 days	102 days	198 days

However, during the initial telephone calls and site visits to the large new sites, while the law enforcement agencies and schools reported that they had indeed received Cops in Schools awards in 1999, they also reported that they had had police officers stationed part time in the schools for 2-1/2 to 25 years teaching various classes (e.g., Drug Abuse Resistance Education [D.A.R.E.], Gang Resistance Education and Training [G.R.E.A.T.]) and mentoring students. Furthermore, most of the "new" SRO officers were the same individuals who had already been working in the schools for several years. Finally, after the grant award the SROs often continued performing many of the same activities that as regular officers they had been conducting previously.

Under these circumstances, the site program supervisors said that a pre/post survey would not make sense without significant changes in personnel posted to the schools or, in some cases, in the officers' responsibilities, because a survey could not link or attribute any change in attitudes toward the officers, fear of crime, or reductions in crime and student suspensions to SRO program effectiveness. Administrators, staff, and students had already become familiar with having officers in their schools for a number of years, and, in some cases, the officers would not be assuming significant new responsibilities that could have been expected to generate any changes in measures of program effectiveness.

In conjunction with NIJ and the COPS Office, we decided to still include these "new" sites in the study because selecting, recruiting, arranging to visit, and visiting substitutes for these programs would have involved a significant delay in the project as well as the need for additional funds. Furthermore, we had every reason to believe that most other large "new" sites we screened for inclusion as replacement programs in the study would likewise have had police officers in the schools prior to the SRO program who performed activities similar to the activities that the "new" SROs were expected to perform and were in many cases the same officers.

A second problem arose with regard to conducting a pre/post impact evaluation of the large new SRO programs. The original research design assumed the administration of the surveys would be based on "passive" informed consent, whereby parents of students would be asked to indicate their opposition to their children's participation and, in the absence of such opposition, informed consent would be assumed. However, Abt Associates' Institutional Review Board (IRB) unexpectedly required that we use "active" consent for the survey. Of particular concern to the IRB was that asking students about past victimization and fear of crime in the schools could have negative emotional effects. Using active consent necessitated that we secure student and parental written assertions of their understanding of the risks associated with the surveys as well as their willingness to participate. Securing these assertions would have greatly increased the amount of time and effort required to ensure even modest response rates.

As a result, we proposed to NIJ and the COPS Office that we abandon the use of a pre/post design and the associated implementation of an impact evaluation in the large new sites because the design and implementation lacked scientific validity and financial feasibility. Instead, we proposed to intensify our efforts with the large new sites to develop especially rich case studies. We further proposed to conduct a single-point-in-time survey involving questioning students.

After meeting with NIJ and the COPS Office in November 2001 to discuss this plan, we submitted a written justification for the proposed modification in January 2002 and engaged in a conference call at NIJ's request to discuss the justification in April 2002. In June 2002, NIJ requested a full-line item budget for the Office of the Comptroller in support of the modification. We submitted the budget in July and received the Grant Adjustment Notice in August 2002 approving the methodology and budget modifications.

DATA ANALYSIS AND FINDINGS

There were two rounds of data analysis and reporting, the first occurring after the first set of site visits and the second occurring after the second (and in some cases third or fourth) set of site visits.

Interim Report: Trust and Fear

For our contractually mandated interim report, NIJ and the COPS Office requested us to summarize our preliminary impressionistic observations concerning (1) perceptions of fear about campus safety among school administrators, faculty, and students and (2) trust in the police among these groups in the 19 sites. The COPS Office was particularly interested in the perceptions of students, school administrators, and other local stakeholders concerning the effects that SRO programs appear to have on fear of crime in the schools. Declines in fear of crime and increased trust in the police are among the principal goals of many if not most SRO programs.

In order to investigate these two issues, the COPS Office and NIJ asked that we attempt to measure these perceptions during the course of the administration of a local survey in each of the four large "new" jurisdictions that had recently received Cops in Schools grants. While these surveys would not be administered until the fall of 2002 and the findings would not be analyzed until the winter, the two agencies expressed interest in our preparing interim observations based on our initial round of site visits to the 19 jurisdictions.

Data Analysis

The interim report represented the combined experience of Abt Associates, the Center for the Prevention of School Violence, and Eastern Kentucky University. Subjective and perceptual information concerning these two potential program effects—fear of crime and trust in the police—were collected during the course of the first round of site visits. The full interim report identifies the types of individuals we interviewed during the site visits whose perceptions (when offered) formed the basis for the report's findings.

Caution should be used in interpreting the observations presented in the interim report and summarized below since they were not based on systematic data collection protocols or instruments. In addition, the findings reflected subjective perceptions of fear and trust on the part of program participants. Furthermore, for respondents to suggest SROs reduced fear in the schools required an admission that students, faculty, administrators or all three were fearful before the SRO program began. For many reasons, some respondents may have been unwilling to report that their schools had once been unsafe or that students and teachers felt they were unsafe. As a result, they may have been reluctant to suggest that the SRO program had been influential in increasing their schools' safety or reducing their schools' climate of fear. Finally, our observations were also very preliminary because we had conducted only one round of site visits and had not yet implemented the surveys of students in the large new programs (see above).

Summary of Findings

A brief synopsis of the full interim report's findings follows.

Large Established Sites. Among those respondents who were willing to give an opinion about whether the SRO program has increased trust in the police, all felt it has done so. No respondent reported that the program had failed to increase trust. However, when asked for empirical evidence of increased trust, most were able to provide anecdotal evidence at best. The same consensus, and lack of definitive evidence, pertained to the question of whether the program reduced fear in the schools. With regard to both questions, many respondents felt that concrete evidence of the program's effectiveness in increasing trust or reducing fear was lacking and, therefore, were unwilling to offer an opinion. In addition, as several respondents pointed out, other changes (e.g., curfews, student uniform policies) occurred just before the initiation of the SRO program or during its operation that compromised any attempt to attribute positive effects to the program alone.

Large New Programs. There was no systematic attempt to measure fear of crime or trust in the police during the initial site visits to the large new sites because questions on the perceptions of these two variables were planned for inclusion in the 2002 surveys of students with presentation of the findings in the final technical report (see below).

Small Established Programs. Overall, the preliminary subjective assessments of the effects of SRO programs were positive across the five small established programs. Generally speaking, trust was reported to increase over time, and the SROs' presence and activities were felt to contribute to a sense of security in the schools.

Small New Programs. Faculty and staff expressed near universal trust in the SROs in their sites. Across all five sites, administrators and faculty reported feeling safer since the SRO programs were implemented. Several said that they did not want to work in a school without an SRO again. Students were also generally supportive of the notion that schools were made safer by an SRO's presence, and most students who expressed an opinion said that as a result they were less fearful.

The respondents in the small established and new sites were more willing than the respondents in the large established sites to express an opinion on the issues of trust in the police and fear in the schools. This discrepancy may have occurred because in the small sites respondents could gain a fairly accurate picture of the effects of the program since SROs were posted in only a few schools, whereas in the large sites the programs were so large that few individual respondents had the ability to generalize about trust and fear across so many schools. There may also have been more events taking place in the large sites than in the small sites that could have affected perceptions of trust and fear independently of the SRO programs. As a result, respondents in the large sites may have been reluctant to attribute any perceived changes in fear and trust to the SRO programs.

Case Studies of 19 School Resource Officer (SRO) Programs

We prepared and submitted to NIJ a report that presented case studies of each of the 19 programs included in the National Assessment.

Data Analysis

Information used in the preparation of the report included:

- the results of the site visit interviews, focus groups, and observations;
- telephone interviews conducted after the site visits to obtain information not available during the site visits (e.g., because a respondent was sick or the data were not yet available); and
- program materials the sites sent us, such as data sets, memorandums of agreement, SRO monthly progress reports, minutes of school board meetings, and public information materials.

We decided to provide separate case studies for each of the five large established and four large new programs since these initiatives were generally complex. By contrast, we merged the write-ups on the five small established programs into a single "case study" that provided a summary of each program followed by a "cross-site" discussion of key features. We took the same approach in reporting on the small new programs. We used this format for the small sites because, as small programs, the sites' lack of complexity precluded the need for a lengthy description of each one.

Abt Associates prepared the case studies on the five large established programs; Northeastern University prepared the case studies of the four large new programs; the Center for the Prevention of School Violence prepared the case studies on the five small established programs; and Eastern Kentucky University together with Abt Associates prepared the five small new case studies.

Summary of Findings

LARGE ESTABLISHED SITE ONE

Large Established Site One, a largely middle class town with a population of 75,000, is located about 25 miles northwest of a large metropolitan area in the Mid-West. The local school district, which includes Large Established Site One and six other towns, consists of 22 elementary and 5 junior high schools (no high schools). Three of the district's 5 junior high schools are in Large Established Site One.

After a pilot test in 1995 involving placement of an SRO in one of Large Established Site One's three junior high schools, the school district placed a second and then third SRO in each of the town's other two junior high schools.

Program Planning and Costs

Planning and implementation of the SRO program proceeded relatively smoothly. The most serious problems related to planning involved disagreements between the school district and the Large Established Site One police department related to using retired officers as SROs, arming the SROs, and working in civilian clothes. Problems related to implementing the program included local school administrators' misconception that SROs were supposed to focus on law enforcement and disciplining students.

Until recently, the school district tapped into its Tort and Immunity Fund to pay for the program, enabling the police department to replace the SROs with new officers. The cost to the school district for the three SROs' salaries in fiscal year 2002 was $193,296.

The SROs

Together, the principal and assistant principal, health teacher, and the police department's SRO supervisor interview applicants whenever an SRO position opens up. The school makes the final selection in consultation with the police department's SRO supervisor. While initially SROs learned their responsibilities by trial and error on the job, today they are trained thoroughly before they begin their new assignment.

Program Activities

With the exception of interviews with school district and police department supervisors, all of the observations and interviews for this case study were conducted at one Large Established Site One junior high school chosen for intensive study. This sample school had a 2001-2002 enrollment of about 700 seventh and eighth grade students. Three quarters of the students were white, 3.6 percent African American, and the rest Asian and Hispanic. Low-income families made up 3.5 percent of the community. In 2002, the school's SRO was in the last year of his four-year rotation.

The SROs in all three Large Established Site One junior high schools devote an estimated 10 percent of their time to law enforcement, 30 percent to advising students, faculty, and administrators, 40 percent to classroom teaching, and 20 percent to other activities (e.g., paperwork). From the outset, the school district has considered teaching and mentoring equally if not more important than the SROs' law enforcement responsibilities.

- *Law Enforcement:* Most SROs make only a few arrests a year because of a low crime rate in the schools, the program's focus on mentoring and teaching, and the juvenile court's discouraging of referrals of minor cases. Instead, SROs sometimes assign students to perform community service in the schools. Teachers, parents, and students, like school administrators, sometimes refer matters directly to the SROs that may involve criminal behavior.
- *Teaching:* Each SRO teaches the G.R.E.A.T. (Gang Resistance Education and Training) curriculum to all seventh graders as well as classes on other topics. In addition to teaching G.R.E.A.T., the SRO at the intensively studied junior high school teaches classes on sexual harassment, babysitting, shoplifting, gangs, driving under the influence, drugs and alcohol, fingerprinting, and the law. Teachers leave a note in his mailbox with requests and dates for him to teach specific topics. Just as the school district intended, a teacher confirmed that the SRO " is like another staff person."
- *Mentoring:* The SROs are constantly available to students for informal chats and serious conversations about problems. The SROs also engage in activities, such as jogging with the track team, where they act as role models. The SRO's office at the intensively studied junior high school is crowded between classes and during all four 20-minute lunch periods with students who want to chat.

Program Monitoring and Evaluation

The program keeps extensive and meticulous qualitative and quantitative records, including a detailed monthly summary form completed by each SRO. The head of the police department's juvenile division supervises the SROs, making sure they complete the activity forms properly, observing them teach, and meeting with them individually.

While there is no empirical evidence that the SRO program is effective in reducing crime in the schools, there is promising evidence of its effectiveness.

- Smoking and possession of cigarettes, and gang activity, appear to have declined.
- Students report that they and their parents feel safer because of the SROs' presence.
- Students in focus groups report small but positive changes in attitude toward the police. Several knowledgeable individuals also report that the SRO program has increased trust in the police department.

The program's planners and current administrators were as interested in the SROs' mentoring and teaching roles as in providing security, and all observers report that the officers are effective in these two roles.

The community's support for the program was indirectly confirmed when a budget crunch forced the school board in 2002 to discuss laying off teachers—and the idea of dropping or cutting back the SRO program was never even raised.

LARGE ESTABLISHED SITE TWO

Large Established Site Two, with a 2002 population of over 500,000, encompasses more th square miles in a State in the Southwest. The police department has nearly 1,000 sworn of while the principal school district within the city has over 50,000 students. Begun in 1962 single SRO, Large Established Site Two's SRO program now has one full-time SRO servin each of 19 of the city's 21 middle schools (one SRO serves two middle schools).

Program Planning and Costs

The police department pays the entire cost of 18 of the SROs and will pick up the cost of the other 3 SROs currently funded with a U.S. Department of Justice COPS in Schools grant. The only source of ongoing dissension is school administrators' concern that the officers are not available enough at the schools—in part because each one serves up to six feeder elementary schools as well as a middle school and works a four-day week.

The SROs

In addition to fixed criteria for becoming SROs, the program prefers candidates with some college education. Several years ago, the program provided incentives to become SROs (take-home cruisers, four-day week, five percent pay increase) because few officers were applying for the posting. SROs take the National Association of School Resource Officers (NASRO) 40-hour basic course as it becomes available, and they receive on-going in-service training, as well.

Program Activities

On average, SROs spend about 25 percent time on law enforcement, 38 percent advising, 25 teaching, and 12 percent on other activities. Over time, they have been spending more time on education and less on enforcement.

- *Law Enforcement:* SROs are responsible for making arrests (generally for drug possession, threats, and fights) and preventing crime (through teaching, dealing with rumors, and cruiser patrols around the schools).
- *Teaching:* Most SROs spend considerable time in the classroom, including teaching the G.R.E.A.T. (Gang Resistance Education and Training) curriculum and other topics ranging from Halloween safety to animal cruelty.
- *Mentoring:* SROs mentor students, especially by talking with students who have gotten into trouble—sometimes establishing ongoing relationships that last two or three years. SROs are also expected to engage in extracurricular activities that afford the opportunity to mentor students outside of school.

Program Monitoring and Evaluation

While the school district collects a great deal of information about school crime, levels of fear, and suspensions, these data cannot be used to evaluate the impact of the SRO program largely because of the program's longevity. However, two knowledgeable school district administrators feel the program has increased trust in the police.

LARGE ESTABLISHED SITE THREE

Large Established Site Three, with a population of 100,000 and encompassing over 2,000 square miles, is located in the South. Begun in 1995, the Large Established Site Three SRO program includes 9 SROs, one each in the county's three high schools, an alternative school, two junior high schools, a "troublesome" middle school, and two who rotate among seven other middle schools.

The sheriff's department has 250 sworn personnel, including 100 correctional officers. About half of the county's 20,000 students are eligible for the Federal Government's free and reduced cost lunch program.

Program Planning and Costs

In 1995, the county established a zero tolerance policy for fighting because of frequent physical altercations—including riots—in some schools. Under the policy, police may arrest and take any student caught fighting to the sheriff's office or jail where a parent must post a $250 bond that is returned after the student performs community service and attends a conflict resolution course. The SRO program was initiated shortly after to enforce the policy and reduce the fighting. Everyone considers the zero tolerance policy and the SRO program to be inseparable: neither one would be effective without the other.

The single most difficult problem getting the program going was disagreement between SROs and local school administrators over the officers' authority to arrest and handcuff students—at one point, an SRO threatened to arrest a principal if he interfered with the officer's arresting a student. By contrast, the relationship between the sheriff's office and school district has always been constructive.

The school district pays the SROs' salaries at two schools (approximately $65,000) and splits the cost with the sheriff's office at the other four schools ($100,000 per agency).

The SROs

A group of command officers decides whom to invite to become SROs. The officers are trained but sometimes not until they have been in a school for several months.

Program Activities

There is no description of the SROs' responsibilities because they vary depending on what each principal wants the SRO do to. However, SROs average spending about 10 percent of their time on enforcement, (much more when the program began), 60 percent mentoring, 10 percent teaching, and 20 percent on other activities.

- *Law Enforcement:* As fights among students declined, the SRO program's law enforcement focus shifted to addressing problems primarily related to drug dealing and possession. Some SROs also enforce discipline. The SROs prevent crime through their presence, tips from students about impending problems, and informally mediating disputes among students.
- *Teaching:* SROs teach several times a month, such as classes as part of a school's law studies course and classes on self defense designed to prevent fights.
- *Mentoring:* SROs spend considerable time mentoring students, and their offices are typically full of students. Some SRO also mentor parents.

Program Monitoring and Evaluation

The school district and police department collaborate in supervising the SROs. Neither party evaluates the program's effectiveness. However, several crimes appear to have declined since the SRO program was instituted, especially fighting, as evidenced in particular by the significant increase in fights that occurred when SROs were pulled out of the schools for eight months due to a budget shortfall. Several individuals felt that the program could take significant credit for a declining level of fear in the schools and an increasing trust in the sheriff's office.

According to the sheriff's department's SRO supervisor, "The voters like it [the SRO program]. People call me 30 times a month thanking an SRO for helping their kid." If there were a budget problem, it would be difficult to end the program.

LARGE ESTABLISHED SITE FOUR

Large Established Site Four, with a population of 50,000—about half minority—is a county seat about 50 miles from a major Southern city. The site's police department has about 150 sworn officers. There are three K-12 school districts in the site. The site's SRO program, begun in 1995, serves the one junior high school in each district.

Program Planning and Costs

After attending a school safety conference, a police lieutenant and school district deputy superintendent, sold on the SRO concept, set up the program. The police department saw—and still envisions—the program as a means of improving the public's image of police and, as a result, enabling officers to do their work more effectively. School district administrators supported the program because of chronic fighting at some schools.

School administrators' uncertainty about the SROs' role, need for the SROs to be constantly availability, and concerns about the officers' authority to decide whether to arrest were the principal sources of friction when the program began. Over time, these problems were ironed out and most SROs now work productively with their schools.

The police department pays the entire cost of the SROs' salaries and fringe benefits, representing about $160,000.

The SROs

Currently, the police chief and captain pick the SROs. However, few officers typically apply for openings because of disincentives involved in the position. While the SROs are eventually adequately trained, some receive the training only after going on the job.

Program Activities

- *Law Enforcement:* Fighting and gang activity have been the SROs' major focuses in terms of their law enforcement role. However, both activities have diminished considerably. SROs' enforcement efforts are helped by parents, program directors, and students who tell them about planned or actual criminal activity.
- *Teaching:* Currently, the SROs devote more time to teaching than to either law enforcement or mentoring. The SROs' most time-consuming teaching responsibility is the G.R.E.A.T (Gang Resistance Education and Training) program, which can take up to one quarter of their time for many weeks.
- *Mentoring:* SROs spend considerable time talking impromptu or by appointment with students who ask for help. Extracurricular activities include after-school tutoring, attending athletic events, and participating in neighborhood meetings.

Program Monitoring and Evaluation

Program monitoring is conducted largely through SRO written reports. Quantitative and anecdotal evidence suggest that the program may have reduced student misconduct, including fights and gang activity, and increased trust in the police department.

LARGE ESTABLISHED SITE FIVE

Large Established Site Five serves a 50-square-mile jurisdiction in the Far West with about 200,000 residents. The police department has over 200 sworn officers. The city's public schools are organized into elementary and secondary school districts of 20,000 and 30,000 students each. The police chief initiated the program in 1993 with two SROs, increasing the number over time to 18 SROs. SROs are assigned to clusters of schools based on geographic grouping rather than grade level.

Program Planning and Costs

The biggest misunderstanding with school administrators was about what the SROs do. Elementary school principals complained when the officers were not present when fights broke out because the officers were at the middle and high schools—yet the elementary school district was sharing the cost of the officers. An occasional ongoing problem is that schools sometimes call for an SRO to handle minor problems that supervisors feel teachers and administrators should be handling.

The elementary and secondary school districts share about half of the $2,078,821 cost of the program with the police department.

The SROs

The department announces each new SRO opening by e-mail and hard copy in every eligible officer's mailbox. School administrators are involved in interviewing and selecting SROs as members of the interview panels.

Every new SRO rides along with an experienced SRO for two weeks. SROs attend COPS in Schools or 40-hour basic SRO training as soon as training becomes available.

Program Activities

The SROs spend on average about 60-65 percent of their time on law enforcement, 25–30 30 percent mentoring, and 5-10 percent teaching.

- *Law Enforcement*: SROs provide full law enforcement coverage to all public schools in the city. School administrators call the department's dispatch center when they need an SRO. While on patrol in the neighborhoods, the SROs also pick up truants.
- *Teaching*: SROs generally do not teach regularly scheduled classes at the secondary school level except for four SROs who teach G.R.E.A.T. at the middle schools each year. SROs teach an annual "Safety on Site (SOS)" three-class course to all 5th grade students.
- *Mentoring*: Because of a number of constraints, SROs do not do as much mentoring as supervisors would like. However, SROs visit campuses to try to get acquainted with kids. The department purchased 11 bicycles for the SROs in part to increase the officers' opportunities to interact informally with students.

Program Monitoring and Evaluation

Two supervising sergeants visit schools to observe SROs interact with students and administrators; review SROs' crime reports; hold a daily special morning roll call; and call special meetings every six months to redistribute and discuss updates of the SROs' roles and responsibilities. The elementary school district examines relevant outcome data over time.

A number of program participants suggested that the program is likely to have created increased trust in the police and reduced student fear in many of the schools. An informed program participant felt that the SROs were a tremendous deterrent to student misconduct.

Despite considerable support for the program among many school administrators, with increased fiscal constraints school district administrators will be considering whether to discontinue or reduce their share of program costs in 2004-2005.

LARGE NEW SITE ONE

Large New Site One, a county in South Central United States, has a population of over 600,000 and occupies approximately 700 square miles. The county seat has just over a half million residents, 35 percent minority. The sheriff's office, with law enforcement authority throughout the county, has 130 sworn officers.

The office's School Resource Officer program began in 1999 with five full-time SROs working in two highly dissimilar school districts. One school system serves a small, urban, largely minority, economically distressed, crime-burdened neighborhood. The other serves a large, rural, affluent, predominantly Caucasian, sparsely populated community.

Program Planning and Costs

The sheriff's office views the program as an opportunity to enhance community outreach, violence reduction efforts, and substance abuse prevention services at county schools. Administrators at both participating school districts see the program as a means of improving school safety, with officials from one emphasizing crime prevention and relationship building, and staff at the other stressing counseling and teaching, particularly around issues of alcohol and drugs. The COPS in Schools grant from the U.S. Department of Justice Office of Community Oriented Policing Services covers the full cost of the five SROs' salaries and fringe benefits.

The SROs

The SRO openings attracted a great deal of interest within the sheriff's office. One school superintendent helped the department with officer screening and selection, interviewing between 10-20 candidates for the initial five positions. All of the officers selected had significant law enforcement experience and had rotated through several divisions within the sheriff's office. In addition to attending training sessions required by the COPS Office, some of the officers attended the National Association of School Resource Officers' (NASRO) 40-hour basic course before starting work. All SROs have received ongoing in-service training from the sheriff's office, and two have attended annual school safety programs at the request of their school district superintendents.

Program Activities

SROs spend roughly one-quarter of their time on law enforcement, one-quarter teaching, and one-half counseling and mentoring.

- *Law enforcement*: Officers at one school district have helped staff to identify potential signs of gang activity. They have interpreted gang graffiti and reduced control of courtyard corners by groups of students. SROs at the other school district coordinate their enforcement-related actions with a private security unit and the schools' administrative staff.
- *Teaching:* The SROs provide drug prevention classes and presentations to students at all grade levels. The officers use considerable creativity in reaching students with this message, in one instance writing and filming a skit. In the program's urban site, officers focus their classes on gang and drug deterrence. In the more rural district, SROs integrate teaching more routinely into their work. Teachers request that they speak to classes on law-related topics and address drug and alcohol use in small teacher-led group discussions.
- *Mentoring:* Informal conversations provide the greatest amount of SRO-student interaction, but officers also use after-school activities as opportunities to mentor students.

They attend athletic events, dances, and class trips. In one school district, the SROs coordinate a "community services" program that gives kids an opportunity to perform SRO-monitored "service" in lieu of more severe disciplinary measures.

Program Monitoring and Evaluation

The sheriff's office uses written reports from SROs and comments from school staff to monitor the program. Schools also provide yearly written assessments of the officers. These resoundingly endorse the initiative. Students also express approval: three quarters that of those who took a written survey said they would feel comfortable reporting a crime to their SRO, and half said their opinion of police had improved since the program began.

Although difficult to attribute reduced crime or increased safety at schools to any one factor, quantitative data from this site show promising trends. In the urban district, police records show a steady fall in the number of calls to send beat officers on campus since the SROs started, while at the rural schools discipline reports suggest achievements in terms of conflict resolution and early detection of criminal behavior.

LARGE NEW SITE TWO

Large New Site Two, with a total population of about 400,000, is a county of roughly 600 square miles in a Mid-Western state. Residents are predominantly white, urban-dwelling homeowners with a per capita income slightly lower than the state average. The sheriff's office employs approximately 100 sworn officers. The office's School Resource Officer program received COPS in Schools' funding for five full-time officers beginning in 1999. These SROs work in five separate school districts that vary in size and in level of urbanization and socioeconomic development.

Program Planning and Costs

Based on needs identified by school administrators at the program's start, SROs planned to work in the areas of dispute resolution, truancy reduction, identification of at-risk students, mentoring, and role modeling. Each school system's SRO and school administrators have collaborated to tailor the program according to their other needs. The COPS in Schools grant covers the full cost of the five SROs' salaries and fringe benefits, with the exception of a small county contribution in year three. Four of the five districts assumed the costs of retaining their SROs when the COPS Office grant expired.

The SROs

The agreements between the sheriff and school districts called for "joint selection" of SROs by the sheriff's office and school districts. Fourteen candidates applied for the initial five openings and were screened through written questionnaires and personal interviews. While the five deputies selected had between 11 and 16 years' experience with the sheriff's office, they found the transition to SRO a difficult and stressful process because they were not trained before taking up their new assignments.

Program Activities

Because each of the school districts has distinct characteristics and needs, the SROs vary in the degree to which they perform activities suggested by the program's triad model. On the whole, however, the county's SROs focus approximately half of their time on counseling and mentoring, a quarter of their time on teaching, and a quarter of their time on law enforcement or other activities.

Program Monitoring and Evaluation

The sheriff's office uses written reports from SROs and comments from school staff to monitor the program. School officials have used different means for evaluating the program's effectiveness in the five school districts. All districts provide written assessments of the SROs, some annually and some quarterly, to the sheriff's office.

Truancy declined and less severe disciplinary measures were imposed in the site after the SRO program began, although numerous other factors may have contributed to these improvements.

LARGE NEW SITE THREE

Large New Site Three, bordering two major east coast cities, has a racially and ethnically diverse population of 45,000. The town employs roughly 100 sworn officers to police its 10 to 12 square-mile jurisdiction. Its public schools serve an annual enrollment of 7,000 in grades K-12. Three School Resource Officers began working in the school system during the 1999-2000 academic year–one assigned to each of the town's two middle schools and high school.

Program Planning and Costs

Planners of the Large New Site Three SRO program viewed it as a vehicle for improving communication and trust between local and youth and for formalizing the long-standing, positive working relationship between town police and schools. Over its three-year duration, a COPS in Schools grant funded approximately 80 percent of the three officers' salaries and benefits, with the town assuming an increasing share from year to year.

The SROs

The police department recruited and screened 11 candidates for the three SRO positions. Police interviewed applicants on their own, although the school district provided a list of criteria for officers to meet. All three officers selected, as well as their immediate supervisors in the police department, attended a 40-hour basic training course offered by NASRO. One of the three officers also completed NASRO advanced "practitioner" courses. The police department includes SROs in all mandatory in-service classes, ensuring that they maintain their law enforcement skills. Supervisors believe that, because the SROs interact with so many students each day, their report writing, interviewing, and other "people-oriented" skills have improved since they have been posted to the schools.

Program Activities

School and police officers favor the triad model of program implementation that incorporates law enforcement, teaching, and counseling activities. The SROs report they concentrate on counseling, with informal conversations with students, guidance appointments, and parental conferences accounting for about two-thirds of the SROs' time. About 20 percent of their time is dedicated to classes or assemblies, and about 15 percent to enforcement-related duties. They also play a vital role in planning and maintaining school safety.

Program Monitoring and Evaluation

SROs discuss their work daily with police supervisors and provide monthly summaries of their activities to the department. Principals routinely share comments and concerns with these supervisors although they have no formal process for evaluating the SROs' performance. Educators at this site resist assessing the program based on changes in disciplinary data. Police records do show, however, an apparent decline in arrests and criminal misbehavior at the three schools hosting SROs. Students say they appreciate the officers' approachability and assistance with personal, as well as law-related, concerns. Principals and teachers strongly advocate for the program's continuation.

LARGE NEW SITE FOUR

Large New Site Four is a city of more than 250,000 in the southwestern United States. Its population is diverse with a significant number of Hispanic residents. The police department employs more than 600 sworn officers to cover the city's more than 150 square miles. The school system has more than 70,000 students in more than 100 schools. Thirty-eight school resource officers assigned to the city's 30 middle and high schools began working in the school system in 1999 with funding from the COPS in Schools program.

Program Planning and Costs

Those involved with the development of the SRO program viewed it as the next phase of a long-standing commitment to having police work in schools. Local police have worked in schools in Large New Site Four for more than 25 years. These efforts have included D.A.R.E. officers, G.R.E.A.T. officers, and now SROs. The city has a significant gang and violence problem in several schools as well as many neighborhoods. As a result, stationing police in the schools has been viewed as a public safety priority. The budget, fully funded by a COPS in Schools grant, had an initial cost of $1,218,269.

The SROs

The police department assigns SROs to schools without consulting school administrators. Most of the SROs have had considerable police experience. They have worked in a wide range of areas within the department including SWAT, white-collar investigation, drug enforcement, juvenile investigation, and patrol. However, except for one SRO and one school administrator who attended a COPS-sponsored training, there has been no other formal training for SROs.

Because of a very high turnover rate, the department has had trouble filling the vacancies; as a result, the department has had to use "reverse seniority," assigning the newest officers to the SRO unit. The program budget, initially $1,218,269, is paid for by a COPS in Schools grant.

Program Activities

The SRO program has is no clear model or structure. As a result, officers perform varying sets of activities. However, the most common forms of interaction with students involve coaching athletic teams, community service, summer camps, and informal contacts during the school day.

Program Monitoring and Evaluation

Because SROs are stationed in multiple schools, school administrators do day-to-day monitoring. A police officer who supervises the SROS deals with problems as they arise.

SMALL ESTABLISHED SITES

Case Studies

All five small established sites are in North Carolina. Two began in 1993, two in 1994, and one in 1995.

Small Established Site One: This program involves a police department with fewer than 40 sworn officers in a county of over 40,000 people. As part of a written agreement, one SRO is stationed at the one high school, which has over 1,500 students. The SRO spends about 50 percent of his time on law enforcement activities, including traffic control, supervising lunch periods, and responding to calls from the elementary schools; 30 percent on law-related education, including teaching Drug Abuse Resistance Education (D.A.R.E.); and 20 percent devoted to 20–30 counseling sessions a week.

Small Established Site Two: The local police department that sponsors this program has fewer than 50 sworn officers serving a town with slightly more than 20,000 residents. The one high school and two middle schools where the three SROs are stationed have between 700–2,000 students. A community panel interviews all applicants for SRO positions, although the chief makes the final choice. SROs receive a five percent supplement to their salaries. The amount of crime in the schools influences the ratio of time the SROs spend on law enforcement, education, and counseling. For example, one middle school SRO spends only 20 percent time on law enforcement, while the other two SROs spend about 60 percent, including investigating crimes, filing petitions, going to court, and patrolling the campuses. All three SROs are involved in mentoring, including coaching sports teams.

Small Established Site Three: In this county of 60,000, two SROs from the sheriff's department (50 sworn deputies) are assigned to two high schools, and a third SRO covers three middle schools.

Student enrollment at the schools ranges from 600 to over 900. The program began in response to an increasing number of bomb threats and drug trafficking at the schools. As the program developed, the SROs' initial primary focus on law enforcement shifted to a more even balance with education and counseling, but the proportion of time each SRO spends on these three areas varies considerably by school.

Small Established Site Four: The sheriff's department that operates this program has about 30 sworn officers serving a community of 27,000 people. The four SROs are assigned to two middle schools and two high schools with student populations ranging from 500–700. When the initial grant that funded the SROs ended, community support for maintaining the program prevented the county commissioners from eliminating it. Initially, SROs spent most of their time on law enforcement, including supervising a deferred prosecution community service and counseling program for students the officers have arrested. Over time, the SROs have spent more time counseling, as well as teaching about date rape, civil law, and other topics at teachers' requests, and D.A.R.E. at the four elementary schools.

Small Established Site Five: The program in this rural county of 35,000 people began in response to the statewide emphasis on school crime prevention and to violent incidents in nearby school districts. Four SROs from the sheriff's department of 30 sworn officers serve two high schools and two middle schools with student bodies ranging from 700–1,000 each. The officers spend about 30 percent of their time on law enforcement, a large portion of it investigating crimes through reviewing surveillance videos; 30 percent on law-related education, including teaching D.A.R.E.; and 40 percent on counseling and mentoring, including participating in PTAs, school plays, and pep rallies.

Similarities and Differences among Five Small Established Programs

In some respects, most or all of the five programs are very similar; in other respects, they differ considerably.

Program Planning and Costs
Program planning and implementation vary among the five sites largely due to different initial community reactions to the programs. Two communities strongly opposed having an armed officer in the schools, forcing one SRO initially to drive his own car and not wear a uniform as well as go unarmed. In two other sites, there was confusion about what the SROs' role should be. However, four of the five sites experienced relatively smooth beginnings, not because of prior planning but because of direct discussions between police chiefs and sheriffs with school superintendents who knew each other and "sealed" their agreements with a handshake.

The State provides funding to all school systems for high school SROs. However, in two of the five programs the funding does not cover the full cost of the officers' salaries and equipment, which the local law enforcement agencies or county or municipal government has to pay for.

In one site, a COPS in Schools grant from the Office of Community Oriented Policing Services (the COPS Office) has funded one of the program's middle school officers for three years, with the school system agreeing to pay the cost in full for the fourth year; school systems fund the middle school SROs in two other sites; and the county pays for the middle school SROs in the two remaining sites.

Program Activities

All five programs require SROs to be trained at the North Carolina Justice Academy, where officers are introduced to a tripartite SRO model that expects them to perform as law enforcement officers, law-related educators, and law-related counselors. However, SROs spend very different proportions of time on each of these roles across—and even within—the five sites. After law enforcement, the SROs devote the most time to counseling. SROs also mentor students by coaching athletic teams, advising extracurricular clubs, and hosting summer camps for at-risk youth. In their education roles, some SROs rarely taught in the classroom while others taught as many as 2–3 days a week for 6–10 weeks just at their assigned schools' feeder schools

Monitoring and Evaluation

The principal means of monitoring the SROs is through informal contact between law enforcement agency officials and school administrators. However, SROs in one site submit a report to their sheriff's department supervisor each month, and principals are asked to fill out a performance review for each SRO in their schools. While each jurisdiction has annual crime incident figures for its schools, the data could not shed light on whether the SRO programs were reducing student misconduct largely because the very few crimes committed by students at most of the schools studied made comparisons between the number of offenses before and after the SROs programs began unreliable. However, several administrators, teachers, and students reported that they felt safer as a result of the SRO program, observing that the officers provided a "comfort level" that they liked. With the exception of the SROs in two sites' middle schools, SRO supervisors from the participating law enforcement agencies along with school district administrators in all five sites felt that their programs would endure, in some cases because the funding sources were stable, there was significant public support for the programs, or both.

SMALL NEW SITES

Case Studies

All five of the small new sites selected for this evaluation were in Kentucky. The programs were recent recipients of COPS in Schools grants from the office of Community Oriented Policing Services (the COPS Office). Three of the programs began in the fall of 1999, and two programs began in February 2000. With the exception of interviews with school district and police department supervisors, all of the observations and interviews for the case studies were conducted at the high schools and middle schools to which the SROs are primarily assigned.

Small New Site One: This program is located in a rural county of about 500 square miles with a population of approximately 25,000. The school district is countywide with a total enrollment of about 4,000 students enrolled in 12 schools, including one high school with about 1,000 students and a middle school with over 500 students. Two SROs are assigned primarily to the high school but respond to calls and occasionally patrol all of the district's schools. The program's host agency is a small-town police department with about 10 sworn officers. The SRO program was designed to deter drug activities, crime, and disorder in the schools. The SROs engage in a variety of safety and enforcement activities ranging from traffic control to criminal investigations, as well as teaching, counseling, field trips, and athletic events, but estimates of the time distribution across activities could not be provided.

Small New Site Two: The county in which this program is located, with about 300 square miles, includes areas categorized as rural and suburban. There are about 4,000 students enrolled in six schools within the county. The program's lone SRO is assigned to the district's only high school, which enrolls approximately 1,000 students. The SRO serves a small sheriff's department of fewer than 20 sworn deputies. The SRO program was intended to address fighting, smoking, drugs, and general disorder among students. The SRO spends most of her time on enforcement duties and patrol. The heavy focus on law enforcement appears to be a result of poor discipline within the school. What little time she spends on teaching and counseling is done on an informal basis.

Small New Site Three: This site is located in a county of about 25,000 residents distributed across about 500 square miles in a rural part of the state. The county school district enrolls approximately 4,000 students in seven schools, including one high school housing the SRO program. The SRO's host agency is a county sheriff's department with about 10 sworn deputies. The SRO program was designed to address problems of disorderly conduct, smoking, truancy, and occasional instances of students bringing weapons to school. An overarching program goal was the presumed deterrent effect an SRO would produce and ability to provide quick response capabilities for serious crimes or other disasters. The original orientation of SRO activities emphasized law enforcement, but the SRO's role has shifted significantly so that he currently spends roughly half his time in enforcement and patrol, with 2-3 hours per week teaching classes and about 12-14 hours per week mentoring students.

Small New Site Four: This site is situated in a rural county of under 300 square miles with approximately 20,000 residents. About 3,000 students are enrolled in the nine schools in the county, including one high school with about 1,000 students. The program's SRO, one of about 20 deputies in the county sheriff's department, is assigned to the high school. The main impetus for the program was the chief deputy's concern about the number of violent incidents in schools across the country. The program began with a focus on enforcement but has evolved incrementally toward a much heavier emphasis on crime prevention, student counseling, and teaching classes. The SRO is also actively involved in disciplinary cases with the assistant principal.

Small New Site Five: This site abuts a small city within a county of 500 square miles, with areas classified as urban, suburban, and rural. Over 10,000 students are enrolled in the district's 25 schools, which include three high schools and three middle schools. The one high school and one middle school participating in the SRO program have approximately 1,300 and 700 students, respectively. The schools are served by one SRO from the local city police department with fewer than 100 sworn officers, and one SRO from the county sheriff's department, with fewer than 10 sworn deputies. The program's initial intent was to help youth develop positive relationships with, and impressions of, the police. Although the schools are perceived to have little serious crime and fewer problems than do most middle and high schools, there were still concerns about drug and alcohol abuse, smoking, truancy, and general discipline that the program was intended to address. The SROs spend about 15 hours per week on law enforcement duties and about 5 hours per week in meetings with school-related organizations and community groups. The rest of the officers' time is spent teaching, counseling, and mentoring.

Similarities and Differences among Five Small New Programs

The program locations were widely distributed throughout the state: two in the west, two in the north, and one in the east. The school and community populations were not racially diverse—the student bodies of four of the five school districts and counties were all at least 85 percent white.

Throughout this capsule description and later in this chapter, many of the observations made about the five small new sites are presented collectively, except where substantial differences merit special attention. On many important dimensions, there are significant similarities in program design and implementation, and widespread agreement about how the programs were regarded by their constituencies.

Program Planning and Costs

Planning and implementation of the SRO programs proceeded in a variety of ways. The sponsors initiating the program varied across sites. In one case, the county sheriff (the host law enforcement agency for the SRO) applied for grant funding and pushed for the school district leadership and high school administration to accept it. In other sites, the programs were advanced initially by district superintendents or principals.

All five programs began without a detailed plan for exactly how the SROs were to be used. There was a general idea that the officers would spend part of their time on patrol and that they would respond to crime and serious disorder, as well as disciplinary incidents. Beyond that, there was a wide range of often-conflicting expectations. Initially, SROs learned their responsibilities by trial and error on the job and over time developed standards for appropriate and inappropriate activities. The most serious implementation problems related to disagreements about where to draw the line between criminal violations and other serious incidents meriting SRO attention, and disciplinary activities more properly handled by teachers and staff. Other common areas of disagreement were whether the SRO would be available beyond normal school hours, direct traffic, or routinely teach or give presentations.

All of the programs were funded by COPS Office grants covering the SROs' salaries. Grant funding was supplemented to various extents by the school districts, the police departments, or both in the form of training, equipment, and office space. Many of the program costs beyond salaries were not precisely recorded as SRO program expenditures.

Program Activities

The SROs in four of the five sites operated in a relatively traditional law enforcement mode: patrolling and responding to calls for service. In the fifth site, the SRO spent the majority of his time teaching, giving presentations, holding meetings, and actively fostering relationships with various constituencies. Partly because each SRO began the program with little initial direction, this range of emphasis evolved primarily as a result of the interests and abilities of individual officers.

Most SROs make few arrests a year because of the relatively low crime rate in the schools. Instead, most enforcement activity addresses misdemeanors, and officers usually issue citations rather than make arrests. Most officer calls for service involve disruptions and suspicious behavior. The SROs in all five programs are very available to students for informal chats and serious conversations about problems. In addition to the obvious mentoring benefit, the significant time the SROs invest in informal conversations with students serves to aid law enforcement by establishing trust and rapport that increases the likelihood that students will report problems, as well as tapping into an excellent source of intelligence about past incidents and potential trouble brewing among students. Most of the SROs periodically teach or give presentations, although the frequency of these activities varied widely among sites and SROs.

Program Monitoring and Evaluation

Police and school district administrators monitor the program on an as-needed basis by reviewing expulsion records of cases in which SROs were involved. Records of SRO activity vary widely across the five small new programs. While all officers keep required records of misdemeanor citations and the relatively rare arrests, documentation of other SRO activities varied from none to the completely and meticulously detailed.

Most SROs make few arrests a year because of the relatively low crime rate in the schools. Instead, most enforcement activity addresses misdemeanors, and officers usually issue citations rather than make arrests. Most officer calls for service involve disruptions and suspicious behavior. The SROs in all five programs are very available to students for informal chats and serious conversations about problems. In addition to the obvious mentoring benefit, the significant time the SROs invest in informal conversations with students serves to aid law enforcement by establishing trust and rapport that increases the likelihood that students will report problems, as well as tapping into an excellent source of intelligence about past incidents and potential trouble brewing among students. Most of the SROs periodically teach or give presentations.

In all five sites, interest in sustaining the SRO programs after COPS Office funding ends is strong among school administrators, law enforcement administrators, and parents.

> Regardless of who initiated the program and who resisted initially, the pockets of resistance soon dissolved, and in all five sites the SRO programs subsequently experienced widespread and strong support. Parental support is very strong for the SRO programs, even in sites in which parents strongly resisted the program initially.

Survey of Students in Three Large New SRO Programs

As noted above, Northeastern University conducted a survey of students in its four large new sites to learn more about perceptions about fear of crime and trust in the law enforcement agency. However, for reasons explained above, the report of the survey results provides information on only three of the programs.

Data Analysis

As part of a the National Assessment, Northeastern University developed, designed, and implemented a 38-item survey instrument to collect information regarding student perceptions of the SRO program in three sites. Within these three sites, 907 students in four distinct school districts were surveyed. The survey was administered to 6th and 8th grade students and/or 10th and 12th grade students in schools in three different sites. Fifty-eight percent of the students from Large New Site 1 were 6th or 8th grade students and 42 percent were either in 10th or 12th grade. Eighty percent of the students surveyed in Large New Site 3 were 6th or 8th graders, and 20 percent of the students were 10th or 12th graders. All the students in Large New Site 4 were either 10th or 12th grade students.

To meet the requirements of the Abt Associates Human Subjects Review Board, Northeastern University used an active consent method of recruiting student respondents. Since all of the potential respondents were minors, the university sent parental consent forms home prior to the administration of the survey. While only students with parental permission were allowed to participate in the survey, students with this consent still retained the right to decline to participate. The potential sampling problems that this method of recruitment can result in are explained Northeastern University's full report.

The process of administering the survey varied slightly in each location. In some schools the survey was distributed in English class. In other schools it was easier for the administrators and teachers to have the research team give the survey in a study period. However, a research team member was present during the administration of the survey at each site. At the start of each survey session, instructions on how to properly complete the survey and a brief synopsis of the purpose of the project were explained to the group of students. Detailed instructions were also printed on the first page of the survey. As part of the instructions, students were informed that their participation was voluntary and that their answers would be kept confidential. Students were also instructed to place the completed survey in the envelope that was given to them with the survey and to pass it in to the proctor or a member of the research team.

Summary of Findings

Relying on past research on SRO and "SRO-type" programs, there were several questions the survey sought to answer. These research questions can be broken down into two basic concerns: (1) what factors in an SRO program affect students' comfort level for reporting crimes and (2) what factors in an SRO program affect students' perception of safety.

Three SRO programs in four schools districts were surveyed. The survey addressed variables that may affect students' comfort level reporting crimes to the SRO and variables that may affect their perceptions of safety. The analysis was based on data obtained through surveys of 907 students across four school districts. Using these data, the analysis addressed seven research questions:

1. Does frequency of interactions between students and SROs affect students' perception of safety?
2. Do positive opinions of the SRO affect students' perception of safety?
3. Is there a relationship between environmental factors such as neighborhood crime or past victimization and students' perception of safety?
4. Does frequency of interaction between student and SRO increase students' comfort level reporting crimes to the SRO?
5. Does having a positive opinion of the SRO increase students' comfort level reporting crimes?
6. Do environmental factors or other variables negate the effects of interactions, positive opinions, or comfort reporting?
7. Does being comfortable reporting crimes to the SRO affect students' perception of safety?

The goal of the survey was to identify factors that affect both students' comfort reporting crimes to SROs and their perceptions of safety in schools. Univariate, bivariate, and multivariate analysis showed that several factors were associated with the dependent variables.

In terms of students' comfort level reporting crimes to the SRO, the analysis found the following:

- There is a statistically significant relationship between frequency of conversations between student and SRO and comfort reporting crimes. However, further examination proved that having frequent conversations with the student may be less influential than initially thought. Perhaps this is true because SROs are able to affect the students' comfort level with their reputations; that is, students who have met with or spoken to the SRO may be "spreading the word" about whether other students should approach them.
- There is statistically significant relationship between having a positive opinion about the SRO and feeling comfortable reporting a crime. Students who hold a positive opinion about the SRO are more apt to feel comfortable reporting crimes. This finding was supported with the regression model, which showed that students' opinion of the SRO remains significant when holding other variables constant. The regression model illustrates that, compared with other students, students who have a positive opinion of the SRO are a little more than 2-½ times more likely to feel comfortable reporting a crime to the SRO.
- The regression model also indicated that students' perception of safety also has a significant relationship with feeling comfortable reporting crimes; students who

reported that they felt safe at school were more than 2-½ times more likely than other students to feel comfortable reporting crime.

In terms of students' perception of safety, the analysis showed the following:

- A larger percentage of students who have a positive opinion of the SRO also report feeling safe at school. Ninety-two percent of students who have a positive opinion report feeling safe compared with 76 percent of students who do not have a positive opinion of the SRO.
- Neighborhood crime and feeling safe at school have an inverse relationship; that is, the lower level of perceived crime in a student's neighborhood, the safer that student feels at school.
- Students who have experienced some type of victimization feel less safe than students who have not.
- Very importantly, even when victimization and environmental factors are introduced into a regression model, having a positive opinion of the SRO and being comfortable reporting a crime remain statistically significant.

Of course, it is important that students report crime occurring on campus. The study findings suggest that students are more likely to report crime if they respect and feel comfortable with the SRO. Overall, the study showed that perhaps the most important and easily modifiable variable in both models is creating a positive opinion of the SRO among the student body. The results suggest that it is important to determine the best method for SROs to create a positive image.

Comparison of Program Activities and Lessons Learned among 19 School Resource Officer (SRO) Programs

This report compares the 19 programs in terms of seven key dimensions, with a focus on lessons learned: choosing a program model; defining specific SRO roles and responsibilities; recruiting SROs; training and supervising SROs; collaborating with school administrators and teachers; working with students and parents; and evaluating SRO programs.

Data Analysis

Information used in the preparation of the report came from the same sources as the information included in the case studies report:

- the results of the site visit interviews, focus groups, and observations;
- telephone interviews conducted after the site visits to obtain information not available during the site visits (e.g., because a respondent was sick or the data were not yet available); and
- program materials the sites sent us, such as data sets, memorandums of agreement, SRO monthly progress reports, minutes of school board meetings, and public information materials.

Summary of Findings

This cross-site report discusses commonalities and differences among the 19 sites with a particular focus on lessons learned—information based on the experience of the sites that could benefit other jurisdictions in setting up or improving an SRO program.

The report focuses on seven issues:

1. Choosing a Program Model
2. Defining Specific SRO Roles and Responsibilities
3. Recruiting SROs
4. Training and Supervising SROs
5. Collaborating with School Administrators and Teachers
6. Working with Students and Parents
7. Evaluating SRO Programs

Choosing a Program Model. In the basic School Resource Officer model, SROs enforce the law, teach, and mentor. Most of the 19 programs included in the National Assessment reflect this model, but *the level of emphasis that SROs devote to each of these three roles varies considerably across and within programs*. As a result, it is more accurate to think in terms of where individual programs and SROs fall along a *continuum* between, at one extreme, engaging in mostly law enforcement activities and, at the other extreme, engaging in mostly teaching and mentoring.

There are several considerations that new—and existing—SRO programs should think about in deciding how their SROs can best allocate their time according to the three basic SRO roles, including *the level of crime and disorder* in a school and *the wishes of the school administration*. However, *the personality and experience of the individual SRO* may ultimately prove the most decisive factor in determining where on the continuum each SRO's balance of activities falls.

Defining Specific SRO Roles and Responsibilities. When SRO programs fail to define the SROs' roles and responsibilities in detail before—or even after—the officers take up their posts in the schools, problems are often rampant—and may last for months and even years. Successful programs have generally followed several steps in developing a list of SRO roles and responsibilities, including:

- identify roles and responsibilities *in writing*;
- *avoid relying on a personal relationship, easy access, and a handshake* between police and school administrators for establishing SRO roles;
- *involve the schools* in developing the SRO roles and responsibilities;
- *distribute* the roles and responsibilities, and periodically *review them*; and
- provide *a mechanism for resolving disagreements* between school administrators and SROs about the officers' responsibilities.

In developing the written description of SRO roles and responsibilities:

- narrow the considerable leeway of *what it means for SROs to engage in "law enforcement"*;

- make clear whether and how SROs will be responsible for *enforcing discipline*; and
- be specific about the SROs' *teaching, and counseling and mentoring, responsibilities*.

Recruiting SROs. Carefully screening applicants and conscientiously supervising them are necessary to recruiting and retaining officers who are—and remain—well qualified by temperament and skills to be SROs. It is especially important to develop written criteria for who can qualify as an SRO, including:

- likes and cares about kids;
- has the temperament to work with school administrators;
- has the capacity to work independently;
- is not a rookie; and
- knows the community in which he or she will be working.

Other keys to successful screening and recruitment include:

- assigning officers with the right personality—someone, as one principal put it, with *"an outgoing, caring, but no-nonsense personality"*;
- when there is a lack of qualified applicants, *using incentives*, such as take-home cruisers and a percent salary increment to help attract qualified candidates; and
- *involving school district and school-level administrators* in the screening process to increase acceptance of the SROs among school personnel.

Training and Supervising SROs. Few of the 19 programs train SROs before they go on the job. Nevertheless, *any delay in training can be a serious problem* because SROs then have to learn their jobs by "sinking or swimming." One program has provided for pre-service training by arranging for a long-standing SRO to become certified as an SRO trainer. Several other programs arrange for new SROs to "shadow" an experienced SRO before going on the job. A number of programs provide in-service training, including sending SROs for advanced SRO training with reputable training organizations. Most SROs and school administrators agree that it would be valuable to train principals and assistant principals along with SROs as a team.

Most programs fail to provide consistent or close supervision of the SROs' work. However, adequate supervision of SROs is important to make sure the officers are working to their full potential and are not experiencing unreported or unacknowledged problems. Typically, programs require SROs to complete monthly activity logs and meet once a year with the supervisor. In some programs, supervisors periodically visit SROs and school administrators at the schools and observe the officers teach.

Collaborating with School Administrators and Teachers. Perhaps the single most troublesome area for most programs has been establishing productive relationships between the SROs and principals and assistant principals, in large part because of a fundamental difference in the law enforcement culture and the school culture in terms of goals, strategies, and methods. Administrators expressed three principal concerns about having an SRO in their schools:

- *Who's In Charge?*
- *Who Makes the Decision to Arrest?*
- *Why Isn't "My" SRO Available All the Time?*

Nevertheless, over time, most administrators developed good working relations with their SROs and came to value the program highly. While sometimes this change in attitude involved just getting used to the program, *many programs found they could expedite the process of improving working relationships* by:

- collaborating with school administrators in planning, operating, and supervising the program;
- explaining program benefits to administrators;
- orienting school-level administrators to the program;
- training SROs before they go on the job; and
- addressing administrator concerns about the SROs' availability.

Gaining the support of teachers is essential if SROs want to get invited to teach their classes—and *teaching is an essential SRO responsibility for improving kids' perceptions about "cops" and taking advantage of a unique opportunity for motivating students to seek out the SROs* outside of class when the youth are having problems. Many SROs are constantly invited by teachers to address their classes because the officers have taken the time to:

- orient teachers to the program before it begins;
- explain how SROs improve student learning; and
- go beyond the normal SRO responsibilities to help teachers.

Working with Students and Their Parents. Program coordinators, SROs, and school administrators all recognize the difficulty SROs experience trying to maintain authority as enforcers of the law while at the same time preserving a helping relationship with students as teachers and mentors. *Walking this fine line plays itself out in two particular areas: counseling and familiarity with students.*

Especially when there is a poor or no relationship between the school guidance counselor and a student, the SRO often fills the gap. However, in addition to the serious risk of giving poor advice, SROs are exposed to the criticism—and even civil liability—of practicing psychological counseling without a license when they help students with personal problems unrelated to the law. Nevertheless, the vast majority of school administrators said they trusted the SROs' judgment to know when to refer a student for professional help with a personal problem and involve the parents.

Most familiarity between SROs and students is harmless, such as students using informal names to refer to the officers (e.g., "Officer Nancy" or "JD"). However, a few SROs have skirted or exceeded the boundaries of appropriate behavior with students. Programs can help SROs balance being supportive while remaining an authority figure by:

- establishing specific guidelines for appropriate and inappropriate behavior;
- arranging to provide formal training for SROs on the topic; and
- instructing SROs to act defensively—for example, never close their office doors when talking with a student of the opposite sex.

Some parents become concerned that an SRO's presence in the schools suggests their children's schools must be unsafe. Programs that used PTAs, other community meetings, newsletters, letters, and newspaper articles to inform parents about the program reported few or no objections from parents. In turn, *parents who support the program often encourage their children to seek out the SRO for help and, in three different sites, have helped pressure city officials to reverse their plans to drop their SRO programs*.

Evaluating the Program. Very few of the 19 programs included in the study conducted useful and valid assessments of their programs. However, *program evaluation is essential* to learn whether and how the program needs improvement and to convince funding sources of the importance of continuing the program.

The first step in any evaluation is to review the program's goals and then *decide what questions to ask about each goal*. For example, if a program's goals include reducing truancy and improving kids' image of the police, the evaluation can ask:

- By how much have truancy rates changed since the program began?
- How have students' opinions of the police changed since the program began?

The second step is to *identify the information to collect* that will answer the questions, and the third step is to *determine how to collect the information*.

The law enforcement agency and school system should collaborate on the assessment by interviewing or obtaining written assessments from principals and assistant principals. One school district conducts annual focus groups of randomly selected students designed to assess their opinions and use of the program.

Program supervisors need to circulate the evaluation findings to the chief or sheriff, the city manager or mayor, and the school board to bolster the case for continued funding. The program also needs to give the evaluation results to each SRO and school for purposes identifying problem areas that need addressing.

In: School Resource Officers
Editor: Andrew O'Murphy

Chapter 3

COMPARISON OF PROGRAM ACTIVITIES AND LESSONS LEARNED AMONG 19 SCHOOL RESOURCE OFFICER (SRO) PROGRAMS[*]

Peter Finn, Michael Shively, Jack McDevitt, William Lassiter and Tom Rich

EXECUTIVE SUMMARY

Abt Associates Inc. and its subcontractors conducted a National Assessment of School Resource Officer (SRO) Programs ("National Assessment") through a cooperative agreement with the National Institute of Justice (NIJ) supported by the Office of Community Oriented Policing Services (the COPS Office).

Section 1. Introduction

The purpose of the National Assessment was to identify what program "models" have been implemented, how programs have been implemented, and what lessons selected programs may have for other programs. To obtain this information, *Abt Associates and its subcontractors collected implementation data by telephone and on site from 19 SRO programs.*

This cross-site report discusses commonalities and differences among the 19 sites with a particular focus on lessons learned—information based on the experience of the sites that can benefit other jurisdictions in setting up or improving an SRO program.

The report focuses on seven issues:

1. Choosing a Program Model
2. Defining Specific SRO Roles and Responsibilities

---

[*] This is an edited, reformatted and augmented version of the National Institute of Justice, dated February 28, 2005.

3. Recruiting SROs
4. Training and Supervising SROs
5. Collaborating with School Administrators and Teachers
6. Working with Students and Parents
7. Evaluating SRO Programs

Section 2. Choosing a Program Model

In the basic School Resource Officer "triad" model, SROs enforce the law, teach, and mentor. Most of the 19 programs included in the National Assessment reflect this model, but *the level of emphasis that SROs devote to each of these three roles varies considerably across and within programs.* As a result, it is more accurate to think in terms of where individual programs and SROs fall along a *continuum* between, at one extreme, engaging in mostly law enforcement activities and, at the other extreme, engaging in mostly teaching and mentoring.

There are several considerations that staff in new—and existing—SRO programs should think about in deciding how their SROs should allocate their time according to the three basic SRO roles, including *the level of crime and disorder* in a school and *the wishes of the school administration.* However, *the personality and experience of the individual SRO* may ultimately prove the most decisive factor in determining where on the continuum each SRO's balance of activities falls.

Section 3. Defining Specific SRO Roles and Responsibilities

When SRO programs fail to define the SROs' roles and responsibilities in detail before— or even after—the officers take up their posts in the schools, problems are often rampant— and often last for months and even years. Successful programs have generally followed several steps in developing a list of SRO roles and responsibilities, including:

- identify roles and responsibilities *in writing*;
- *avoid relying on a personal relationship, easy access, and a handshake* between police and school administrators for establishing SRO roles;
- *involve the schools* in developing the SRO roles and responsibilities;
- *distribute* the roles and responsibilities, and *periodically review them*; and
- provide *a mechanism for resolving disagreements* between school administrators and SROs about the officers' responsibilities.

In developing the written description of SRO roles and responsibilities:

- narrow the considerable leeway of *what it means for SROs to engage in "law enforcement"*;
- make clear whether and how SROs will be responsible for *enforcing discipline*; and

- be specific about the SROs' *teaching, and counseling and mentoring, responsibilities*.

Section 4. Recruiting SROs

Carefully screening applicants is usually necessary for recruiting and retaining officers who are well qualified by temperament and skills to be SROs. It is especially important to develop written criteria for who can qualify as an SRO, including choosing someone who:

- likes and cares about kids;
- has the temperament to work with school administrators;
- has the capacity to work independently;
- is not a rookie; and
- knows the community in which he or she will be working.

Other keys to successful screening and recruitment include:

- assigning officers with the right personality—someone, as one principal put it, with "an outgoing, caring, but no-nonsense personality";
- using incentives, such as take-home cruisers and a salary increment, when there is a lack of qualified applicants; and
- involving school district and school-level administrators in the screening process to increase acceptance of the SROs by school personnel.

Section 5. Training and Supervising SROs

Few of the 19 programs train all their SROs before they go on the job. Nevertheless, *any delay in training can be a serious problem* because SROs then have to learn their jobs by "sinking or swimming." One program has provided for timely pre-service training by arranging for a long-standing SRO to become certified as an SRO trainer. Several other programs arrange for new SROs to "shadow" an experienced SRO before going on the job. A number of programs also provide in-service training, including sending SROs for advanced training with reputable SRO training organizations. Most SROs and school administrators agree that it would be valuable to train principals and assistant principals along with SROs as a team.

Most programs fail to provide consistent or close supervision of the SROs' work. However, adequate supervision of SROs is important to make sure the officers are working to their full potential and are not experiencing unreported or unacknowledged problems. Typically, programs require SROs to complete monthly activity logs and meet once a year with the supervisor. In some programs, supervisors periodically visit SROs and school administrators at the schools and observe the officers teach.

Section 6. Collaborating with School Administrators and Teachers

Perhaps the single most troublesome area for most programs has been establishing productive relationships between their SROs and principals and assistant principals, in large part because of fundamental differences in the law enforcement culture and the school culture in terms of goals, strategies, and methods. Administrators expressed three principal initial concerns about having an SRO in their schools:

- *Who's In Charge?*
- *Who Makes the Decision to Arrest?*
- *Why Isn't "My" SRO Available All the Time?*

Over time, most administrators developed good working relations with their SROs and came to value the program highly. While sometimes this change in attitude involved just getting used to the SRO, ***many programs found they could expedite the process of improving working relationships*** by:

- collaborating with school administrators in planning, operating, and supervising the program;
- explaining program benefits to administrators;
- orienting school-level administrators to the program;
- training SROs before they go on the job; and
- addressing administrator concerns about the SROs' availability.

Gaining the support of teachers is essential if SROs want to get invited to teach their classes—and ***teaching is an important SRO responsibility for improving kids' perceptions about "cops" and for taking advantage of a unique opportunity for motivating students to seek out the SROs*** outside of class when the youth are having problems. Many SROs are constantly invited by teachers to address their classes because the officers have taken the time to:

- orient teachers to the program before it begins;
- explain how SROs improve student learning; and
- go beyond the normal SRO responsibilities to help teachers.

Section 7. Working with Students and Their Parents

Program coordinators, SROs, and school administrators all recognize the difficulty SROs experience trying to maintain authority as enforcers of the law while at the same time preserving a helping relationship with students as teachers and mentors. ***Walking this fine line plays itself out in two particular areas: (1) counseling and (2) supportive interpersonal relationships between SROs and individual students.***

Especially when there is a poor or no relationship between the school guidance counselor and a student, the SRO often fills the gap. However, in addition to the serious risk of giving poor advice, SROs are exposed to the criticism—and even civil liability—of practicing psychological counseling without a license when they help students with personal problems unrelated to the law. Nevertheless, the vast majority of school administrators said they trusted the SROs' judgment to know when to refer a student for professional help with a personal problem and involve the parents.

Most familiarity between SROs and students is harmless, such as students using informal names to refer to the officers (e.g., "Officer Nancy" or "JD"). However, a few SROs have skirted or exceeded the boundaries of appropriate behavior with students. Programs can help SROs balance being supportive while remaining an authority figure by:

- establishing specific guidelines for appropriate and inappropriate behavior;
- arranging to provide formal training for SROs on the topic; and
- instructing SROs to act defensively—for example, never closing their office doors when talking with a student of the opposite sex.

Some parents become concerned that an SRO's presence in the schools suggests their children's schools must be unsafe. Programs that used PTAs, other community meetings, newsletters, letters to the home, and newspaper articles to inform parents about the program reported few or no objections from parents. In turn, *parents who support the program often encourage their children to seek out the SRO for help and, in three different sites, have helped pressure city officials to reverse their plans to drop their SRO programs.*

Section 8. Evaluating the Program

Very few of the 19 programs included in the study conducted useful and valid assessments of their programs. However, *program evaluation is essential* to learn whether and how the program needs improvement and to convince funding sources of the importance of continuing the program.

The first step in any evaluation is to review the program's goals and then *decide what questions to ask about each goal*. For example, if a program's goals include reducing truancy and improving kids' image of the police, the evaluation can ask:

- By how much have truancy rates changed since the program began?
- How have students' opinions of the police changed since the program began?

The second step is to *identify the information to collect* that will answer these questions, and the third step is to *determine how to collect the information*.

The law enforcement agency and school system should collaborate on the assessment by interviewing or obtaining written assessments from principals and assistant principals. One school district conducts annual focus groups of randomly selected students designed to assess their opinions and use of the program.

Program supervisors need to circulate the evaluation findings to the chief or sheriff, the city manager or mayor, and the school board to bolster their case for continued funding, and distribute them to each SRO and school for purposes identifying problem areas that need addressing.

SECTION 1: INTRODUCTION

Abt Associates Inc. conducted a National Assessment of School Resource Officer (SRO) Programs ("National Assessment") through a cooperative agreement with the National Institute of Justice (NIJ) supported by the Office of Community Oriented Policing Services (the COPS Office).

Background to the Report

There has been growing interest in placing sworn law enforcement officers in schools as School Resource Officers (SROs) to improve school safety and improve relations between police officers and youth. By 1999 there were at least 12,000 law enforcement officers serving full-time as SROs. Thirty percent of local police departments, employing 62 percent of all officers, had full-time SROs during 1999. Local police departments had about 9,100 full-time SROs assigned to schools. A majority of the departments serving 10,000 or more residents had SROs.[1] An estimated 38 percent of sheriffs' departments, employing 63 percent of all officers, had deputies assigned full-time as SROs. Nationwide, about 2,900 sheriffs' deputies worked as SROs during 1997.[2]

However, when the National Assessment began in May 2000, relatively little was known about SRO programs. The purpose of the project was to identify what SRO program "models" have been implemented, how SRO programs have been implemented, and what lessons selected programs may have for other programs. To obtain this information, *Abt Associates collected implementation data by telephone and on site from 19 programs*:

- 5 large established programs;
- 4 large new programs;[3]
- 5 small established programs; and
- 5 new programs.

We defined "large" SRO programs as those operated by law enforcement agencies with 100 or more sworn officers and "small" programs as those operated by agencies with less than 100 officers (the Bureau of Justice Statistics' definitions for large and small agencies). We defined "established" programs as those that had been in existence since at least 1995. The definition of "new" that we used was that the site had not reported SROs in schools in the past on the 1999 Bureau of Justice Statistics Law Enforcement Management and Administrative Statistics (LEMAS) survey, and the site was the recipient of a COPS in Schools grant in 1999 from the COPS Office for hiring SROs.

This cross-site report discusses commonalities and differences among the 19 sites, representing a combined total of 104 SROs. The report focuses especially on lessons learned—that is, information based on the experience of the sites that could benefit other jurisdictions in setting up or improving an SRO program. The box "Basic Site Information for 19 SRO Programs" presents selected features of each program.

Program/ Jurisdiction	Location	Population of Community Served*	Agency Size (sworn)*	Date Begun	Number of SROs	Number of Schools Served and Grade Levels
Basic Site Information for 19 SRO Programs						
Large Established Programs						
Large Established #1 city	Mid-West	75,000	140	1995	3	3 junior high
Large Established #2 city	Southwest	500,000	1,000	1962	21	21 elementary middle
Large Established #3 county	South	100,000	250	1995	9	14 junior high middle senior high
Large Established #4 city	South	50,000	150	1995	3	3 junior high
Large Established #5 city	West Coast	200,000	200	1993	15	70 K-12
Large New Programs						
Large New #1 county	South Central	600,000	130	1999	5	5 K-12
Large New #2 county	Mid-West	400,000	100	1999	5	9 -- varies by county
Large New #3 city	Northeast	45,000	100	1999	3	3 middle high school
Large New #4 city	Southwest	250,000	600	1999	38	10 middle 20 high school
Small Established Programs						
Small Established #1 city	South	40,000	40	1995	1	1 high school
Small Established #2 city	South	20,000	50	1993	3	3 middle high school
Small Established #3 county	South	60,000	50	1992	3	5 middle high school
Small Established #4 county	South	27,000	30	1994	4	4 middle high school
Small Established #5 county	South	35,000	30	1995	4	4 middle high school
Small New Programs						
Small New #1 county	South	25.000	10	1999	2	1 high school
Small New #2 county	South	24,000	20	1999	1	1 high school
Small New #3 county	South	25,000	10	2000	1	1 high school
Small New #4 county	South	20,000	10	2000	1	1 high school
Small New #5 city	South	20,000	10	2000	1	2 middle high school

Other Reports Prepared for the National Assessment

The cross-site report is one of six reports that Abt Associates and its subcontractors (see the box "The Research Team") have prepared for NIJ as part of the National Assessment. The other five reports, all available from NIJ, are summarized briefly below:

1. The *National Survey of SRO Programs and Affiliated Schools* summarizes the results of 322 responses to a mail survey of law enforcement agencies with SRO programs and 108 responses from affiliated schools.

2. An *Interim Report: Fear and Trust* summarize preliminary impressionistic observations concerning (a) perceptions of fear about campus safety among school administrators, faculty, and students among 15 of the 19 sites and (b) trust in the police among these groups in the 15 sites.

3. *Case Studies of 19 School Resource Officer (SRO) Programs* provides in-depth descriptions of each program's history, SROs, program activities, and program monitoring and evaluation efforts.

4. *Results of a Survey of Students in Three Large New SRO Programs* presents the results of a survey of nearly 1,000 students designed to identify the relationship between perception of safety and the SRO program.

5. The *Final Project Report* describes the activities Abt Associates conducted for the National Assessment and summarizes the study findings. The report has five sections: the mail survey; the process of selecting the 19 study sites; the site visits; modifications to the research methodology; and data analysis and findings.

Information from the first four reports—in particular, from the case studies report—has been integrated, as appropriate, in the present cross-site report.

THE RESEARCH TEAM

Three subcontractors assisted Abt Associates Inc. in collecting, analyzing, and reporting the data for the project:

- The Center for Criminal Justice Policy Research at Northeastern University
- The Justice and Safety Center, College of Justice and Safety, at Eastern Kentucky University
- the Center for the Prevention of School Violence in North Carolina

Two consultants assisted Northeastern University in collecting and analyzing the data:

- Timothy Bynum, School of Criminal Justice at Michigan State University
- Scott Decker, Department of Criminology and Criminal Justice at the University of Missouri-St. Louis

---

Topics the Report Addresses

Rather than trying to address every issue the 19 programs have confronted, the cross-site report focuses on a selected number of areas where new programs may run into serious problems or where many existing programs could still use help. Five criteria guided the selection of the topic areas that the report addresses:

1. *A number of the 19 programs* in the study experienced difficulty with the issue.
2. The problem area is not a trivial one but rather *can have a serious effect* on preventing a program from achieving its goals.

3. There are ***documented solutions*** to the problem—that is, some of the 19 sites overcame the obstacle.

4. Program planners and participants ***are likely to implement*** the solutions these programs came up with.

5. ***No existing materials*** present the solutions to the problem as comprehensively or present solutions based on actual program experience.[4]

Based on these criteria, the report focuses on seven issues:

1. Choosing a Program Model
2. Defining Specific SRO Roles and Responsibilities
3. Recruiting SROs[5]
4. Training and Supervising SROs[6]
5. Collaborating with School Administrators and Teachers
6. Working with Parents and Students
7. Evaluating SRO Programs.

The report does not purport to present the problems or solutions of the "typical" SRO program or of a random sample of programs. Indeed, because of the criteria used to select the programs for study (see the separate project report, "Final Project History," for the complete study methodology), the programs selected are likely to be exemplary rather than representative. However, while the study lacks generalizability because we did not randomly select the programs, it represents the most intensive study of programs to date—involving a total of 198 person days (almost 8 months) spent on site.

SECTION 2: CHOOSING A PROGRAM MODEL

SECTION SUMMARY

The basic School Resource Officer model involves SROs in enforcing the law, teaching, and mentoring. Most of the 19 programs in the National Assessment reflect this model, but the level of emphasis that SROs devote to each of these three roles varies considerably across and within programs. For example, some SROs focus primarily on law enforcement, while one SRO spends 80 percent of his time teaching and mentoring. As a result, it is more accurate to think in terms of where individual programs and SROs fall along a ***continuum*** between, at one extreme, engaging in mostly law enforcement activities and, at the other extreme, engaging in mostly teaching, mentoring, or both.

However, the relative emphasis devoted to each of these three roles changes in most programs because ***implementation is often an incremental process in which what an SRO actually does is developed over time rather than representing a response to a preconceived conceptual model.***

In particular, most of the 19 sites focused initially on law enforcement and evolved only later into a more balanced approach with increased teaching and mentoring. Why?

- Many law enforcement agencies and schools did not provide their SROs with either instructions on how they should spend their time on campus or training in how to teach and mentor. As a result, most SROs fell back on doing what they *were* trained to do and *did* know how to do—enforce the law.
- Many school administrators wanted the SROs to do nothing but enforce the law, while, at the same time, many SROs were nervous about talking in front of a class or mentoring students.
- Teachers were often initially uncomfortable inviting SROs into their classrooms—or were not even aware that the officers could teach.

In most programs, SROs and school administrators alike came over time to realize the benefits of officers teaching classes and mentoring students.

There are several considerations that new—and existing—SRO programs should think about in deciding how their SROs should allocate their time.

- The *level of crime and disorder* in a school should influence the proportion of time the SRO spends on law enforcement compared with teaching and mentoring.
- Programs need to consider—although by no means always or completely accede to—*the wishes of the school administration* in establishing the SROs' focuses.
- *The personality and experience of the individual SRO* may ultimately prove the most decisive factor in determining where on the continuum each SRO's balance of activities falls.

Programs should expect that, *after SROs have been trained* in how to teach and mentor, they may increase the proportion of time they spend teaching and mentoring. Often, it is a matter of the SROs establishing their credibility with administrators, faculty, and students *over time* that results in a balance among the SROs' three roles.

Because programs evolve over time, and because schools' needs may change, SROs and school administrators should not feel they have to stick with their program's initial or current position on the continuum. Furthermore, some programs, within certain limits, encourage their SROs to emphasize one or another of the three roles at any given time based on changes in the schools' needs, turnover among school administrators, and alterations in student behavior.

The basic School Resource Officer model supported by the Office of Community Oriented Policing Services (the COPS Office), the National Association of School Resource Officers (NASRO), Corbin and Associates, and the Center for the Prevention of School Violence (CPSV) expects SROs to engage in three types of activities: law enforcement, teaching, and mentoring. Most of the 19 programs included in this study reflect this model—but the level of emphasis in terms of priority and time that SROs devote to each role varies considerably across and within programs. As a result, *it is more accurate to think in terms of where individual programs and SROs fall along a continuum within the tripartite model* between, at one extreme, engaging in mostly law enforcement activities and, at the other extreme, engaging in mostly teaching, mentoring, or both.

How the Programs Fall on the Three-Focus Continuum

Abt Associates' survey of SRO programs conducted at the beginning of this study (see the separate report, National Survey of SRO Programs and Affiliated Schools) found that, among 322 law enforcement agencies that returned the questionnaire, SROs on average divided their time as follows:

- 50 percent on law enforcement activities;
- 25 percent on counseling or mentoring;
- 13 percent on teaching; and
- 12 percent on other activities (e.g., meetings).

SROs who responded to a survey from the Center for the Prevention of School Violence at the North Carolina Department of Juvenile Justice and Delinquency Prevention reported that they typically spent about:

- 50 percent performing the law enforcement role,
- 20 percent teaching, and
- 30 percent counseling.[7]

There is considerable variation in the proportion of time the SROs in the 19 sites included in this study devote to each of the three roles. Two SROs, for example, spend nearly 100 percent of their time doing law enforcement.

- Two years into the program, the lone SRO in a small new site had not started any teaching duties or collaborated with any outside groups or organizations. While police and school administrators would like to see the SRO develop teaching and mentoring activities, she has been so busy with law enforcement activities, especially investigations and case preparation, that she has been unable to do anything else. During one two-day period, she was working on 10 theft reports, an armed robbery report, a drug possession and trafficking case, and a first degree criminal mischief investigation involving slashed tires and cut phone lines.
- The SRO at the high school in a large new site spends almost all his time on law enforcement in part due to personal choice and in part because of school administrator instructions. Because the SRO views his role as addressing criminal issues, and because as a single father he refuses to give up his evenings, he rarely attends after-school events with its opportunity to mentor kids. For her part, the principal has not included the SRO in staff meetings and sees no need for officer involvement in the classroom. As a result, the SRO has almost no interaction with teachers. In terms of mentoring, the principal expects the SRO to refer students with emotional or family issues to counselors rather than address the problems himself.

At the other end of the continuum, the middle school SRO in a small established site spends about 80 percent of his time teaching and mentoring, and only 20 percent of his time doing law enforcement. Furthermore, even when they devote a plurality of their time to law enforcement activities, many SROs spend a *majority* of their time on the *combined* activities of teaching and mentoring.

SROs in the same school district—even though they are all participating in the same SRO program—may spend very different percentages of time on each of the three roles. In one jurisdiction, the high school and junior high school SROs do more counseling than do the two middle school SROs because the latter lose so much time traveling among the several middle schools. In one large new site, the specific needs of each school, as well as the particular preferences and operating style of each SRO, have led to diverse emphases in each of several school districts.

School level can also influence the ratio of time SROs spend on law enforcement versus teaching and mentoring. In general, SROs assigned to middle and elementary schools are able to spend more time teaching because of the reduced need for enforcing the law with younger students. In addition, some SROs and school administrators feel that younger students are more amenable to educational approaches than are "jaded" high school students.

There are widespread differences, too, in the proportion of time SROs spend on teaching versus mentoring. In some school districts, officers rarely teach in the classroom, while in other districts officers teach frequently at feeder schools in addition to their assigned schools.

- In three jurisdictions, SROs spend considerable time teaching because all of the SROs are certified D.A.R.E. instructors. In one of these three jurisdictions, the SROs are also trained as Child Abuse Resistance Education (C.A.R.E.) instructors, a local program created to curb the high rate of child abuse. Over a period of 6 to 8 weeks, these dually certified SROs spend as many as three days a week devoted almost entirely to teaching at elementary schools.
- SROs in two large established sites are responsible for teaching the Gang Resistance Education and Training (G.R.E.A.T.) curriculum, which alone can take up to one-quarter of their time for many weeks. One of these SROs estimates he spends 40 percent of his time in the classroom, sometimes teaching seven straight periods a day.

The relative emphasis devoted to the three types of activities changes over time in most programs. *Many program participants described implementation as an incremental process in which what an SRO actually does is developed over time rather than representing a response to a preconceived conceptual model.* In particular, many of the 19 sites had an *initial* focus on law enforcement that *evolved* into a more balanced approach with increased teaching and mentoring (although law enforcement may still remain the highest priority). For example, most of the SROs in the five small established sites shifted over time from doing primarily or almost exclusively law enforcement to spending increased time on education and mentoring.

This evolution of role emphasis is consistent with the findings of research conducted by the Center for the Prevention of School Violence[8] that found that an initial focus on law enforcement often evolves into a more balanced approach, although law enforcement typically remains the single highest priority among the three types of activities as it did among several of the 19 sites in the present study. The COPS in Schools training manual used by the COPS Office also observes that SRO non-enforcement roles tend to develop more fully over time.

Many programs began with a major emphasis on law enforcement at the expense of teaching and counseling for reasons that had nothing to do with advance planning on the parts of either the law enforcement agencies or schools.

- Many law enforcement agencies and participating schools did not provide their SROs with instructions or even guidance on how they should spend their time on campus except, perhaps, for a vague mandate to enforce the law, teach classes, and mentor kids. Some law enforcement executives in the small established sites applied for grant funding because the money was available—and then did not give the SROs *any* assignments. As a result, SROs did what they knew best—enforced the law.
- Because few SROs received training how to teach in the classroom or mentor kids, they again fell back on doing what they *were* trained to do—enforce the law.
- SROs were also significantly guided in what they initially did by what their local school administrators wanted or would allow them to do. Some principals were receptive to—and facilitated—the idea of SROs teaching classes; however, most principals initially wanted SROs to limit their activities to enforcing the law and, in some cases, enforcing discipline.
- Many teachers were initially uncomfortable inviting SROs into their classrooms because faculty objected to an armed presence in their rooms or assumed that the officers had nothing of educational value to offer students.

For several reasons, over time SROs tend to devote a larger proportion of their time to teaching and mentoring.

- As principals, assistant principals, and teachers become comfortable with their particular SROs and aware of their skills, administrators and faculty increasingly support the SROs' spending more and more time in the classroom.
- SROs, many of whom are initially nervous—even terrified—about teaching, become more comfortable with the role after giving it a try, especially if they receive training in how to teach young people.
- SROs do more mentoring as students come to trust them. Because of this trust, students approach the SROs to share personal problems, offering the officers an opportunity to mentor and counsel.
- As crime (e.g., fights) and other student misconduct decline as a result of the SROs' presence, consistency, and firmness, the officers find they have more time to devote to teaching and mentoring.

How to Select a Position on the Continuum

Despite the strong tendency to begin the SRO program on the law enforcement end of the continuum, it is clear from the experiences of these and the other programs that *there are several considerations that new—and existing—SRO programs should think about in deciding how their SROs should allocate their time.*[9]

- *Level of crime or disorder.* Not surprisingly, most SROs concentrate more or less on the law enforcement role depending on the level of crime or disorder in the schools to which they are assigned. For example, an SRO reported that fights and assaults occur every day at his school and they involve as many as 50 students. As a result, almost all of his time is taken up stopping them and then dealing with the aftermath. Of course, there are exceptions. In one large new site, the longest active SRO working at a highly distressed, inner-city school district where gang involvement abounds has focused on counseling and mentoring activities. Conversely, the SRO in another school in the same school district uses an almost "SWAT-like" approach even though the school is perhaps the least troubled of all the high schools in the district. Despite these exceptions, *the level of crime and disorder in a school should at least influence the proportion of time the SRO spends on law enforcement compared with teaching and mentoring.* It should have this influence for several reasons:
  - SROs will not have time to teach or do mentoring in a school with many serious discipline problems because administrators will be constantly calling on them to deal with fights, weapons, drugs, and other situations on campus that require a law enforcement response and then may require follow-up paperwork and court time. Regardless of administrators' preferences, several SROs reported that they had to get control over miscreant students before they could do almost anything else because they would be derelict in their duties if they ignored the serious misconduct the students continued to engage in when the officers first arrived at their schools.
  - SROs will lose all credibility with administrators, faculty, and students if they turn a blind eye to serious misbehavior in the school—credibility they need to establish to be effective as teachers and mentors.
  - By addressing serious student misconduct, SROs get the opportunity, if they handle the problem correctly, to gain respect from students. On the one hand, many troublemakers whom the SRO arrests, issues a citation to, or turns in to administrators realize that—unlike the past when they would only be suspended or given detention—there will now be consistent and strict punishment for misbehaving. On the other hand, when "good" kids see that there are real consequences for misbehavior, they may become more willing to report rumored or observed misconduct confidentially to the SROs.
  - By arresting, citing, or turning in students to school administrators, SROs get to know the troublesome kids and can then concentrate some of their effort on mentoring them. A number of SROs reported they ended up mentoring kids

whom they had initially gotten to know by punishing their unacceptable behavior in a firm but respectful manner.

- **Wishes and culture of the school.** Programs need to consider—although by no means always accede to—*the wishes of the school administration* in establishing the ratio of time that SROs spend on law enforcement, teaching, and mentoring. In a large established site, school administrators made education and mentoring the SROs' principal focus from the beginning, with enforcement always considered a distant third.

  However, in many sites school administrators initially preferred—or even required—that SROs spend almost all their time doing law enforcement. Interested SROs can work to expand their role in schools whose administrators want them to do nothing but enforce the law. Of course, disobeying a strong-willed administrator's instructions can be difficult. For example, a principal in a large new site forbids her SRO from engaging in any other activity than addressing criminal manners. She instructs her staff *always* to contact parents before turning a child over to the SRO. She expects the SRO to "know his limitations" and refer students to counselors rather than handle difficult emotional or family issues himself. She also sees no need for SRO involvement in the classroom. By the time students reach high school, she claims, "They have become bored with law-related education, tired of hearing the same old messages so many times. By high school, kids see the officers as law enforcers and expect them to act as such." However, SROs can sometimes *eventually* turn more attention to teaching and mentoring if they can craft a collaborative relationship with administrators and faculty; acceding temporarily to administrator wishes that the officers concentrate on enforcing the law can help forge this relationship.

  Using that positive relationship as a foundation, SROs can then educate administrators to the importance of the officers' teaching and mentoring roles. Indeed, as administrators and teachers became comfortable with their particular SROs, in almost every site they increasingly supported the SROs' spending more and more time teaching and mentoring.

- **Personality and skills of the SROs. The style and orientation of the individual officer** may ultimately prove the most decisive factor in determining where on the continuum each SRO's balance of activities falls.

  - An SRO in a large established site who taught extensively when she was a physical education instructor before becoming a police officer chose to spend considerable time teaching kids because she was comfortable with the role and felt that at the elementary and middle school levels where she worked the kids were more impressionable than kids at the high school level would be.
  - An SRO in a large new site who always wanted to teach and who is married to a teacher has made classroom activities a standard in his daily routine.
  - An SRO in a small established site had jumped at the opportunity to serve as an SRO mostly because, before becoming a sheriff's deputy, he had hoped to pursue a teaching career.
  - The SRO in a large new site reported that he spends most of his time on investigative and follow-up activities at the district's high school and three middle schools. Even though a lot of his work involves investigating alleged

sexual assaults, he has not offered any classes or presentations focused on the prevention and consequences of date rape. He stated that he enjoys working "big cases."

- A high school SRO in a large new site, unlike the other SROs in the program, attends almost no after-school events (where he would be able to mentor kids) because, as a single father of a 5-year-old, he wants to spend as much time as possible with his child.

- In a large new site in a highly distressed, inner-city school district, one of the school district's SROs prefers to relate to kids in the formal setting of the classroom rather than mentor them in his office or in the corridors. A second SRO in the district focuses more on mentoring activities than on teaching because of his interest in the field of counseling. Objectively, without knowing the personal preferences and individual personalities in play, one might have expected that *neither* the education *nor* the counseling role would have held such significance for the SROs in this school district where the burdens of gang activity and violence might easily have elicited a greater emphasis on enforcement. However, individual SRO preferences and personalities trumped school safety conditions.

- *Training.* The relative emphasis SROs place on the three basic SRO program components is affected by whether and how soon they develop teaching and mentoring skills. While many SROs learn how to perform both of these activities by trial and error, training SROs in how to perform them can expedite by months their devoting serious attention to teaching and mentoring.

- After an SRO in a large new site learned at a NASRO training about the significant potential for classroom teaching, he expanded his teaching load considerably.

- After they had attended a COPS in Schools conference, which has a 90-minute segment on "classroom strategies," the SROs in a small new site dramatically increased their teaching and counseling.

Whatever the initial mix of roles a program's SROs start out with, one large new site implemented a policy that all programs can consider adopting. The site produced a brochure that presents the triad of roles but emphasizes that any given SRO in any given school may emphasize one or another of the three elements at any given time or continuously based on several factors, including changes in the school's needs, administrator turnover, and alterations in student behavior (e.g., less fighting).

Deciding the relative emphasis the program should place on law enforcement, teaching, and mentoring is a relatively broad issue. Programs still need to decide what *specific* responsibilities SROs will have *within* each of these three program focuses—the subject of the following Section.

SECTION 3: DEFINING SPECIFIC SRO ROLES AND RESPONSIBILITIES

SECTION SUMMARY

One the most frequent and destructive mistakes many SRO programs make is to fail to define the SROs' roles and responsibilities in detail before—or even after—the officers take up their posts in the schools. When programs fail to do this, problems are often rampant at the beginning of the program—and often persist for months and even years.

Successful programs have generally followed several steps in developing a list of SRO roles and responsibilities.

(1) Identify roles and responsibilities *in writing*.
(2) *Avoid relying on a personal relationship, easy access, and a handshake* between police and school administrators for establishing SRO roles because:
   - key personnel change;
   - verbal agreements are subject to misinterpretation and distortion; and
   - written role descriptions make it easier to evaluate SROs' performance.
(3) *Involve the schools* in developing the SRO roles and responsibilities.
(4) *Distribute the list* to SROs and to school district and school building administrators, and *periodically review them*.
(5) Provide *a mechanism for resolving disagreements* between school administrators and SROs about the officers' responsibilities.

In developing the written description of SRO roles and responsibilities, keep the following considerations in mind:

   - Narrow the considerable leeway in *what it means for SROs to engage in "law enforcement."*
   - Make clear whether and how SROs will be responsible for *enforcing discipline*.
   - Be specific about the SROs' *teaching and mentoring responsibilities*.
   - Specify which responsibilities *apply to* all *SROs in* all *schools* (e.g., patrolling the cafeteria at lunch) and which responsibilities *are negotiable* between individual SROs and their local school administrators (e.g., standing in the corridors between classes).

There is a close relationship between determining the proportion of time SROs should spend on law enforcement, teaching, and counseling, on the one hand, and defining their specific roles and responsibilities, on the other hand. However, deciding the proportion of time SROs spend in each of these three areas is a broad issue. Specifying roles and responsibilities is a "micro" issue where attention to detail is critical.

A Critical Early Step—but It's Never Too Late to Do It

One of the most frequent and destructive mistakes many SRO programs make is to fail to define in detail the SROs' roles and responsibilities before the officers take up their posts in the schools. *Even though the SROs' specific responsibilities may change over time and may vary from school to school, it is still essential to define them at the outset.* As the following observations by program participants attest, when programs fail to specify roles and responsibilities, problems are often rampant at the beginning of the program. Moreover, because of turnover among SROs and local school administrators, these problems can persist—for years—until they are finally addressed.

- *Last school year was . . . consumed by trying to figure out what the role of the officer was to be. The actual role continues to evolve.* – small new program
- *The biggest early problem was figuring out what the SRO should do. They [program participants] were given no "game plan," and he had to figure it out as he went along. The principal and the SRO "played it by ear."* – small new program
- *There was a major gap in understanding about the SRO's and school administrators' duties, responsibilities, and legal obligations to act in certain situations.* – large new program
- *The lack of defined roles caused a great deal of tension and frustration at the high school where the SRO and principal both reported they routinely "butt heads."* – large new program
- *SROs recounted feeling uncomfortable and even alarmed by the inactivity and uncertainty of their early days.* – large new program

The potentially damaging effects of failing to clearly establish SRO responsibilities are illustrated in a large new site where there was major gap in understanding about the SROs' and school administrators' respective duties, responsibilities, and legal obligations to act in certain situations. Monthly logs written by all three SROs highlight this problem. The following account of a reported child molestation, taken from one of these logs, exemplifies the degree of tension that can erupt at particularly troubling or stressful times if roles are not clarified in advance. In this case, a teacher had given the SRO a letter left behind by a student in which the student describes having been sexually abused at home. The SRO conferred about the letter with both her police supervisor and the school's principal. She wrote:

> *[The principal] informed me that the Aunt of the female student who wrote the letter would be at the school at 1130hrs. I informed [the] Capt. of this meeting and asked if he wanted me to attend, Capt. stated he did. . . . [The principal] expressed wanting me to do lunch duty instead of attending the meeting with the Aunt. I informed him that I needed to be involved in the meeting due to the seriousness of the letter. He was upset at my decision. After the meeting adjourned at 1215hrs I left the office to help with lunch duty. Upon leaving the office there was a boy on the phone who was crying and told [the principal] that he was jumped at lunch. [The principal] looked at me and stated that "this is why I needed you at lunch . . . I knew this was going to happen!" As I began to enter his office [he] yelled, "I don't need your help . . . this doesn't concern you . . . this doesn't have anything to do with law enforcement! I will contact your supervisor . . . !" I informed him that I realized as an administrator that lunch duty is important because of*

liability reasons and that I try to understand his job as an administrator. However, he needed to try to understand my role as a law enforcement officer and that it was my duty to act on the female student's letter. I realize that he does not understand my position and if he needed to contact my supervisor that was okay. I told [the principal] that I am trying to help him the best I could. [He] calmly told me that he knew I was trying to help, but that he needed a line drawn and he would contact my supervisor.

Programs have followed several important steps in spelling out their SROs' roles and responsibilities.

Put the Roles and Responsibilities in Writing

Developing a memorandum of agreement (MOU) or contract is of critical importance for minimizing conflict related to:

- who is in charge of the SROs,
- who pays the SROs salaries, training, and equipment,
- when SROs are expected to be in school,
- who evaluates the SROs (and how), and
- how conflicts will be resolved.

A detailed discussion of roles and responsibilities can also form part of the MOU or contract. For example, the draft memorandum of agreement in a large new site (which the school district never signed) specified the conditions under which SROs may:

- detain individuals;
- question individuals, including minors;
- conduct pat downs and searches; and
- respond to incidents that violate school policy.

The SROs' roles and responsibilities can also be a stand-alone document. Indeed, *identifying roles and responsibilities in writing may be more important than having an MOU or contract*.

- Four of the five small new sites had MOUs concerning the SROs' deployment in the schools, but the agreements described the officers' activities in very general terms, such as stipulating that the officers worked for the law enforcement agency and noting who paid them and who supervised them. Because the MOUs did not elaborate on the SROs' day-to-day operations, many of the small new sites experienced moderate to serious start-up problems.
  - In one site, because the SRO initially established his role on his own according to his experience and interests, there was tension in his relationships with school administrators as working arrangements developed.
  - In a second site, the first year of the program was problematic in large part because it was primarily consumed by trying to figure out what the SRO's role

was to be. The most important tension has been the changing nature of the SRO's role: the officer has had to assume a wide variety of tasks, with his workday often consumed pursuing minor incidents typically handled in the past by teachers or other school staff (such as finding students who have skipped class).

- In a small established site, the formal contract between the school system and sheriff's department merely states that the department agrees to supply officers for the SRO position. Serious problems with the program resulted.

Program coordinators in some small sites insist that informal verbal understandings are sufficient or even desirable for establishing SRO roles and responsibilities (see the box "Sealing Agreements with a Handshake"). However, there are several critical advantages to developing a *written* and *detailed* description of SRO roles and responsibilities.

(1) A written list forces participants to iron out many potential conflicts in advance. As a former SRO wrote, "Will the officer, for example, be expected to routinely provide lunchtime coverage in the school cafeteria or bus loading and unloading duties? Most agencies believe that these are *not* law enforcement functions and are the responsibility of the school's administrative team. Yet what happens when the principal *insists* that the officer comply with a directive to work these specific assignments?"[10]

(2) The list serves as written record everyone can refer to when in doubt. Verbal agreements are subject to misinterpretation and distortion, especially as time passes.

(3) Even if the initial verbal arrangement works smoothly, key personnel change, and new law enforcement executives, SROs, and school administrators have nothing written to guide them regarding the previous arrangement (unless they talk with their predecessors).

(4) With a specific written list of SRO responsibilities it is much easier to evaluate whether SROs are performing their jobs properly. One assistant principal observed that she could not evaluate her SRO's performance because there was no list of responsibilities she could refer to.

In developing a written description of SRO roles and responsibilities, programs should keep the following considerations in mind.

- The document should *narrow the considerable leeway in terms of what it means for SROs to engage in "law enforcement."* Does the SRO's responsibility include enforcing the law just on campus or also in the school neighborhood? Does the role include traffic control? For example, the SRO in one small new program regularly helps out with traffic before and after school, while the police supervisor in a small established program prohibits his SRO from doing traffic control. The operations manual for a large established site's program stipulates under "Security Responsibilities" that the SROs will:
  - Maintain a high level of visibility during school entrance and dismissal times as well as during passing periods.
  - Supervise parking lots before school and at dismissal periods.

- Make clear whether SROs will be responsible for *enforcing discipline* on campus and, if so, which violations of school rules they will be responsible for enforcing and what their options are for enforcing them (see the box "To Enforce or Not to Enforce Discipline").

SEALING AGREEMENTS WITH A HANDSHAKE

Especially in small programs, police and school administrators sometimes feel that their personal acquaintanceship and easy access to each other make it unnecessary to document anything about the program in writing.

- In several small established sites, the discussions that occurred before the placement of the officers took place directly between sheriffs or police chiefs and school district superintendents. The agreements they developed were often sealed with a handshake. As one rural law enforcement chief executive said, "We handle these things with a handshake here."
- In most of the small new sites, the solution to poor articulation of SRO duties and expectations that was used was simply to proceed with the hope that the SROs, the schools and the host law enforcement agencies "would work it out as we went along." Initially, SROs in these programs learned their responsibilities by trial and error on the job, while over time the schools developed unwritten standards for appropriate and inappropriate use of the SROs.

Program staff in two small new sites said that an MOU or contract could be harmful:

- A school system and police department both felt that adding procedures and written agreements might hamper the collaborative process in the future.
- An assistant principal said that written guidelines and formal contracts "may only add an excessive amount of unnecessary paperwork."

However, as explained in the text, relying on informal understandings, even in small sites, can lead to trouble from the start. Reflecting these dangers, an article entitled "An Analysis of Interagency Communication Patterns Surrounding Incidents of School Crime" that looked at how schools and law enforcement agencies communicate concluded that, while in rural settings there is a network of interpersonal acquaintanceships formed between law enforcement and school officials, " . . . it is important to realize that the . . . network [of interpersonal acquaintanceships] sometimes impaired communication and interaction."[*]

A good example of the unreliability of relying on informal relationships occurred at a large new site. The local police chief had a good rapport with the superintendent of schools, and together they planned a police-school collaboration. However, shortly after the SRO program began, the school superintendent left his position after a series of incidents that were described as "gross misconduct," including allegations of widespread "kickbacks" and problems relating to alcohol use.

Several board members openly criticized and actively opposed the superintendent. Other members defended him and his suggested policy changes. The struggle polarized opinion around most aspects of the superintendent's "agenda," including the SRO initiative, which was badly stigmatized.

* Minor, Kevin L., Fox, James W., and Wells, James B. "An Analysis of Interagency Communication Patterns Surrounding Incidents of School Crime," *Journal of School Violence*, V. 1, No. 4: 2002.

- *Be specific about the SROs' teaching responsibilities*. For example, even when there is agreement that SROs will teach, SROs may *unnecessarily limit* themselves or be limited by school staff to engaging only in *law*-related education, as they tend to in some of the five small established programs. By contrast, without something in writing, SROs may *inappropriately expand* their teaching. SROs in one large established program range far afield from the law in their classroom presentations, such as teaching about the importance of good writing skills. It may also be desirable to stipulate a range in the SROs' hours or proportion of time that they will be expected to devote to teaching on average over the course of a week or month or year—for example, between 4-8 hours a week or 10-20 percent time. Especially for new SROs, it may be sensible to stipulate an increasing proportion of time—for example, between 5-10 percent from September through November, 10-15 percent from December through February, and 15-20 percent from March through May.
- *Specify the nature of the counseling* SROs will do. In the area of counseling, many SROs in the 19 programs talk with students who are (or think they are) pregnant, say they are suicidal, or are having conflicts with parents—areas that go well beyond providing counseling "about the law." Concerns about SROs, as unlicensed mental health practitioners, engaging in "counseling" as opposed to mentoring should also be explored (see Section 5, "Collaborating with School Administrators").
- Because responsibilities can vary by school depending on the personal preferences of individual principals and SROs, as well as the legitimate needs of the individual school, the list of responsibilities should *specify which ones apply to all SROs in all schools* (e.g., no SRO will patrol the cafeteria at lunch) and *which responsibilities are negotiable between individual SROs and their local school administrators* (e.g., each SRO and principal may decide whether the officer will stand in the corridors between classes). For example, the SRO procedures manual in one site calls for SROs to "Perform preventive patrol for students en route to and from school. Attention will be directed to observations pertinent to the safety and well being of children." While it makes sense to leave SROs and principals some latitude in specifying the officers' responsibilities on their own, this can be carried to an extreme. The five SROs in a large new site agreed that, although they understood that the sheriff's office had deliberately avoided providing them with firm guidelines so that the officers could better respond to particular problems in each school district, this lack of direction created stress for the deputies.
- The agreement needs to *provide a mechanism for resolving disagreements* between administrators and SROs about the officers' responsibilities.

- The police or sheriff's department immediate supervisor—and his or her supervisor—should *sign the document* along with the SRO.

TO ENFORCE OR NOT TO ENFORCE DISCIPLINE

School discipline involves dealing with students who break school rules as opposed to handling students who violate state statutes and local ordinances. Examples of misconduct that is not illegal but may violate school rules include tardiness, inappropriate dress, going to the parking lot without a pass, swearing, verbal bullying, and defiance.

The topic is important because it is a source of repeated friction between SROs and school administrators in many sites. How the SRO handles discipline can also hamper establishing rapport with students and teachers. For example, while the program planners in a large new site did not intend for SROs to handle matters of discipline, it took two years to establish the policy firmly in the minds of all school administrators and faculty. Some administrators asked SROs to send students to the assistant principals for punishment and to recommend penalties for school rule violations such as not getting to class on time. Two administrators used their SROs as substitute building administrators, leaving them in charge when the administrators left the building. The program's supervisors resorted to repeated written and verbal communication with these administrators to end these practices.

There are also numerous gray areas that administrators and SROs need to iron out—for example, is shoving to be treated by the SRO as a criminal matter (battery) or by the assistant principal as a violation of the school discipline code?

Programs vary considerably in the latitude they allow SROs to enforce discipline.

- At one extreme, the memorandum of agreement in a large established site makes clear that the SRO "shall not act as a school disciplinarian as disciplining students is the responsibility of the school district and their faculty." Similarly, two sample SRO job descriptions of programs in another state stipulate, "Refrain completely from functioning as a school disciplinarian. The School Resource Officer is not to be involved in the enforcement of disciplinary infractions that do not constitute violations of the law."
- At the other extreme, some SROs in some sites consistently enforce discipline—or enforce it on a case-by-case basis on their own initiative or at an administrator's request. The SRO in a large established program learned what to do by trial and error—"playing it by ear," as he put it. For example, when some students began to challenge his authority to tell them to tuck their shirts in ("You can't make me do that"), in order to enforce his authority he filled out and turned in a discipline slip form not knowing whether the school administrators would honor it—but the student was suspended. The SRO continues to sometimes write discipline reports on students who are in the parking lot during school hours without a pass. He also writes up students who fail to tuck in their shirts in violation of the school uniform policy after he has asked them three or four times the same day to do so.

> Finally, there is a separate but related issue not of *whether* SROs do discipline or of *how often* they do discipline but *whether they want to handle punitively through the criminal justice system school rule violations that are also minor offenses.* In particular, an individual SRO's previous orientation as a law enforcement officer may impel the officer to handle minor infractions either informally or by referral to school administrators, or by making arrests and handing out citations. For example, if an SRO as a street officer practiced a "legalistic" style of policing, punishing every type of misconduct (whether through personal choice or department philosophy) and carries over this previous enforcement orientation into the school setting, the officer may continually come into conflict with school administrators (and parents) who are used to handling most minor violations through the school discipline process.
>
> Like their other roles, the SROs' role in enforcing discipline can change over time. When one large established program began, the chief made clear that "the Police Officer would not involve himself in violations of school rules. He would confine himself to the problems which normally fall within the police jurisdiction." However, the current Intergovernmental Agreement calls for SROs "to enforce the school district's student disciplinary process, utilizing police involvement where appropriate . . . ."

Even with a written list of roles and responsibilities, there can be problems because no one can anticipate every possible area of disagreement and because some activities are gray areas that could legitimately be more than one person's responsibility. For example, some school administrators may consider a group of students who are "picking on" a student by calling him names to be the principal's responsibility, but some SROs may feel that students who bully need to be told that their behavior could have legal ramifications if it involves sexual harassment or physical contact. SROs may also feel that they need to step in because victims of bullying sometimes end up taking revenge on the students who taunt them—or on innocent parties in the school. However, it is possible to avoid many of these areas of potential conflict between SROs and administrators by discussing them in advance and committing agreed-upon resolutions to them to paper.

Involve the Schools in Developing the Responsibilities

A consistent theme in this cross-site report is that SRO programs work most successfully when they address the concerns and needs of both partnering agencies—law enforcement and education. Because in most sites the law enforcement agency takes the lead in setting up the program, an early crucial step in this collaboration for police is to involve the schools in the process of establishing the SROs' roles and responsibilities.

The chief deputy in a sheriff's department spearheaded the SRO program in one small new site. When he saw the availability of COPS Office funding for SROs, he approached reluctant school district administrators and sold them on the idea. However, he gained invaluable support for his ideas through an advisory committee he established consisting of a school board member, teacher, parent, and community member. This committee remains active, holding monthly meetings to share information about the program and develop new ideas.

SOME SCHOOL DISTRICTS HAVE INITIATED THE SRO PROGRAM

The school district assistant superintendent in a large new site was the driving force behind the SRO program and the COPS in Schools grant application. The assistant superintendent introduced the community to the idea of having police officers in schools in the early 1990s when he was principal of a local elementary school. He had a number of friends who were law enforcement officers and, because he believed there were benefits that officers could bring to schools (especially, increased interactions between kids and the officers), he started inviting them to come to his school. He developed a curriculum for a program intended to teach elementary school students respect for officers, and he initiated a CrimeStoppers program at the school.

After he became assistant superintendent, he heard about the COPS in Schools grant program from a regional school administrator. He asked the city's police department to partner with the county school district in submitting an application. Of course, he wanted his former elementary school to be included. In the end, four schools—one high school, two middle schools, and his elementary school—were included in the program.

A particularly effective approach to involving schools is through joint training attended by both the SROs and local school administrators. The assistant superintendent in a large new site attributed early tensions about the SRO program to lack of role definition. When should administrators "pull in the SRO" for discipline problems? What situations posed potential violations of student rights if the SRO gets involved? How could the district approach the integration of the two distinct cultures of law enforcement and school administration? These questions remained "sticking points," she said, until the SROs, together with a principal or superintendent's representative from each of the five school districts, attended a full-day seminar on school law. The presenters, a law group from a nearby city, distributed a handbook on safety, order, and discipline in American schools. The SRO and district officials have referenced this handout countless times for guidance on Federal and state law and "best practices" concerning police involvement in schools. They consider it an essential resource.

Similarly, program staff in a small new program who attended a COPS in Schools conference reported that they found it extremely helpful for both the SROs and school administrators to have the opportunity to specifically define the SROs' roles during the conference. Indeed, according to the terms of the grant, each new grantee *must* send one school administrator, along with the SROs, to a COPS in Schools conference.

Distribute the List of Roles and Responsibilities, and Periodically Review Them Administrators—and SROs—may forget that an agreement even exists. In one large established program, some school administrators seemed not to be aware of the agreement signed by the police department and their school district; others knew of it but either had not seen it or could not lay a hand on a copy. An SRO called it "defunct." As a result, programs need to take steps to keep the document "alive."

- An SRO in a small established site who wrote his own list of duties meets with each new school administrator to review them before the school year begins.

- At the beginning of the program in a large established site, the principal who coordinates the program reviewed the SROs' responsibilities for several months at each bi-monthly coordination meeting attended by the SROs, the police department SRO supervisor, and other school administrators.

Developing written SRO roles and responsibilities is essential for recruiting candidates for the position—officers need to know what their work in the schools will entail if they are to make an informed decision about whether to apply for the posting—and if program supervisors are to be able to make wise decisions about which candidates will be suitable for the job. This recruitment process is the focus of the following section.

SECTION 4: RECRUITING SROS

SECTION SUMMARY

Perhaps the single most important component of an SRO program is recruiting and retaining officers who are well qualified by temperament, skills, and motivation to be SROs. This requires careful screening of applicants and then conscientiously supervising them.

Developing Application and Selection Criteria

While most programs included in the study do not have written criteria for who can qualify as an SRO, without written criteria different people involved in deciding whom to approve as an SRO may be applying different—even contradictory—criteria. In addition, *officers* need to know what the job criteria are.

A number of programs in the study use similar criteria in selecting officers, including:

- likes and cares about kids;
- has the temperament to work with school administrators;
- has good communication skills;
- has the capacity to work independently;
- knows the community in which he or she will be working; and
- is not a rookie.

Although applying written criteria to the selection of SROs will help ensure they are suitable for the position, almost every program participant agreed that it was the SRO's personality that enabled the officer to be effective—as one principal put it, "*An outgoing, caring, but no-nonsense personality* is needed."

Recruitment Methods

Programs use roll call and department bulletins to publicize the availability of SRO openings. However, one program found that *stuffing every patrol officer's mailbox with the announcement was the most effective approach*. A few sites, because of a lack of interested applicants, have offered incentives such as take-home cruisers and a five percent salary increase to attract candidates.

The Screening Process

Because not all applicants may have appropriate motives for wanting to become an SRO—for example, they want the daytime, weekday hours—many programs require a written application and an oral interview (often with a panel of individuals). *Involving school district and school-level administrators in the screening process increases acceptance of the program and the SROs among school personnel.*

Programs have taken several steps to reduce rapid turnover among SROs, such as:

- implementing a careful screening procedure to weed out inappropriate officers;
- telling candidates about the drawbacks to the position (for the same reason); and
- providing SROs with timely and adequate training and supervision.

As with many occupations, the *qualifications and the personality of the SRO are likely to make or break the program*. Even the most detailed written list of SRO roles and responsibilities, or the most supportive local school administrators, will be of little importance if the SROs are not qualified by skills and temperament for the position. For example, all five small established programs reported making at least one mistake in assigning an officer who was inappropriate for the position. As a result, perhaps the single most important component of an SRO program may be staffing it properly *by developing criteria for selecting qualified officers and then screening applicants carefully*.

Solicit Volunteers for the SRO Positions

Precisely because SROs have to have some skills and personality characteristics that are different than those required for patrol duty, programs that have assigned officers to be SROs involuntarily have found that this can result in officers doing a poor job because they did not have the ability or desire for the position. While some officers assigned to the position grow to enjoy and become good at it, some of the least effective programs involved officers who had been forced become SROs.

By contrast, several programs reported that *allowing officers to volunteer to serve as SROs seems to result in a higher level of commitment to the program*. (The Center for the Prevention of School Violence report, "An Effective Practices Outline for the School Resource Officer Approach," also recommends using only volunteers.)

When candidates for SRO positions are invited to apply for the job, the selection process begins by *developing explicit, written criteria for who qualifies for the position*.

Developing Application and Selection Criteria

Most programs included in the study do not have written criteria for who can qualify as an SRO. This is a mistake. Without written criteria, different people involved in making the decision about whom to post to the schools may be applying different—even contradictory—criteria. In addition, *officers* need to know what the job criteria are—and have the criteria provided in writing, not just verbally.

As discussed below, there are two types of criteria most programs in the study use to select officers to become SROs:

- core competencies—or minimal requirements—and
- desirable qualities and skills.

Core Competencies

Most programs agreed on the following minimal set of criteria for selecting officers as SROs:

- likes and cares about kids;
- communicates well;
- has the ability to teach or the capacity to learn how to;
- has the flexibility to work with school administrators;
- has the capacity to work independently, especially important for SROs in rural areas; and
- is not a rookie.

While the first four criteria are self-evident, the last two require comment.

- In terms of **having the capacity to work independently**, while all patrol officers (unless they have shift partners) function largely without direct supervision or in collaboration with other officers, programs have reported that SROs are particularly isolated. In part, they are out of sight (literally—inside the school building) and therefore out of mind. Usually, they do not even appear for roll call. They are also isolated inasmuch as their direct (if unofficial) supervisor for day-by-day activity is typically a principal or assistant principal, not the police or sheriff's department SRO supervisor. As a result, SROs must be capable of and comfortable working alone, with minimal contact with the department.
- In terms of **assigning only experienced officers to be SROs**, the rationale is that, because rookies do not have experience in enforcing the law, do not know how statutes, local ordinances, and department general orders are applied in practice (especially in relation to juveniles and children), and have not gotten to know their colleagues and supervisors well, they will be at a serious disadvantage working in schools where this experience is critical to their law enforcement role. (The Center for the Prevention of School Violence report, "An Effective Practices Outline for the School Resource Officer Approach," recommends that "An **effective** practice is to

choose an experienced street officer, although a set number of years' experience cannot be realistically identified for all programs [emphasis in the original].")

Desirable Qualities and Skills

Several programs use additional criteria for selecting SROs. For some of these programs, SROs may not be selected unless they meet these criteria but, in most programs, these criteria are more of a "wish list" that departments add to the minimal criteria identified above. Among these desirable qualities and skills departments look for are the following:

- has completed some college (one program prefers candidates with some college because, according to an SRO supervisor, "that means they are connected to education, and the SROs' work is prevention more than anything else");
- is willing to put in overtime—including uncompensated overtime;
- is a good listener and problem solver;
- prefers to—and knows how to—resolve disputes by deescalating tensions rather than by using force as a first resort;
- is skilled in and comfortable exercising discretion;
- can put up with being teased by other officers (e.g., as a "Kiddie Cop"); and
- has ties to the local community.

The final criterion in the list can be extremely beneficial. In some programs, the SROs were students of the principals with whom they were working. In others, they went to school with many of the students' parents. *This familiarity with the school and community makes it much easier for the SROs to establish credibility and rapport*. In one small established program, all but one SRO position was filled with "home-town" boys who had graduated from the schools they now serve. Program supervisors and SROs in this site believe that their understanding and knowledge of the people and families in the community was essential to their effectiveness.

Minimum and Maximum Tours of Duty

Some programs require candidates to agree to remain SROs for a minimum number of years. One large established program requires a two-year commitment and another a five-year commitment, while a small established program requires a three-year tour of duty. The Center for the Prevention of School Violence report, "An Effective Practices Outline for the School Resource Officer Approach," recommends that "The first year should evolve into assignment to a particular school for a minimum of three years [which] . . . allows the SRO to go through high school with a given tenth-grade class."

On the one hand, requiring a minimum tour of duty has the advantage of helping to ensure consistency among SROs and avoiding the problems of frequent turnover (see below). On the other hand, requiring an SRO who no longer wants the position to continue serving as an SRO is likely to create resentment, resulting in poor job performance. Programs should reassign SROs who truly "want out."

A few other programs *restrict SROs from serving for more than a specified number of years*. Police chiefs and sheriffs who have instituted mandatory rotation sometimes want to have periodic SRO openings so they can reward other officers with the position. However, limiting the number of years SROs can remain in the position can be harmful because the program may lose officers who are happy and effective, and create temporary gaps in effectiveness as new SROs who replace the seasoned SROs take time to learn the job and win the confidence of school administrators, faculty, students, and parents. In one large established site, however, the collective bargaining agreement requires that all officers rotate out of specialized posting, and the SRO program qualifies as a special post.

The Key: The SRO's Personality

Although applying written criteria to the selection of SROs will help ensure they are suitable for the job, almost every program participant agreed that it was the SRO's personality that enabled the officer to be effective or rendered the officer ineffective:

- An assistant principal: "We are lucky to have an SRO with his personality."
- A principal: "Without a doubt, the personality of the officer . . . is key to the success of the position."

While program coordinators and school administrators do not always agree on what "the right personality" refers to, an assistant principal summed up *three attributes that seem to be the core of the personality characteristics that make an officer an effective SRO* when he said, "*An outgoing, caring, but no-nonsense personality* is needed."

Recruitment Methods

Recruiting SROs involves advertising the position and considering offering incentives.

Announcing the Position

Programs use one or both of two methods of announcing the SRO openings:

- roll call announcements and
- department bulletins (regular bulletins or special notices).

Roll call announcements have the advantage of enabling officers to ask questions (if the SRO program supervisor or an SRO makes the announcement), while department bulletins ensure that every officer has an opportunity to learn about the opening (some officers may be on vacation, in court, sick, or in training on the day the opening is announced at roll call). Ideally, programs should announce the opening both ways.

One large established site uses two additional methods of announcing openings: stuffing every patrol officer's mailbox with the announcement and e-mailing it to them. This site has found that using officers' mailboxes is the most effective of the four methods for drawing officers' attention to the job openings.

Using Incentives

In most programs, there have usually been more than enough applicants to fill the available openings. In one large new site, the 5 SRO positions initially attracted interest from over 10 candidates. When 6 additional SRO positions were created, 53 deputies bid for the positions.

In a few programs, not enough officers have applied. No one at all volunteered for the position initially in one small new site. In another jurisdiction, the number of candidates declined from 18 to 4 after they saw that SROs were required to teach and work one-on-one with students. As a result, 4 of the 19 programs in the National Assessment provide one or more incentives to attract applicants:

- take-home cruisers, which eliminate the time SROs have to spend each day going to and from the station house to pick up and return a cruiser each day— and also save wear and tear on the SROs' personal cars;
- opportunities for paid overtime not available to patrol officers;
- a salary bonus (five percent in one small established site); and
- making it known that the position can be a stepping stone to eventual promotion and other coveted assignments.

However, using incentives was not commonplace among the programs. (Similarly, among the 658 SROs and SRO supervisors polled in the 2002 NASRO School Resource Officer Survey, only 19 percent reported receiving additional benefits.) Furthermore, incentives have to be used with caution because they may attract inappropriate candidates who are more interested in the "perks" than in working with youth.

Finally, although no examples were found among the 19 programs included in the study, agencies can try to increase the number of applicants, especially well-qualified applicants, by *minimizing or neutralizing what officers may perceive to be disincentives to becoming SROs*, such as anxiety about teaching in front of a class, being seen as a "Kiddie Cop" by other officers, or closing off promotional opportunities. Program coordinators—and the chief or sheriff—can make clear that candidates will receive training in how to teach and that the position is a valued posting in the department.

Finally, if current SROs make informal brief presentations describing the program at trainings or roll call, they can specifically address any perceived disincentives in question and answer sessions either by explaining them away or pointing out how the advantages of being an SRO outweigh any actual drawbacks. SROs can also accomplish this by talking informally about the program with officers they run into.

The Screening Process

A thoughtful screening process can significantly improve the chances of assigning qualified officers as SROs. For example, the vast majority of SROs contacted in the 19 programs reported that they had applied for the program at least in part because they enjoy working with kids—clearly a prerequisite for becoming an effective SRO. However, some applicants did not have any appropriate motives for wanting the position. Screening can help to weed out these individuals.

- In one large new site, some officers reported they went after the position only because they viewed it as a good opportunity to get away from paperwork or to get on the same schedule as their children's.
- An SRO in a large established site said he joined just because he would not have to work nights or weekends.
- Some older officers view the position it as a "cushy" job until they retire.

Sometimes SROs who accepted the position for the "wrong" reasons (e.g., to have evenings and weekends free) came to like the work and became good at it. However, more often than not inappropriate motives for applying resulted in problems working with school administrators and students, tarnished the reputation of the program and of the law enforcement agency—and resulted in frequent SRO turnover.

Careful screening can also often avoid embarrassing appointments. A vocal parent in one large established site went through court records and discovered that an SRO had had a child out of wedlock and had never paid child support. The sheriff had to replace the officer.

Programs follow as many as three steps in screening candidates. While only one program requires candidates to take *a written examination* to become an SRO, a large established program requires applicants who apply to submit an essay explaining why they want the position and what they expect to accomplish on the job. Most programs also conduct *an oral interview*. Oral—and especially panel—interviews provide a unique opportunity to observe candidates':

- demeanor;
- ability to communicate clearly and fluently;
- comportment under pressure; and
- responses to problem scenarios SROs might encounter in the schools.

Much more controversial—and a source of potential conflict—is the issue of *whether and how school personnel should be involved in the screening process*. In one small established program, the sheriff has refused requests from the principals to participate in the selection of the SROs. While the police in a large new jurisdiction have worked in the local schools for more than a decade, they still assign officers without consulting with school officials.

Leaving schools out of the screening process can damage the program. For example, at the large new site cited above, officers in some schools are left on their own, having little interaction with school administration. Furthermore, despite frequent police department reservations about sharing the screening process with schools, *the law enforcement executives in the study that involved school district and school-level administrators in the screening process uniformly said it was advantageous because it increases acceptance of the program and the SROs among school personnel*. School administrators in these program also said they valued the opportunity to play a part in the selection process.

- The school superintendent in one large new site served as the school representative for officer screening and selection. She interviewed over 10 candidates for the initial five slots. With so few adult role models for the many minority students in her district, this superintendent wanted at least one African-American or Latino(a) officer placed there. She also believed it best to have one male and one female SRO available to her students. She made a specific request for one of the two officers she interviewed and approved of the second, as well.

- In a small established site, a community panel interviews all applicants for the SRO position. The panel consists of school officials, parents, the chief of police, the department head for the community policing division, and a representative of the North Carolina Center for the Prevention of School Violence. The chief of police considers the recommendations of the panel but makes the final choice.

A more contentious issue is whether schools should have veto power over which candidates are chosen. In the small established program cited above, the sheriff maintains ultimate decision over which officers will be posted to which schools. Occupying a middle ground, one large established program allows individual school principals to reject candidates for their schools—but not for the program as a whole.

Retaining SROs

Many SROs have remained in their positions for years—as long as 8 in two sites. In one site, all three SROs stayed the maximum four years the chief allows except for one who was promoted after three years. The majority of SROs in the large new sites had been in their schools since the programs' inception more than two years before. Two reported they hoped to stay in the program until they retired.

Other programs have had severe problems with turnover. One school district had five different SROs in less than three years. At another program, a school had four different SROs in four years—they all quit because of an authoritarian principal. When the principal retired, the next SRO remained in the position.

Of course, circumstances beyond anyone's control sometimes result in turnover, including promotions, retirements, and resignations. However, high turnover may also reflect "burnout" of officers who confront severe problems coupled with a strong desire to help students, limited supervision, and scarce support from—or worse, conflict with—administrators, such as the dictatorial principal noted above.

Minimizing turnover is important because replacing an SRO makes the program less effective for several months as the new officer learns how to do the job. The new SRO needs to develop teaching and counseling skills, and school administrators, faculty, and students must begin the process all over again of learning to trust and rely on the officer. A few programs have taken one or more of the following steps to help reduce turnover among SROs:

(1) *Implement thorough screening procedures* to help make sure officers are not chosen who will not work out and therefore have to be replaced.
(2) Straightforwardly *inform candidates about drawbacks to the position* they may not have considered, such as:
   - the need to overcome their fears about standing in front of a classroom and

- working harder than they ever thought the position would require—or harder than they ever worked as patrol officers.

(3) **Provide SROs with timely and adequate training and supervision**, as suggested in section 4 below, so the officers do not become disappointed in the position as they flounder around ill equipped to teach and counsel students.

(4) Be willing to **consider changing some agency policies** that can interfere with job satisfaction.

- The union contract or department policy may require giving overtime assignments to the most or least senior officers, which can make it impossible for SROs—who know their students best—to be assigned to school events.
- In some programs, SROs cannot be promoted to sergeant as long as they work in the schools.
- The program supervisor in a large new site allowed SROs to ignore a department rule on the purposes for which cruisers may be used in order to let the officers drive students home to retrieve medication they had forgotten to bring to school.

Once SROs have been recruited, programs need to thoroughly train and conscientiously supervise the officers—as discussed in the following section.

SECTION 5: TRAINING AND SUPERVISING SROS

SECTION SUMMARY

The vast majority of the 19 programs included in the study provide adequate training, but frequently not in a timely manner. Most programs do not conscientiously supervise their SROs.

Training SROs

Few of the 19 programs train SROs before they go on the job, not usually because of the expense but because training is generally not offered after SROs have been selected and before they go on the job. Nevertheless, *any delay in training can be a serious problem* because SROs then have to learn their jobs by "sinking or swimming" with the possible consequences of providing ineffective services and making serious mistakes on the job.

A few programs have found ways of providing pre-service training:

- A large established program arranged for its most long-standing SRO to become certified as an SRO trainer.
- A few programs arrange for each new SRO to "shadow" an experienced SRO before going on the job.

A number of programs arrange in-service training, including advanced SRO training. SROs funded by COPS in Schools grants receive mandatory comprehensive training provided by the COPS Office. Program supervisors in one large program provide in-service training for SROs every two or three months. Training in problem-solving techniques is especially needed because most SROs are not familiar with the approach.

Most SROs and school principals and assistant principals agree that *it would be valuable to train principals and assistant principals along with SROs as a team*. One program requires new local school administrators to attend a week-long basic SRO training course.

Supervising SROs

One of the weakest components of many SRO programs in the study is the lack of consistent or close supervision of the officers' work. Typically, the supervisor has other, higher priority responsibilities, feels that little monitoring is necessary, or, because lack of understanding of what SROs are supposed to do, would find it awkward or embarrassing to supervise them. However, *adequate supervision of SROs is important to make sure the officers are working to their full potential and are not experiencing unreported or unacknowledged problems.*

In most programs, SROs complete monthly activity logs and meet with their supervisors for an annual job performance assessment. In some programs, supervisors periodically visit SROs and school administrators at the schools and observe the officers teach.

There are compelling reasons to involve school personnel in supervising SROs, not the least because assistant principals have by far the most contact with SROs. In one site, an advisory committee of SROs, a teacher, a school board member, and school administrators meets monthly to review problems and develop new ideas.

Almost all the programs included in the study provide SROs with training, but few do this in a timely manner. Most programs fail to adequately supervise their SROs. However, for a number of reasons training and supervision are extremely important to a program's success.

Training SROs

Training falls into two categories: pre-service and in-service. Both are essential for a number of reasons.

- Because few SROs have experience teaching in the classroom or practicing counseling and mentoring youth, they need to be trained in basic teaching and counseling skills.
- SROs need training in child psychology and behavior in order to be most effective as counselors and mentors—and to know when to refer students for professional help.

- There are complex issues associated with enforcing the law in a school that many SROs are not initially ready to handle, such as legislation and case law related to search and seizure involving minors, interrogating juveniles, and privacy.
- SROs may need help to "unlearn" some of the techniques they learned to use on patrol duty that are not appropriate in dealing with students (for example, resorting too quickly to using handcuffs or treating misconduct as part of a person's criminal make-up when in a student the behavior may be an example of youthful indiscretion).
- SROs need guidance in how to collaborate with local principals and assistant principals from whom they will receive day-to-day instructions, requests, and complaints.
- SROs need to learn how to work effectively with parents.

Pre-Service Training

Almost all programs provide SROs with adequate training—eventually. Sooner or later most of the 19 programs send SROs for training to one or more of reputable training programs, including:

- the Office of Community Oriented Policing Services COPS in Schools training, mandatory for grantees, held several times a year in different parts of the country);
- the National Association of School Resource Officers (NASRO) basic and advanced SRO training;
- Corbin and Associates basic and advanced SRO training; and
- the North Carolina Justice Academy whose course all SROs in the state must attend.

However, few programs train SROs before they go on the job. Some SROs have been on the job for as long as a year before they receive training. As a result, the National Assessment's mail survey of 322 law enforcement agencies (see section 1) found that many SROs engage in activities for which they have not been trained, especially teaching and mentoring. The 2002 NASRO School Resource Officer Survey also found that "between 17% and 34% (depending on the topic) [of responding SROs] have not received specialized training in topics such as adolescent child behavior, counseling skills, . . . and related issues." Rather than the cost of the training, the delay typically reflects the problem that training is offered only periodically, often not during the interval after SROs have been selected and before they go on the job.

The Center for the Prevention of School Violence report, "An Effective Practices Outline for the School Resource Officer Approach," recommends that officers be sent for training in the summer before they go on their new assignments. However, only a large established site among the 19 programs follows this guideline. The SRO procedures manual in another large established site requires new SROs to call the training academy to attend the next available general instructors' course (if they have not already taken it) and to arrange to be certified to teach the G.R.E.A.T. curriculum by contacting the department's G.R.E.A.T. staff.

The delay in training is often a serious problem. First, when SROs learn their jobs by "sinking or swimming," for several months—even the entire first year—the schools may be poorly served by the program. Second, without proper training, SROs can make serious mistakes related to their relationships with students, school administrators, and parents that at best cause short-term crises and at worst jeopardize the entire program in the school. An SRO in a large established site reported that:

> I learned what to do by trial and error, playing it by ear—for example, bringing parents in with their children to talk with me. When students began to challenge my authority to tell them to tuck in their shirts ("You can't make me do that"), to enforce my authority I filled out and turned in a discipline slip form not knowing whether the school administrators would honor it. But the student was suspended. But I could have made serious errors without the training. I could have been overzealous or apathetic, doing too much or not enough. Plus, you need training to cover you in court—training *is* policy in court.

A large established program solved the timing problem by arranging for its most senior SRO to become certified as an SRO trainer. The SRO then developed a week-long training syllabus, which he teaches during the summer to officers who might apply for any SRO openings the following school year. In the long run, this approach saves the agency money by avoiding the registration fees and travel expenses involved in sending SROs out of town for training by professional organizations (except for COPS in Schools training, which is paid for by grant funds—up to $1,200 per required participant).

A few programs arrange for each new SRO to "shadow" an experienced SRO before going on the job much in the way new recruits ride with field training officers before they are "let loose" on their own. This approach has the considerable advantage of providing some orientation to being an SRO before a new SRO goes on the job. It also makes it possible for new SROs to gain indispensable real-world, on-the-job knowledge of the position that formal training typically cannot provide. Nevertheless, shadowing is an essential supplement, not a substitute, for formal pre-service training. Furthermore, if the established SROs whom the new SROs shadow are not doing their jobs properly or give poor guidance, the experience may be at best worthless and at worst harmful.

In their curriculum materials, the COPS Office, the Center for the Prevention of School Violence (CPSV), the National School Safety Center, and NASRO have identified the topics that new SRO training should focus on. As a result, the list of training topics below only summarizes the most frequently addressed and important topics (taken from the COPS in Schools training manual) that should be covered in pre-service training:

- legal issues;
- classroom teaching skills and strategies;
- mental health interventions;
- understanding the child's perspective;
- cultural fluency;
- collaborative problem solving applied to the school setting;
- safe school preparation; and
- mentoring and counseling skills.

New SROs should also receive training, or at least advice, in how to remain a visible part of the department while being isolated in the schools—a frustrating experience for some SROs who feel they suffer from the "out of site, out of mind" phenomenon.

In-Service Training

Most SROs in the study's 19 programs did not attend regularly scheduled in-service SRO-related training. The Florida Attorney General reported in its 2000 School Resource Officer Survey that 82 percent of 156 programs indicated that SROs had missed in-service training opportunities, 54 percent because they could not leave during the school day and 46 percent due to lack of funding. The 2002 NASRO School Resource Officer Survey suggests that many programs are unaware of sources of funding for training: "Almost two-thirds (65%) of SROs were unaware that U.S. Department of Education's Safe and Drug-Free Schools Program funds can be used to pay for SRO training . . . ." However, even awareness of such funding does not necessarily result in a request for money: "[O]f those [SROs] who are aware [of the funding from this source], over half indicated that their district does not use the funds for such purposes." One reason some departments do not apply for training funds is that they may still have to pay overtime for other officers to substitute for the SROs while the SROs are being trained.

A few programs provide funds for SROs to attend advanced SRO training after they have been on the job a year or two. One large established program with over 20 SROs provides in-house, in-service training at regularly scheduled intervals. Every two or three months, each of the three SRO supervisors holds trainings for the 6-8 SROs under his supervision, typically to explain a new technology, vendor, or piece of legislation or court ruling.

Florida's 2000 School Resource Officer Survey reported that the top three types of training *SROs request* are school law, conflict resolution, and emergency management. The SROs contacted in the National Assessment identified three other areas that in-service (and basic) training should address:

- working collaboratively with school administrators;
- establishing boundaries in terms of getting involved with students and determining appropriate and inappropriate issues to address with students; and
- engaging in collaborative problem solving.

The importance of addressing the first two of these three issues is discussed in detail in sections 5 and 6 below. A brief discussion of collaborative problem solving follows below.

Training in Collaborative Problem Solving

The 19 programs in this study engage in very little, if any, collaborative problem solving—working with other agencies to implement the SARA model (*S*canning, *A*nalysis,

*R*esponse, *A*ssessment) or some other model of collaborative problem solving. Of course, the collaboration between law enforcement and the schools inherent in the SRO position is a major example of collaborative problem solving. But within that framework, SROs rarely involved other individuals and groups outside the schools in implementing a permanent solution to get at root cause of a chronic problem such as bullying or vandalism. This was true even of SROs whose law enforcement agencies had adopted community policing or who had attended COPS in Schools conferences (which devote an entire module to "Bringing SARA to School").

The COPS in Schools training manual, "Keep Our Kids Safe," suggests that failure to use the SARA model may reflect lack of support from the school principal, difficulty accessing school records, lack of support from the police chief or sheriff and the agency SRO supervisor, and the inability to get free from immediate problems to engage in problem solving. This last explanation is consistent with the findings from the present study. *The SROs in the 19 sites generally do not have the time to pursue the steps of the SARA model*—for example, examining school records and meeting with potential collaborators. Many SROs cannot even complete their paperwork during normal business hours but must do so at night at home—when they are not doing a detail at a school athletic event or attending a PTA meeting. In one of the only two good examples of problem solving involving non-school organizations that the study discovered (see the box "Two Examples of Collaborative Problem Solving by SROs"), the officer had to find the time to meet individually with the owners of three homes adjacent to the school whose fences were being vandalized by students; solicit help from and develop a plan of action with the town code enforcement officer; and meet again with each homeowner accompanied by the code enforcement officer. To be sure, because the approach solved the problem, the SRO no longer had to deal with complaints from the neighbors. But for most SROs, an uncertain future benefit, even if it may ultimately involve saving time and frustration in the long run, is probably outweighed by the necessary initial investment of time and energy.

That said, if the obstacle to collaborative problem solving lies with school administrators and not with the SRO, the officer can explain the SARA model to them and point out how implementing the process will provide a return on their investment of time that will be well worth the effort.

The second most important reason the National Assessment found for the lack of collaborative problem solving is SROs' lack of familiarity with the SARA (or any other) model for implementing joint solutions to chronic problems.

Training for School Administrators

Although none were involved themselves in such an activity, several program coordinators and school administrators suggested that *it would be valuable to train principals and assistant principals along with SROs as a team*, focusing especially on cultural differences between law enforcement agencies and school systems, supervision of SROs, and decisions about what SROs will and will not do. Even the SRO supervisor in a large established site in which the SROs engage predominantly in law enforcement recommended joint SRO training with school administrators, because "The biggest thing about being an SRO is not the criminal side but being able to work with assistant principals."

TWO EXAMPLES OF COLLABORATIVE PROBLEM SOLVING BY SROs

In a large established program, for over two years a few students on their way home at the end of the school day had been damaging the fences (already in a state of disrepair) around neighbors' front yards. After talking with the suspected students failed to resolve the problem, the SRO learned that there was a safety issue involved because of the loose and jagged boards and nails.

As a result, the SRO invited a city code enforcement officer to join him in visiting the three complaining homeowners to ask them to help solve the problem by repairing their fences. The SRO, in turn, said he would see to it that the students stopped damaging them. One neighbor replaced his fence entirely, and the other two had theirs repaired. The vandalism stopped.

In a large new site, the police department received several complaints from senior citizens about high school students speeding in the area of the high school. The SRO discovered that the senior center's chess club met near the school and ended just as students were dismissed. The SRO spoke with a few kids, who agreed to drive more respectfully, and worked with the chess club to modify its schedule, thereby solving the problem.

The COPS Office already requires grantee agencies to send one school administrator from a partnering school district along with the SROs supported by the grant to one of its three-day training conferences. (However, participating school districts are reimbursed for sending only one administrator.) One large established program requires new assistant principals and principals in schools with SROs to attend the week-long basic NASRO training course. According to one school administrator who attended, "Since these trainings are attended primarily with SROs, the administrators have a tremendous opportunity to hear about the program from the officers' perspectives and to gain information on a number of strategies from different jurisdictions for solving program- related problems." In a large new site, a statewide legal aide group offers classes and materials about education-related law to school boards and police departments that participate in SRO programs.

Supervising SROs

One of the weakest components of many SRO programs in the study is the lack of consistent or close supervision of the officers' work. Most law enforcement agencies assign a ranking officer to supervise the program, but typically the supervisor (often the same person as the program coordinator) has other responsibilities to which he or she gives higher priority. For example, in one large established site, the supervisor was also responsible for community and public relations, which occupied nearly all of his time.

Some program coordinators believe there is no need to supervise SROs—or at least not *their* SROs. The program supervisor in a large established program reported he does not need to monitor the SROs because "principals monitor them and tell me if there's a problem." For example, a principal called him to report that an SRO was constantly late for things. The supervisor spoke to the SRO and "he shaped up." The only formal monitoring the program conducts is a three-hour meeting involving the SROs, sheriff's department, and school administrators at the end of every school year to review problems and progress. In the small sites in particular, "supervision" occurs through informal conversations between the police chief or sheriff and school superintendent. In a few jurisdictions, it was clear that *experienced* SROs no longer did need close supervision because they knew their job and its limitations, were conscientious, and were self-motivated.

Finally, some supervisors, because they lack understanding of what SROs are supposed to do (never having been trained themselves in what the SRO program is all about or in how to monitor SROs' performance), take a "hands-off" approach because they would find it awkward or embarrassing to supervise them.

Importance of Supervision

Adequate supervision of SROs is important to:

- assist new SROs in making the transition from patrol officer to school-based resource;
- obtain information from school administrators and SROs that may suggest an impending or possible problem before it develops;
- identify existing problems that SROs or school administrators are reluctant to bring to the supervisor's attention;
- make SROs feel that their work is important and valued by the department;
- impress upon school administrators that the agency considers the program an important collaborative initiative; and
- identify disaffection among SROs that needs to be addressed to avoid turnover among officers who are performing well in the position.

Barriers to Supervision

There are several obstacles to effective supervision:

- Lack of time on the part of the police supervisor. Only 2 of the 19 sites in the present study—both large established programs—had more than one supervisor: one had three supervisors for 22 SROs, and the other had two supervisors for 18 SROs. (The Florida Office of the Attorney General reports in its Year 2000 "School Resource Officer Survey" that there was approximately one SRO supervisor for every 5 SROs among 156 responding programs in the State.)
- SROs' geographic separation from the rest of the department that can result in an "out of sight, out of mind" state of mind.
- The logistics and time involved in supervising SROs who serve multiple schools.
- Objections from principals to SROs leaving the campus (one supervisor considered calling monthly meetings to improve the flow of ideas and information among her six SROs, but school administrators refused to allow the SROs to leave campus during the school day).
- Lack of any written SRO roles or responsibilities that can provide a basis for supervision—knowing what to look for.
- Rapid turnover among program supervisors due to promotions or transfers, forcing SROs to adjust to each new supervisor's approach to program monitoring.
- Failure to train supervisors in how to monitor SRO performance. (Although a number of supervisors had been SROs, no site trained its program supervisors in how to monitor SROs. Similarly, the 2002 NASRO School Resource Officer Survey also found that "school-based law enforcement supervisors are not specially trained in the supervision of school-based officers.")

Approaches to Supervision

Programs do not follow any one model in how they go about supervising SROs. For example, among the four large new sites:

- in one program, the SROs begin and end each day at headquarters, touching base with their commanding officers;
- in the second site, the department relies on daily telephone or radio contact with the SROs, as well as weekly visits by a sergeant to each school district;
- in the third site, the SROs see their supervisor at roll call each day at 6:30 a.m.; and
- in the last site, the SRO supervisors hold a weekly unit meeting at their division offices.

In one small new site, the SRO calls in his activities to the law enforcement dispatch center. When a new activity starts, he radios in and the dispatcher records the precise time and activity category (e.g., "going on patrol now"; "responding to call to investigate possible drug use"; "going to teach driver ed now"). The dispatch system calculates time spent on each activity and can aggregate time spent on various activities on a weekly or any other basis.

Typically, program supervisors use a combination of two or more approaches to monitoring SROs, among them:
- requiring SROs to submit monthly activity logs with summary counts of various activities;
- periodically meeting with each SRO individually;
- meeting with SROs as a group at fixed intervals;
- fielding calls from SROs experiencing problems or concerned about potential future problems;
- visiting SROs, school administrators, or both at the schools; and
- observing SROs teach.

In many programs, supervision is limited to review of the SROs logs and an annual discussion with each SRO (or a meeting with all SROs as a group), with active intervention the rest of the year taking place only when the school, SRO, or parent brings a problem to the supervisor's attention. For example, in one large established site SROs log in their activities in a monthly activity report that they submit to the department's SRO coordinator, who compiles the reports for the department's service division captain. The report tracks activities each SRO undertakes according to the type of activity (e.g., fingerprinting class, PTA lecture on child safety), who requested it (e.g., teacher, coach, community person), date and place offered, and number of participants. For example, the SRO at one of the site's junior high schools documented that from January 1, 2001, through May 31, 2001, in addition to participating in an after-school program 21 times, he:

- presented 64 programs involving 1,798 attendees;
- attended 10 civic meetings and functions;
- devoted 2 hours to a newsletter;
- issued 11 misdemeanor citations;

- took 7 reports; and
- engaged in a number of other law enforcement-related activities.

The SRO coordinator prepares a yearly written evaluation of each SRO, but it is based only on the supervisor's own contacts with the SROs, not on contacts with school administrators. Otherwise, the SROs are largely on their own. For example, no one observes them teach.

Two large established programs had the most formal supervision.

- In one program, every new SRO is assigned to one of three full-time supervisors, all sergeants. New SROs must sign and submit a sheet to their supervisor documenting that they have read and are familiar with the department's SRO Procedures Manual. The Procedures Manual requires SROs to "Provide the supervisor with monthly activity sheets." SROs fill out the sheets weekly on their computers and e-mail them to their supervising sergeant at the end of each month. Supervisors observe their SROs teach and meet at least once a year with the SROs' school administrators. SROs call their supervisor periodically either for advice with a problem or to keep them apprised of something important that took place—for example, an angry parent who is thinking about filing a complaint.
- In another large established site, SROs complete a detailed monthly activity form but, unlike in most other programs, *the program supervisor circulates the reports to command staff, school district administrators, and the school board*. The school district superintendent of schools reads the reports carefully to monitor the officers' activities. SROs meet every other month for two hours with the school district's program coordinator, police department supervisor, and the middle school administrators at whose schools the SROs are stationed to make plans and address problem areas. Meetings have a written agenda and meeting notes are kept and circulated. The police department program supervisor meets every year with each SRO individually and with the SRO's school principal or assistant principal. He has observed each SRO teach. Finally, the school district conducts annual focus groups with middle school students to obtain their perceptions of individual SROS and the program as a whole.

The SRO in a small new site uses an incident tracking software program developed with funding from the National Institute of Justice called *School COP*, distributed at COPs in schools conferences and available for free at www.schoolcopsoftware.com. The software enables him to produce graphs showing incident trends and other displays of crime data at the request of the sheriff or school board. At one point, he became concerned because he had issued 35 drug possession or sales citations to date during the 2003–2004 school year compared with only 11 issued at the same time the previous school year—while the middle school SRO had issued only 2. This is an illustration of performance-based (self-) supervision that another study of SRO programs has investigated in depth (see the box "Supervisors in Five Programs Use Performance-Based Measures to Monitor SROs").

SUPERVISORS IN FIVE PROGRAMS USE PERFORMANCE-BASED MEASURES TO MONITOR SROS

With funding from the COPS Office, Circle Solutions, a professional services firm in the Washington, D.C., area, piloted an outcome-oriented SRO performance evaluation process with five law enforcement agencies in six schools. For each SRO for the coming year, a group of SROs, their supervisors, and program "consumers"—students, faculty, staff, and parents—identified goals specific to the crime and disorder problems in the officer's school and designed measures to determine whether the SRO achieved the goals. Throughout the school year, SROs implemented activities designed to achieve the goals and tracked their activities. At the end of the year, the consumer group reconvened to assess how well the SROs had achieved their goals. The purpose of these efforts was *to integrate the findings into the SROs' performance evaluation* and to use the findings to adjust the activities the SROs would implement during the following school year.

Involving School Personnel in Supervising the SROs

Several sites involve school personnel in supervising SROs. *There are compelling reasons for bringing principals and assistant principals into the supervision process.*

- Principals and assistant principals can usually assess SROs' performance in ways that program supervisors cannot because school administrators have vastly more contact with SROs. In effect, because of their daily contact with the SROs, they are the police agency's on-site "eyes and ears."
- Principals and assistant principals have a much better grasp than the law enforcement agency could ever have of the problems in their schools that the SROs need to address.
- Insofar as SRO programs represent a collaboration between law enforcement and the schools, it is only logical that there should be collaboration in terms of supervision.
- As with other attempts to involve the schools in the operation of the program, including school administrators in the supervision of SROs conveys the message that they are valuable partners in a joint initiative.

Several sites have formal procedures for involving school administrators in helping to supervise SROs.

- In a small new site, an advisory committee consisting of parents, a teacher, a community group member, and a school board member, as well as SROs, the chief deputy, and school administrators, meets monthly to share information about the program's operation.
- School administrators in a large new site contribute to ongoing supervision of SROs by preparing regular performance reviews at the police agency's request.
- A sheriff's department in another large new site encourages administrators from each of its five partner school districts to review, at least annually, the performance of its SROs. Two of the school districts developed specific reporting forms for this

purpose, while administrators from the other three districts submit their evaluations in letter form.

- At yet another large new site, the program supervisor requests annual SRO evaluations from teachers, administrators, and other key staff members at each participating school. She collects these assessments personally, then reviews them individually with the officers. The school district assessments address performance factors ranging from attendance and appearance, to willingness to work with others, to interpersonal communication skills. The following excerpts illustrate the overall tone of the comments:

[He] embodies professionalism in law enforcement. His presence in the school provides an avenue for exposure to trust, safety, knowledge, and experience . . . . School conflicts have been reduced through his constant, positive interaction with the student body. – A faculty member writing about a high school SRO

Students who previously held a negative opinion of law enforcement now ask if they may go speak to the officer. He has developed a rapport with teachers as well. – A school guidance counselor writing about a high school SRO

As this section has suggested, training and supervision of SROs is most effective when school administrators are involved. This aspect of the collaboration between the law enforcement agency and the school system is part of a much larger issue of developing good relations between SROs and principals and assistant principals—the focus of the next section.

SECTION 6: COLLABORATING WITH SCHOOL ADMINISTRATORS AND TEACHERS

SECTION SUMMARY

Perhaps the single most troublesome area for most programs has been establishing productive relationships between SROs and principals and assistant principals. The underlying problem behind many conflicts between them stems from a fundamental difference in the law enforcement culture and the school culture in terms of goals, strategies, and methods.

Working with School Administrators

Administrators expressed three principal concerns about having an SRO in their schools:

- *Who's In Charge?*
- *Who Makes the Decision to Arrest?*
- *Why Isn't "My" SRO Available All the Time?*

These and other administrator concerns were commonplace mostly when the programs had been in operation less than a year. Over time, most administrators developed good working relations with their SROs and came to value the program highly. While much of this change in attitude can be attributed to administrators seeing that their worst fears were not materializing and that the SROs were in fact valuable assets, many programs found they could expedite dramatically the relationships between officers and administrators by taking the following steps.

- *Collaborate*, through joint planning and open and frequent communication, in establishing SRO roles and responsibilities, screening candidates, and supervising the officers.
- *Explain program benefits to administrators*, showing that they have a lot to gain by having an SRO in their schools, such as:
  - an immediate response to incidents requiring police intervention;
  - an increase in everyone's sense of security and actual safety;
  - being spared at least in part the hassle and time of handling incidents of serious student misconduct; and
  - assistance in preparing security assessments and emergency plans.
- *Orient administrators to the program*—do not rely on school superintendents or SROs to do this.
- *Train SROs* before *they go on the job*, to help SROs appreciate and learn to deal with the differences in organizational procedures and cultures between law enforcement agencies and educational institutions.
- *Address administrator concerns about SROs' availability*, for example, by minimizing calling SROs away from the schools for special assignments.

Gaining Support from Teachers

Gaining the support of teachers is essential if SROs want to get invited to teach their classes. Teaching, in turn, is an important SRO responsibility (1) because of the opportunity it provides to educate kids about the law and improve kids' perceptions about "cops" and (2) because teaching offers a golden opportunity for *motivating students to seek out the SROs outside of class* when students are having problems.

Programs have been able to gain faculty support in a variety of ways to the point that in some schools teachers are constantly requesting SROs to take over their classes.

- *Orient teachers* to the program before it begins—or as soon as possible thereafter.
- *Explain how SROs can improve student learning* by teaching classes and by reducing any fear students may have about being safe at school.
- *Go beyond the normal SRO responsibilities to be of help to teachers*, such as answering their legal questions and handling property crimes committed against them.

The single most troublesome area for most SRO programs may be establishing productive relationships between the officers and principals and assistant principals. According to the COPS Office training manual, COPS in Schools: Keeping Our Kids Safe, ". . . perhaps there is no more significant challenge than the development of an effective working relationship between the primary players." The discussion below summarizes the problems SROs have experienced in working together in the 19 sites and suggests methods of collaborating positively.

The Basic Problem: A Culture Clash

The underlying problem behind many of the difficulties SROs and administrators experienced in developing a viable collaboration stems from a fundamental difference in the law enforcement culture and the school culture. *Law enforcement agencies and school systems function in different worlds with different communication patterns, objectives, and methods.* As a result, conflicts are inherent in the SRO position in balancing the enforcer role as a member of a police or sheriff's department with the educational and nurturing role of a school system. For example, a high school principal in a large new site recalled that he had had early misgivings about the SRO's ability to blend into a school culture—how could a police officer approach and interact with students in a positive manner, he wondered. Compared with the criminal justice system, which he perceived as focused on law, order, and punishment, the educational system would require much more flexibility. "Dealing with kids," he stressed, "means you have to understand that youngsters make mistakes—they make them all the time. You have to expect that kids make mistakes and use their blunders as an opportunity to work with them, not slam them."

In a few cases, jurisdictions have been able to minimize these problems from the outset because of unusual circumstances that fostered a positive relationship between the law enforcement agency and the school system before the SRO program even began (see the box "Capitalize on Serendipitous Conditions").

However, in most instances program participants must make a concerted effort to overcome the barriers to collaboration because, as the COPS in Schools training manual points out—and as was confirmed in several of the programs included in the National Assessment—"While the school superintendent and the sheriff or police chief may have reached an agreement about the implementation of the SRO program, individual principals . . . may not be as open-minded regarding the assignment of a law enforcement officer to their school."

CAPITALIZE ON SERENDIPITOUS CONDITIONS

In a few jurisdictions, preexisting conditions made it possible to avoid in part or entirely the culture clash between the law enforcement agency and the school system that have plagued so many other programs.

- In one large new site, the police department's juvenile division and school department administrators had occupied the same building for many years. This close physical proximity increased opportunities for staff from the future partnering agencies to interact and to experience the operating norms and culture of the other organization.
- In a large established site, the police department's sworn SRO program coordinator had a master's degree in education (indeed, he later retired from the force to become a school principal). This not only gave him an understanding of the perspective of school administrators but also enabled him to establish a quicker rapport with them than other SRO supervisors without a higher education background could have achieved.
- In another large established program, a school principal had known the sheriff for "years and years," and he also knew the high ranking officer who was slated to run the SRO program. As a result, this principal spearheaded 90 percent of the program. For example, the sheriff came to him asking how he should go about recruiting SRO candidates. The sheriff had planned to arbitrarily tell road deputies they were going to be SROs. The principal instead suggested the sheriff ask for volunteers and set up an interview process with the principals and let them choose from the pool. The sheriff agreed.
- As a former elementary school teacher for four years, a school system's assistant superintendent in a large established program had worked closely with the SRO in his school before the program expanded to the secondary level.

Other jurisdictions can look closely to see whether there are individuals in the police or sheriff's department, and in the school system, who are uniquely equipped to help overcome the cultural barriers between the two organizations and then involve them in the planning and running of the program.

However, high level collaboration frequently does not extend to the grass roots where individual SROs and principals and assistant principals can be at serious loggerheads regardless of a positive relationship between their chief executives.

School Administrator Concerns about the Program

The vast majority of sites reported that initially there were conflicts between the SROs and school administrators at the local school level.

- Police program supervisors or SROs in four of the five small established sites told of at least one poor experience they had had with at least one school administrator.
- In several sites, conflicts between SROs and school administrators led to the SROs' replacement.
- At two schools, administrators resisted the SROs' involvement in school activities so firmly that teachers and students would not even acknowledge the officers' presence.

Administrators expressed three principal concerns about having an SRO in their schools:

- "Who's in charge?"
- "Who makes the decision to arrest?"
- "Why isn't 'my' SRO available all the time?"

Who's in Charge?

Many school administrators initially fear they will lose control over running their schools or, at least, over the disciplinary process. Realizing that sworn officers have tremendous discretion and power, these administrators wondered whether the SROs would in effect take over the school when it came to all student misbehavior. As a result, when the SRO programs were in the planning stages in several large new sites, administrators felt the need to announce several times that they intended to maintain authority and control over discipline issues in their schools.

Who Makes the Decision to Arrest?

Closely related to the issue of who has control is the concern of many administrators to be the only persons to decide whether a student is arrested. In a few cases, *administrators wanted differential treatment for students*—they wanted to proceed gently with some students whom they saw as "good kids" by not arresting them.

- There have been serious conflicts in one large established site whenever school administrators want some students arrested but not others, although all the students have committed the same offense. According to the program coordinator, this usually happens "because one kid is 'good' and the other 'bad', or because of [a history of] more problems with one kid than another."
- In another large established site, an SRO had arrested three students who admitted to writing lewd graffiti in a bathroom because, according to State law, criminal damage committed in a school is a felony. The principal objected because the students were members of a gifted and talented group. As a result, the principal developed a policy that graffiti writers would not be arrested unless the markings were gang related.
- In a number of school districts, school administrators want SROs to be lenient with special education students who act up, while SROs want to be consistent in their arrest practices regardless of the students' status. "The biggest initial problem," the SRO in a large established site reported, "was that administrators did not want special education students arrested, while the police said, if it is a battery, we have to make an arrest."

Other administrators *wanted students to be arrested* without realizing that officers lack the legal authority to make an arrest under the circumstances.

- In a large established site, some school administrators initially wanted SROs to arrest students for alcohol possession or carrying pagers after administrators had already confiscated the items. The administrators did not realize that an officer in the State may not arrest offenders for most misdemeanor offenses unless the officer witnesses the crime.

- In the same site, the police program coordinator had to rescind an SRO's arrest for criminal trespass because there had been no prior warning (an essential element of a trespass offense). The police department's SRO coordinator said he had tried to explain officers' arrest powers to the administrators, "but we were reading from different sheets of music," so the department pulled the SRO out of the school for a couple of weeks and sent over a new SRO when the removed officer said he did not want to return.

Why Isn't "My" SRO Available All the Time?

The third concern many administrators expressed reflects their appreciation for the program—*disquiet and even anger when "their" SRO is not available in their schools* all the time. This was the most frequent source of conflict at the four large new sites, but it was also a problem at the large established sites.

- An assistant principal complained to the SRO because the officer went off campus to drive a student home. The SRO answered that he was always available by cell phone and was gone only five minutes—the student's home was a two-mile round trip on open roads.
- When the program began in another site, administrators at one school complained that, because the SRO was not staying on campus to teach, they were not sure if they wanted to continue the program.
- According to the SRO at a junior high school, a high school administrator would call the officer once or twice a week to come over to help with vandalism, fights, or unruly parents because the high school was walking distance from the junior high. Because the police department supervisor sanctioned this assistance, the SRO ended up spending considerable time at the high school, which annoyed the junior high school administrators.
- An early implementation problem in another site involved school administrator complaints that the SROs were not always available because the original four SROs were stretched among three schools and could not, as a result, operate proactively— for example, they could not patrol all three lunches. The program supervisor reported that some administrators complained to the SROs, "Why aren't you in *my* school now?" Complaints about SROs' not being constantly available persisted for several years even after the program had demonstrated its value.
- A principal insisted that the SRO station herself in front of the school before classes began and in another location during lunch. If she were not there, an argument ensued. When the SRO came back from a training, the principal asked her, "Why weren't you in school? You report to me. I'll tell you what you can and can't do." Whenever she left the school, he paged her to return. Because of the principal's attitude, the police department almost decided not to replace the SRO when she left the department.
- Administrators wanted the SRO at their school year-round; the police department refused, instead assigning the officer to regular police duty when school was closed.

For the police department, the reintegration of the SROs into regular assignments during school vacations helps avoid the problem of other officers viewing the SROs as "no longer real cops." In addition, many departments want their SROs back on the streets during the summer so that they do not lose their skills as patrol officers. Finally, in smaller communities, SROs who go back to being beat officers during the summer can keep in touch with some of their troublesome students and continue to mentor them.

Although some administrators had unreasonable expectations about SRO's constant and immediate availability, resisting the temptation to leave the campus unnecessarily can be difficult for new SROs, as well. Patrol officers, used to roaming their sectors with considerable freedom when not responding to a call, must adjust to remaining in a specific location—inside a building or in its immediate vicinity. It can take time for some new SROs to adapt to this new job condition.

Other School Administrator Concerns

Although less common, some administrators expressed three other concerns when the programs were in their early stages.

- Creating a "police state" atmosphere. While some administrators in one school district were delighted that there were new SROs available to make arrests, other administrators wondered if the officers' presence would create a "police state" atmosphere within the schools. A high school principal in a small new site reported that, when the program began in his school, he had difficulty reconciling the functions of arrest, suppression, and intelligence gathering, which he attributed to police, with the functions of counseling, teaching, and skill building that he associated with educators. "After all, regardless of what you call a police officer," he reasoned, "he or she still will view most situations through the criminal justice lens."
- Not focusing sufficiently on security. Conflicts arose between SROs and a number of school administrators who—far from being concerned about creating a police state atmosphere—*wanted* to use SROs primarily or even exclusively for security purposes rather than allowing—much less encouraging or facilitating— the officers to act as teachers and mentors. For example, a principal in a large established site wanted the SRO to patrol the parking lots and watch students getting on and off the buses. The SRO, with his police supervisor's backing, refused. According to the program supervisor in another large established site, "The biggest problem was–and still is–that school officials want SROs to be security, but it [the SROs' purpose] is education and getting kids to see cops as friends rather than enemies—it's not security only."
- Creating unnecessary parental concern about school safety. A number of school administrators were apprehensive that parents would associate a law enforcement presence in the schools with the existence of serious problems.
    - A superintendent in a large new site said he did not want to unreasonably alarm parents or students by projecting an image that his school district had dangerous or "bad" schools.

- School administrators in another large new site were concerned about unduly alarming parents who, with media coverage of the SROs' activities, might think there had been a sudden increase in discipline problems and begin to fear for the safety of their children.
- Administrators in yet another school system worried that minority parents might view the new police presence on campus as a reaction to "white flight" and the need for increased enforcement because minority school enrollment had increased.

While these concerns may suggest that most school administrators have negative attitudes toward their SRO programs, for the most part these apprehensions were commonplace only when the programs were first starting and had been in operation less than a year. *Over time, most school administrators developed good working relations with their SROs and came to value the program highly* (see the box "After Initial Skepticism, Most School Administrators Support the SRO Program"). Supporting this finding from the 19 sites, the National Assessment mail survey of schools that host SRO programs found that the vast majority of the 108 administrators who responded rated their collaboration with both the SROs in their schools (79 percent) and with the participating law enforcement agency (81 percent) as "excellent."

AFTER INITIAL SKEPTICISM, MOST SCHOOL ADMINISTRATORS SUPPORT THE SRO PROGRAM

The vast majority of school administrators in the study support the continued presence of SROs in their schools. In fact, most administrators express concern or apprehension about possibly *losing* their officers.

Reasons administrators give for their ringing endorsement vary, but they include:

- more order in schools;
- a greater sense of safety from possible outside threats;
- having an authoritative helping hand in situations in which irate parents confront teachers or administrators;
- the benefits to students of having another adult role model in the schools;
- having a legal resource available to teachers and other staff; and
- having handy access to a knowledgeable resource for addressing staff misconduct.

In all jurisdictions, principals and assistant principals appreciated the marked improvement in police response time that having an officer on campus afforded. In a large new site, the superintendent of a somewhat rural school district mentioned that she rarely saw deputies on patrol before the SRO program began. She worried about how long it might take police to reach her schools in the event of a crisis or tragedy.

In more than one site, administrators suggested that in the past whenever they had a disruption they had two options: call the police and perhaps wait all day for a response (depending on service needs in other parts of the jurisdiction) or handle the situation without law enforcement intervention, anticipating that the police would assign a low priority to their call. With an SRO working specifically in each school, administrators can access police assistance more quickly.

Many administrators believe that the presence of a police officer on campus has helped diffuse tense situations and prevented the escalation of problems. For just these reasons, administrators of two schools in a small new site threatened to quit if the SRO were not retained.

At least two school districts in the study "put their money where their mouth was" when budget constraints appeared to be about to end their SRO programs.

- When a sheriff's department in a large new site could no longer pay for the SROs, four of the five school districts agreed to contribute 100 percent of their deputy's salary for the nine-month academic calendar, with the department picking up the cost for the remainder of the year.
- When a sheriff in another large new site reported he could no longer fund the two SROs for one school district, the school superintendent informed the sheriff that her district would pay for maintaining one of the two full-time officers.

Ways of Gaining School Administrators' Support

There are a number of steps programs can take to prevent or minimize conflict with school administrators.

Collaboration Is the Key

The steps programs have taken to promote collaboration demonstrate above all that joint planning and open and frequent communication between the local police agencies and school districts at every phase of program development and implementation contribute to successful integration of SROs into the schools. The superintendent of one school district in a large new site played an active role in the SRO program from its earliest stages of development. Because the administrator previously had served in other districts with thriving SRO programs, she offered invaluable insight and experience to the applicant police agency during its proposal writing process. By involving her in the planning phase, the law enforcement agency gave her a sense of ownership for the program and, once the jurisdiction received COPS in Schools funds, allowed her to more readily explain and "sell" the program to school district principals and parents.

It is especially important for the police agency and school district—with the involvement of school principals and assistant principals—*to collaborate in establishing the SROs' roles and responsibilities*. As discussed in section 3, a number of sites learned that they could avoid many potential conflicts if the law enforcement agency and school district developed a *detailed* and *written* description of what the SROs would and would not be responsible for doing—for example, stipulating when the SROs may leave the campus. As many principals and assistant principals as possible should be included in this exercise. In addition to creating "buy-in" from all participants, a written list becomes a document to which SROs and administrators can refer when there is misunderstanding or disagreement over an SRO's behavior or an administrator's request to the SRO. It is important to redistribute the job description periodically because, as with similar documents in many professions, participants misplace them or even forget they exist. One assistant principal said she was not aware her jurisdiction had a memorandum of agreement (it did). Another principal in the same site said he knew one existed but claimed she had never seen it. Turnover among school administrators also makes it necessary to keep circulating the job specifications.

In addition to collaborating in planning the program, there are two other significant program activities on which the law enforcement agency and the schools should work together:

- *Screening candidates.* Section 4 addressed the importance of involving school administrators in developing criteria for selecting SROs and screening them for suitability.
- *Supervising SROs.* This is another opportunity for collaboration that should be seized when the program starts (see section 5).

Collaborating in these areas has helped police supervisors to better understand the expectations and needs of each school in hosting an SRO.

Explain the Potential Program Benefits to Administrators

In any collaboration, all the parties have to have something to gain by working with the other groups. However, the benefits of an SRO program to administrators are not always self-evident. Even when the benefits are obvious, they may initially be overshadowed by the perceived negative aspects of the program. Despite the importance of making sure school administrators understand how the program can benefit them, *no site took the time to explain these advantages.*

Most administrators will recognize from the list below that they have something important to gain by having an SRO in their schools. Indeed, these benefits are not hypothetical—at least two principals or assistant principals in the 19 sites said they had personally experienced each of the benefits listed below.

- Many satisfied school administrators pointed out that principals and assistant principals gain the advantage of *an immediate response to an incident requiring police intervention* rather than calling 911 and waiting for a beat officer to appear.
  According to one school administrator, the immediate response by an SRO helps diffuse tense situations and in some cases prevents the escalation of problems. It also relieves administrators from having to hold and pacify an often agitated, accused student for long periods. Furthermore, as another administrator reported, "SROs can also respond globally right away to incidents that happen in the school. For example, when a boy recently touched a girl in an inappropriate way, [the officer] held

separate assemblies for the 6th grade, 7th grade, and 8th grade classes to speak about sexual harassment and immediately set parameters for their behavior."

- Many administrators observed that *SROs can increase their—and their faculty's and students'—sense of security and probably actual safety.*

- A principal in a large established site pointed out that *SROs can save principals considerable time.* "The SRO is another resource—administrators are drowning in paperwork, so he can do some of the work we would otherwise have to do as well as prevent incidents through mediation and talking with kids—which reduces the number of times administrators have to intervene." Another principal reported that, because administrators can call on the SROs to handle underage smoking incidents, "This relieves me from handling them—and it's more effective."

- Several principals reported that they find *it is simpler to ask the SROs to arrange coverage for extracurricular student events* than coordinating coverage through the police or sheriff's department. In addition, they reported, SROs are better able to prevent misconduct at school events than regular officers can. According to an assistant principal, "The SRO takes charge [at these events]. He knows the kids and where the other deputies should be stationed."

- Administrators in a large established site and in several new sites said they like that they can *go to the SROs for legal information.*

- Several assistant principals reported they had discovered that *irate parents show more respect to SROs than to administrators.* Some administrators call in the SRO to mediate disputes between a furious parent and an assistant principal.

- SROs sometimes *take on special responsibilities that benefit administrators.* One SRO registers student and faculty cars so that, if there is a problem with a vehicle, administrators can go to him to find out whose car it is. When an assistant principal saw a shotgun in a car in the school parking lot, he asked the SRO to investigate. Using his registry, the SRO was able to learn in a matter of minutes that the student and his father had gone hunting together and had simply forgotten to remove the gun.

- Several SROs have helped school administrators to *prepare security assessments* and safe school plans, as well as collaborate in preparing emergency response protocols. SROs also practice preparedness drills with students and staff.

- SROs can help administrators *quash rumors.* One superintendent of schools religiously reads the SROs' monthly reports not only to monitor the officers' activities but also "because board members may call me about an incident at a school and ask for more information about it. For example, when drugs were detected at a junior high school, there was a rumor that they were being distributed freely at a soccer field. I knew this wasn't true—just one kid was involved and he was arrested—because of what I read in the SRO's monthly report."

Orient Administrators to the Program

As noted above, even though the chief or sheriff and the school superintendent agree on the value of the program and plan it together, programs cannot rely on school superintendents to orient these local school administrators—or even to expect them to have the leverage to motivate principals and assistant principals to collaborate with the program. Nevertheless, few programs in the study adequately oriented school administrators to the program. All the

SROs in a large established program agreed that "We needed more orientation for administrators." At the beginning of every school year in a large new site, local police administrators request an opportunity to address all the principals at a superintendent's districtwide summit to explain the overall goals of the program and to begin discussing how best to use the officers at each school. However, one year the school department denied the request As a result, the lieutenant who oversees the SRO program reported that individual SROs had to "train" their principals as they worked together over time. While some SROs forged excellent relationships with administrators, others floundered or even dramatically clashed. Some principals called the lieutenant as late as March or April asking, "Just what is your officer supposed to be doing here?"

Orientation for school administrators (even after the program has been in existence for years) can reduce conflict and increase collaboration because *most principals and assistant principals know little about the goals of the program or about how they can make the best use of the officers in their schools.* If possible, one or two local school administrators should co-lead the training to give it added credibility. One large established program provides in-service training for school administrators whenever a new SRO joins a school. When a teacher in another site became an assistant principal, he sat down with the SRO for two hours to discuss what he felt were the officer's job responsibilities.

The orientation can focus on a particular issue in addition to the entire SRO program. Time should be devoted especially to *discussing the SROs' legal responsibilities and limitations* with regard to search and seizure and making arrests involving minors in the school setting. Few school administrators are aware of the tremendous discretion police officers have in terms of responding to criminal behavior—or of the circumstances in which officers have no discretion (e.g., when state statute makes an arrest mandatory for violating a civil order of protection). In a large established site, a police captain had to call a meeting with the principal and assistant principals at one junior high school to explain that the SRO has arrest discretion and the right to follow through. The school administrators had been insisting on making their own decisions about how to address criminal matters. The captain distributed a memo identifying when SROs could make an arrest and explaining why, if administrators did not want the SRO to make an arrest, the SRO still had the right to make one anyway once the officer had been brought in on the case. Although this memorandum comes close, no site sought to reduce conflict in these areas by distributing available guidebooks on school-related law before the program began.

School administrators should attend SRO training. Faculty and board members at a large established site were concerned that "uneducated SROs would be running down the corridors 'kicking butt'." As a result, the school district paid for—and the school board required—all school administrators to attend at least one 40-hour training offered by NASRO. Within two years, most had already attended.

Train SROs before They Go on the Job

Pre-service training may help SROs to appreciate the differences in organizational procedures and cultures that exist between law enforcement and educational agencies. A sheriff's deputy in a large new site who attended basic NASRO training before beginning his new assignment as an SRO reported that the training improved his understanding significantly of how SROs and administrators were meant to work together. The training helped him learn about the teaching component, communication with administrators, and relationships with the community. Moreover, meeting and talking with officers from other SRO programs outside of class was as important as the curriculum itself for learning about how to interact with principals and assistant principals.

Because principals set the tone for leadership within their schools, SROs assigned to different campuses can end up working in different environments with different expectations. As a result, programs should orient SROs to the specific schools to which they have been assigned before their first day on the job. In many sites, SROs are placed in the schools with no introduction to their particular schools and principals, and must somehow attempt to integrate themselves with the administration, faculty, and students without any understanding of their cultures, habits, or perspectives.

Address Administrators' Concerns about SROs' Availability

Programs have used a number of approaches to **address administrators' concerns about SROs' availability**. As the examples below illustrate, some solutions require flexibility on both sides (see the box "Both Sides Need to Be Prepared to Compromise") because, on the one hand, there will be times when the SRO cannot be available but, on the other hand, there will be times when it is important that the SRO be close at hand.

- In a large established site, an SRO radios the civilian security staff and the assistant principal whenever he is going off campus. He always tries to be in school during lunch. If he is off campus and the assistant principal needs him, she can page him and he comes right back—for example, when a fight broke out just as he was beginning a computer training class.
- A large new site arranges for SROs to get their training in the summer to avoid pulling them out of their schools during the academic year.
- Administrators at a school in a large established site complained that, because the SRO was not staying on campus to teach, they were not sure they wanted to continue the program. The police captain replaced the SRO, assuring the administrators that "if an SRO is supposed to teach a class, he will be there to teach it." The captain then held a mandatory meeting with all the SROs and told them they had to be in school— and to start checking in and out whenever they left campus, as well as timing in and out with the dispatcher when taking a student to the juvenile detention center.
- In another program, school administrators objected to the police department's frequently calling out SROs for special assignments, for example, to participate in a fingerprinting exercise at a store or help provide security when the Governor or a business exposition came to town. As a result, the captain issued an order to pull out the SROs last among all specialized officers for these special events—for example, pulling D.A.R.E. officers out of the schools before calling out the SROs.
- In a large established site, the importance with which the SROs regard their teaching responsibilities is illustrated every time they call for a beat officer to transport a student they have arrested to the juvenile justice center so they do not miss teaching a class they have agreed to conduct. (They go the center later to complete the paperwork.) An SRO who received a call on his pager from his captain during a class was observed returning the call only after class was over.

- A large established site avoided problems of availability by including language in a department general order that "this officer is considered an employee of the . . . [town] on special assignment to the school district, and the officer may not be used for other purposes by the police department except by mutual agreement between the principal of the assigned school and the Chief of Police. . . .."

BOTH SIDES NEED TO BE PREPARED TO COMPROMISE

A principal who relied on his SRO to keep the peace at athletic events wanted the other officers on duty to take orders from the SRO—regardless of rank—because the SRO knew the students personally and knew how to handle them. The principal met with the SRO supervisor in the sheriff's department and got verbal agreement that, regardless of rank, the SRO would be in charge. This rankled a few ranking officers, but the SRO supervisor "took care of" their concerns.

In another large established site, school administrators objected to SROs taking vacation while classes were in session. While the police department observed that the SRO would need to be exempted from the collective bargaining agreement's policy of letting regular officers pick their vacation times based on seniority, it eventually relented.

A principal in a large new site said he felt frustrated with his SRO's early absences when the sheriff's department needed her to testify or complete outstanding cases. The principal met with the SRO's supervisors to discuss the problem but became convinced that he had no choice other than to accept that "county business comes first."

The proposal to the COPS Office in a large new program called for all five SROs to serve their schools districts full time during the nine-month academic year but to remain available for other assignments by the sheriff's office during school breaks. However, school administrators from two of the five school districts requested that their SROs work with them for the balance of the year to help with summer school, camps, and other vacation programs. The sheriff agreed to this change.

Accept—and Work with—the Likelihood of Some Initial Conflict

Realistically, even with close early collaboration and communication, there may still initially be conflict between law enforcement agencies and schools given their divergent cultures and the sensitive nature of sharing responsibility for a police officer on campus.

- Even with the significant efforts made by police in one large new site to include school representatives in the planning and screening phases of the program's start-up, the officers all recounted feeling uncomfortable and alarmed by the inactivity and uncertainty of their early days. One SRO estimated that it took about six months for him to settle into the SRO role and for school staff to begin to trust him.
- Even though the sheriff's office in another large new site made significant efforts to include school administrators in the grant application and SRO screening process, all five SROs recall the actual start-up of the program as a difficult and stressful experience. Four of the five started in their districts after the academic year had

begun. This meant that students, teachers, and principals in their schools had already developed schedules and routines, making the SROs' integration into the school even more awkward.

- Despite several efforts by ranking police officers in a large established site to explain the program to school administrators, the principals and assistant principals "still wanted to do things the old way—the school department way [of sweeping embarrassing incidents under the rug]."

Sometimes *school administrators need time to see that what they feared about the program is not going to happen and that SROs do have things to offer.* For example, administrators may not lose their concern about anticipated and real negative reactions from parents to having a police officer in the school until, with the passage of time, parents begin to report that they are *not* upset about the SROs' presence and in fact *like* having a uniformed officer in the school—and a marked cruiser visible on campus. An administrator in a large new site reported that community acceptance grew as students began telling their parents, "Officer ------------ teaches us and helps us." All of this takes time. An eight-year veteran SRO reported, "It took me three years to get this school to work smoothly."

In some instances the law enforcement agency has to take a hard line about what the SROs must do or cannot do. School administrators, if they accept an SRO onto their campuses, must accept that there may be instances in which they may not control the officers' actions.

- In a large new site, the sheriff made it known that he was considering filing obstruction of justice charges against principal who withheld information about an alleged rape. The principal gave in.
- In a large established site, the police program supervisor radioed an SRO who was in the process of confronting a principal who would not let him arrest a student, "If the principal gets in the way of making an arrest, tell him you'll arrest *him* for obstruction of justice—and do it." The principal relented.

Similarly, there may be times when school administrators need to take a firm stance about what SROs cannot do—for example, provide certain types of "counseling" to students (see section 6).

While early and ongoing collaboration and communication may not prevent every problem between SROs and school administrators, these approaches are likely to prevent many difficulties from blossoming into brouhahas that delay or endanger the program's effectiveness.

Gaining Support from Teachers

Gaining the support of teachers is essential for SROs to get invited to teach their classes. Teaching, in turn, can be a critical SRO responsibility.

- Teaching classes offers SROs the opportunity to impart important information about criminal behavior and the criminal justice system that may discourage some students from committing offenses like fighting, shoplifting, vandalism, and bullying.
- Teaching enables SROs to improve students' image of police officers.
- Teaching offers a golden "marketing" opportunity for *motivating students to seek out the SROs outside of class* when students are having problems they feel the officers can help with—or when they want to report misconduct by other students.

Teacher Concerns about the Program

Some teachers feel the SRO shifts the atmosphere and mission in the schools from one of education to one of fear and safety. When an SRO first came to her school, one teacher stated, "I found it hard to have him in my class with the gun because I want my room to be a place for nurturing and sharing.

An armed officer brings a different atmosphere." In a small established site, the most daunting implementation issue was teachers' refusal to allow SROs into the classroom because they did not understand the role SROs perform in the schools. Some teachers at a large new site worried that the SRO would interfere with their "time-tested" ways of dealing with discipline problems.

Ways of Gaining Teacher Support

Programs have gained teacher support in a variety of ways.

- *Orient teachers to the program before it begins*—or as soon as possible thereafter. Arranging for local school administrators to join the SRO in gaining support from faculty can be especially helpful.
  - In a large new site, the principal and SRO dispelled many teacher concerns by attending staff meetings together to clarify that the officer's roles in the school included being an educator and mentor as well as police officer.
  - In another large new site, school administrators early on asked teachers at faculty meetings to brainstorm about presentations the SRO might offer to students and teachers.
  - An assistant principal in a large established site arranged for the SRO to explain to faculty that, with their permission, he might occasionally walk into classes. Ever since, the SRO pokes his head in classroom doors if the door is open. Sometimes the teacher invites him in. While many teachers might find the interruption annoying, when the SRO was walking by a disruptive classroom being taught by a new teacher, he went in and calmed down the class. Later, the teacher told the assistant principal how much she appreciated the SRO's help.
- *Explain how SROs can benefit teachers*.
  - Most social studies, citizenship, and history teachers are attracted to teaching about law-related issues—especially, controversial ones—that most students enjoy learning about and that most SROs are prepared to teach. Driver education instructors like having the SRO explain driving while impaired laws to students. Physical education and health education teachers call on SROs to explain the effects of illicit drugs on the body and mind.

- SROs can improve learning in other subject area classes by making the subject matter fascinating to students in a way that teachers often cannot. In algebra classes, one SRO takes the class outside to look at "skid marks" that he draws with chalk and then has them calculate the speed of the cars by the length of the skid marks on grass and pavement. He teaches about dating violence in family and consumer science classes. In English classes, he explains the importance of a well-written police report—and gives tips on how to write one.
- Many teachers and students report they have a pervasive low-level fear that a "Columbine-like" incident could happen in any school. While most feel it is unlikely to happen in *their* schools, many report that having an SRO on campus can significantly reduce these fears. Program staff can remind teachers that students who are fearful may have difficulty learning. To the extent that an armed officer on campus reduces student fears, he or she may also improve student learning.
- The presence of a police officer or deputy sheriff can free teachers who are concerned about serious discipline problems from worrying about and taking the time to handle students who might become aggressive, because faculty know they can call on the SRO for help in these challenging situations.
- Most of the teachers in one small established program reported that they get a better response from students who have engaged in serious misconduct by sending them to the SROs than by sending them to the office.
- *Go beyond the normal SRO responsibilities to help teachers.*
  - One teacher reported, "The SRO is a computer whiz. He helped me with some computer programming using photos with a digital camera."
  - Teachers in several sites ask SROs personal legal questions, such as what to do with a child on drugs. One teacher approached an SRO for help with a daughter who husband was battering her.
  - Several SROs deal with property crimes against school staff—for example, when a cafeteria worker's car window was smashed during a drive-by, the employee went to the SRO, not the 911 system, for help.

Even with early planning, it can take months of persistently but patiently explaining the SROs' role before officers get an invitation to teach. In one high school, teachers did not feel comfortable allowing the SRO into the classroom until halfway through the school year. However, the wait is worth it—many SROs report they get the most satisfaction from the position when they teach a class to eager students.

SROs must learn to work harmoniously not only with school administrators and teachers but also figure out how to interact with students and their parents—the focus of the following section.

SECTION 7: WORKING WITH STUDENTS AND THEIR PARENTS

SECTION SUMMARY

Program coordinators, SROs, and school administrators all recognize the difficulty SROs experience trying to maintain authority as enforcers of the law while at the same time preserving a helping relationship with students as teachers and mentors. Walking this fine line plays itself out in two particular areas: counseling, and supportive interpersonal relationships with students.

Counseling

Especially when there is a poor or no relationship between the school guidance counselor and a student, the SRO often fills the gap. Indeed, some administrators and many students report that students lie less to SROs, whom they come to know and trust, than to school counselors.

However, in addition to the serious risk of giving poor advice, SROs are exposed to the criticism—and even civil liability—of practicing psychological counseling without a license when they help students with personal problems unrelated to the law. Some administrators and guidance counselors expressed concern about SROs getting involved in students' personal problems. However, the vast majority said they trusted the SROs' judgment to not overstep their bounds. *The key is for SROs to know when to refer a student for professional help with a personal problem and perhaps involve the parents.*

Interpersonal Relationships with Students

Most familiarity between SROs and students is harmless, such as students using informal names to refer to the officers (e.g., "Officer Nancy" or "J.D.") and SROs passing out free soda to students. However, in a few sites SROs and some students hug each other, opening the possibility for students to misconstrue the officers' intentions. There have been SROs who lost their positions because they flirted with students.

Programs have taken several steps to help SROs balance being supportive yet remain an authority figure.

- Establish specific guidelines for appropriate and inappropriate behavior.
- Arrange to provide formal training for SROs on the topic.
- Instruct SROs to act defensively—for example, some male SROs never close their office doors when talking with a female student.

Working with Parents

Vocal parents can damage a program by complaining about it to the chief law enforcement executive or school board. Conversely, *strong support from parents can provide important benefits.*

- Many parents who appreciate the program encourage their children to seek out the SRO for help—in effect, these parents are performing "outreach" for the SROs.
- In three different sites, support from parents and other members of the local community led city officials to reverse their plans to drop their SRO programs.

Some parents become concerned that an SRO's presence in the schools suggests there must be a serious danger to their children. Occasionally, parents object to their child having been arrested. *Programs that used PTAs, other community meetings, newsletters, letters, and newspaper articles to inform parents about the program before and as it began reported few or no such objections from parents.*

A basic dilemma for SROs is combining the role of enforcer of the law and resource to and supporter of students in need.

Walking the Fine Line

Program coordinators, SROs, and school administrators all recognize the difficulty SROs experience in trying to maintain authority as enforcers of the law along with maintaining a helping relationship with students as teachers and mentors.

- An assistant principal said, "SROs have to walk a fine line which can become a thick wall: being kids' friend but enforcing the law."
- Another assistant principal reported that "A few students become attached to the SRO and show up too often in his office, so I run them out and send them back to class. But the SRO is glad I do it: he walks a tightrope—he wants to maintain rapport with kids to get information, but he also needs to be firm with them— even arrest them."
- A program supervisor confirmed that "The hardest thing for them [SROs] is that they have to be friends with everyone but never know if they will have to arrest them [students]—so SROs need to be friendly but not friends."
- An SRO in a large new site who devoted most of his time to teaching and mentoring reported that at times he has felt genuinely "conflicted" when he has had to take punitive action against students. For example, when he learned about a New Year's Eve party one year, he became heavily involved in the investigation that led to numerous charges filed against students for unlawful sexual activity and underage drinking. The SRO felt "embroiled" in these matters and had difficulty separating his emotions as a police officer and mentor.

The challenge of balancing the law enforcement role with the mentor role is exacerbated by the lack of contact many SROs have with other SROs and with patrol officers.

Historically, police have always had to balance how much discretion to exercise in any given encounter with the public, but officers usually look to peers for where the boundaries are on their behavior, for example, through gossip of what happened to police officers who stepped over the line. But, *because SROs are largely isolated from their peers—sometimes for days on end—they are left on their own when it comes to determining how to act.* Furthermore, SROs have taken on new roles and responsibilities for which beat officers—and even the SROs' supervisors—may be able to offer little guidance.

Some SROs go out of their way to avoid casting themselves in a negative light to students (sometimes assisted by school administrators—see the box "Some School Administrators Help SROs Maintain their Mentoring Role"). "Because my position as an SRO requires me to build confidence and trust with students," one SRO said, "I have tried to stay out of enforcement or suppression activities." As a result, this SRO has chosen in certain instances to make school administrators aware of situations he has heard about from students rather than trigger a police investigation. Principals can then resolve the matter using the school disciplinary process. Another SRO reported that "I often find myself in a balancing routine of my own, weighing possible risks to school safety and security against potential risks to my reputation and rapport among students."

SOME SCHOOL ADMINISTRATORS HELP SROS MAINTAIN THEIR MENTORING ROLE

Two school administrators use a variation of the "good cop, bad cop" routine, in which the principal or assistant principal plays the "bad cop" meting out the punishment in order to protect the SRO's role as the student's confidant and mentor.

- According to an assistant principal, "We can play the good guy/bad cop routine, with me being the bad guy. The SRO calms the situation and the kids before I take over."
- Another principal said that "He [the SRO] can play the good guy and I the bad guy. I'm very authoritarian—not a negotiator, ex-army. But the SRO has become friends with many kids—he jogs with the cross-country team and repaints the parking lot stripes with kids on his own time. I don't want to jeopardize that relationship."

Some administrators go even further in helping to shield the SROs from having to be too tough on students.

- In the rare cases when a student needs to be arrested, a district school superintendent instructs the SRO or principal to call a different law enforcement officer to make the arrest rather than have the SRO arrest the youth.
- When incidents rise to the level of criminal misconduct in a large new site, the SROs and school administrators follow an unwritten policy of having the SROs file only preliminary reports, turning over any further investigative duties to the department's juvenile detectives. This "division of labor," all parties say, helps the SROs maintain their positive rapport with students that they feel is necessary in order for the officers to remain effective teachers and mentors.

On two separate occasions, SROs who had to arrest or verbally chastise students were observed making an attempt to maintain good rapport with the youngsters by affectionate but appropriate physical contact.

- After sending a student to be tested for drugs, an SRO swatted him with a rolled-up newspaper and squeezed his shoulder. Later, the SRO explained, "I don't come down too hard on the kids so they will come to me later on [with their problems]."
- After sternly chastising an elementary school student privately in the corridor who had asked during class to see the SRO's gun, the officer sent him back into class with a gentle tap on his shoulder.

Walking the fine line plays itself out in two in particular areas: counseling, and supportive interpersonal relationships between SROs and individual students.

Counseling

Because SROs are trained to be problem solvers, they naturally fall into the practice of giving advice. Especially when there is a poor—or no—relationship between the school guidance counselor and a student, the SRO often fills the gap. Indeed, a number of SROs and school administrators agree that many students often lie less to SROs, whom they come to know and trust, than to school counselors or administrators. A student in a large established site reported, "Officer--------- is totally trustworthy. We can go in at lunch and talk about anything. We don't go to [a] counselor as often because they may call your parents." SROs in a number of sites have been taken aback by the personal nature of problems that students share with them. In one case, a student said that she would speak *only* with the SRO about the fact she was pregnant.

However, in addition to the serious risk of giving poor advice, SROs are exposed to the criticism—and even civil liability—of practicing psychological counseling without a license.

- In a large established site, an SRO got into trouble for talking with a girl about her sexual relationship with her boyfriend after a friend of the girl's mother complained to the sheriff, who then called the SRO and the program supervisor into his office for an explanation.
- A principal in a large new site expressed concern about the amount of time the SRO spent counseling students rather than referring them. The principal became alarmed because the SRO was not a certified mental health care provider. Three students had revealed to the SRO their plans to attempt suicide.

As these vignettes suggest, while SROs may receive training on "law-related" counseling (e.g., explaining the legal consequences of a student's behavior), many SROs attempt to help students with personal problems unrelated to the law.

SROs who get involved with students' personal problems justify their involvement on a variety of grounds.

- Some SROs point out that if *they* do not at least listen empathically to these students, the alternative is not for the students to decide to talk with a counselor or administrator or even teacher—what they will do is *not tell anyone*. The SROs argue that at least *someone* learns about the problem before it is too late.
- One SRO reported that many counselors are too busy to counsel because "they are drowning in paperwork."
- SROs and school administrators observe that the officers have more contact with students because SROs are constantly up and around, while school counselors are largely confined to their offices.

Although some administrators and guidance counselors expressed concern about SROs getting involved in students' personal problems, the vast majority said they had a high level of trust in the SROs' judgment not to overstep their bounds. Some administrators said that they approved of the students' preference to share problems with SROs, adding that this trust in the SROs was beneficial to students and the school.

The key, of course, as several SROs and school administrators suggested, is *knowing when to refer the student for professional help with a personal problem and perhaps to involve the parents*. Some SROs seem to be able to know when and how to do this. For example, the SRO in a large established program brought a female student who was not getting along with her mother to the assistant principal because "I didn't know how far it would go in terms of getting into female problems." When a student gave him a suicide note from another student, he searched and found the girl in a bathroom. He then arranged for her parents come over immediately to take her to a mental health center. When a student will not seek needed professional help, one SRO shares the problem with the school counselor, who then tells the SRO what to tell the student.

Supportive Interpersonal Relationships with Students

There were many examples among the 19 sites of familiarity between SROs and students designed to develop or maintain rapport. In some cases, the familiarity at worst does no harm and at best results in students perceiving the SRO as a valuable and trustworthy source of support. For example, students in some schools—and faculty and administrators, as well—use informal names to refer to the SROs, such as their initials (e.g., "D.D.," "P.A.") or their first name preceded by "Officer," as in "Officer Nancy."

Several SROs keep small refrigerators stocked with soda that they pass out to students (and sometimes to parents), as well as pretzels and other "goodies." Local businesses give coupons to all the SROs in one large established jurisdiction to distribute to students for free products and services. One SRO alone gets 500 coupons each year. Some SROs give students money.

- In one large established site, students sometimes ask the SRO for small amounts of money, which he occasionally provides—"but," he says, "I always get it back."
- An SRO in another site lends some students small amounts of change, when they ask. In his case, however, "Some return it, others don't."

- The same SRO gives a few selected students significant amounts of money that he collects selling pizzas at the school during lunch. For example, he gave money to a student who had been invited to the National Junior Olympics because the boy could not afford to go. "Parents thank me for doing this kind of thing."
- In another site, the SRO gives students his business card with 40 cents or a $1.00 written on the back, which the students hand to the cashier at lunchtime. The SRO goes to the cafeteria every week to pay the total amount on the cards.

In a few sites SROs and students hug each other.

- In one large established site, the SRO hugs students several times a day—but so do some faculty and administrators. It is part of the school culture.
- Another SRO instituted a "hug-a-day program" for students he felt needed that kind of support. He told one student, "I'm putting you in my 'hug-a-day' program—I'm going to see you every day for a hug and, if I don't see you, I'm going to find you." Now that she is a junior in high school, whenever the SRO happens to run into her there, they still hug.
- A female SRO practices what she calls "assertive caring and support—make the kid [e.g., a bully] feel responsible for his or her behavior and then give the child a hug the next day." When she visits the elementary schools, several children gleefully rush up to her in the corridors to hug her.

In no instance did the hugs that were observed appear to be unwanted behavior on the part of the students—indeed, in many cases it is the students who initiate them. However, the potential for students to misunderstand the behavior exists. In addition, some SROs—like some teachers and school administrators—may have mixed motives in engaging in physical contact.

- According to a former school board member, "We made some bad choices for SROs at the beginning—one was tapping girls on the rear end to be their buddy—SROs can't be a playmate; friendly, yes."
- In two sites, SROs lost their positions because of allegations that they were flirting with female students.

Finding the Right Balance

To some extent, the limits on the extent and nature of SROs' interpersonal relationships with students depend on such considerations as the school culture (e.g., the constant hugging with students by faculty and administrators in one school), the SROs' motives (which, however, can be easily misconstrued), the manner in which familiarity is expressed (e.g., allowing students to call the SRO by his or her first name or initials versus touching a female student's fanny), and the SROs' willingness to take risks (as long as no one but the SRO is in harm's way). In this latter connection, an assistant principal expressed concern about an SRO's exposing himself to criticism or charges of molestation after the officer drove a female student home alone. But the SRO feels, "If it's the right thing to do, do it. I need to take risks for these kids. I'm always taking kids home, but only if I have a personal relationship with them and I feel comfortable doing it."

One obvious solution to becoming inappropriately friendly with students is to avoid all physical contact and all discussions that could remotely be perceived as suggestive or extending beyond the SRO's realm of expertise. Most SROs in this study were more flexible because they know when things might be getting out of hand. For example, when a few students over the years have hinted to one long-term SRO that they would like to see him off campus, he has told them in no uncertain terms, "You have a bad idea," in order to confront the issue right away and "shut it down." Two different SROs were observed immediately "shutting down" students' efforts to talk about the officers' sidearms:

- A boy in an elementary school class the SRO was teaching asked to see her gun. The SRO immediately requested the teacher's permission to pull him into the corridor, where she lectured him grimly on not talking about her gun—"It offends me."
- A student in a middle school asked an SRO during class if he had ever used his gun. The SRO answered, "I don't like guns—and you can be expelled for a year if you get caught in school with a gun. The only thing I ever used it for was to break a window—and I hope that's all I ever do with it." End of discussion.

Programs have taken several steps to help SROs walk the fine line between being supportive yet remaining an authority figure.

- ***Establish specific guidelines for appropriate and inappropriate behavior.*** For example, in a large established site the SRO procedures manual says a department Parental Permission/Waiver of Liability should be used whenever students are transported by officers in non-arrest or non-urgent situations.
- ***Arrange to provide formal training for SROs on the topic.*** Some SROs in a large new site pointed out the need for training in how to manage conflicts that sometimes develop between their role as student advocate and their role as law enforcer. The training should include a discussion of developmental issues among children and youth, especially in terms of ***how youngsters can become confused about the meaning of adults' signs of affection*** or be afraid of expressing objections to these displays.
- ***Instruct SROs to act defensively.*** A principal felt uneasy about a male SRO counseling female students with his office door closed. "Just because you have a gun and a badge doesn't mean that you don't have to cover yourself just like we do," she observed. Another SRO always makes it a point to keep his office door open when he has a girl inside talking with him.

Working with Parents

While it is very important that parents not oppose the program, active parental support can benefit the program in several respects.

Why Working with Parents Is Important

Vocal parents can complain about the program to the chief law enforcement executive. Sheriffs, in particular, as elected officials, may be understandably reluctant to antagonize a significant constituency. Parents can also complain to the school board and to elected or appointed city officials. Parents in one large established site went to court to challenge the zero tolerance policy for fighting in the schools that SROs were enforcing by arresting all parties involved in a fight. Such complaints and lawsuits can cripple a program; at a minimum, they require program participants to divert valuable time and energy to "putting out the fires" that they could be spending on teaching and mentoring.

Conversely, *strong support from parents can provide several benefits.*

- Many parents who appreciate the program encourage their children to seek out the SRO for help; some parents themselves contact the SRO for guidance in dealing with their own children. In effect, these parents serve an "outreach" function for the SRO by referring—or becoming—"clients."
- When parents support the program, they are less likely to object when the SRO punishes *their* children.
- Support from parents and other community groups can save rescue a program that town officials plan on reducing or dismantling. In three different sites, city officials reversed their plans to drop their SRO programs because of widespread objections from parents and other members of the community.

Concerns Some Parents Have about the Program

When SRO programs first begin, some parents initially question the need for an officer in the school and wonder whether an SRO's presence suggests a serious danger they were not aware of or do not believe exists. Both initially and later on, some parents object to their child having been arrested—or because another student was *not* arrested. In a large established site, parents call the program supervisor three or four times a month, usually to ask that the SRO arrest a student who is allegedly bothering their children.

Addressing Parental Concerns

Many programs experienced opposition from parents in part because program coordinators and school administrators failed to orient them to the program before—or even after—it began.

- According to a school principal in a large established site, "Parents' misperception of the SROs' role was a major problem—cops on campus was unheard of. We needed to prepare parents on what the SRO does."
- Program staff at a large new site reported they had made no effort to introduce the program to the community. Once on the job, however, the SROs realized the need to explain their goals and functions to parents. They gained permission to speak at various PTA meetings and at parent-teacher night.

Programs that took steps to inform parents about the program before and as it began reported few or no objections from parents.

- In a large new site, a principal reported that parents have never complained about the SRO program in general, or about his district's assigned officer in particular.
    - The superintendent of schools had notified parents of the school district's participation in the program ahead of time and explained his decision.
    - Each school sent letters to parents explaining the program.
    - Program organizers arranged for the high school newspaper and a districtwide newsletter to print favorable and comprehensive stories about the program.
- A school district in a large new site announced plans for the SRO program in a newsletter to area residents, held meetings with community groups, and had the SRO attend school functions and community events on a regular basis.
- A high school principal in a large new site called a parent meeting as the program was getting under way in order to introduce the SRO and explain the purpose of having an officer stationed among their children. The SRO outlined his communication-building and role-modeling responsibilities, which allowed parents to see him in positive terms as a proactive presence rather than as a response to "a problem at our high school." The principal asked parents who attended to "spread the word" to others in the community, which he believes they did.

Even before the program began in one small established site, parents strongly objected to officers carrying guns on campus. The planning process was careful to address this concern. For example, in the beginning the officer drove his own car and did not wear a uniform or carry a gun. Most people in the community did not realize there was an officer working at the school for the first two years of the program's existence.

Programs should implement several of these approaches to building support among parents because any one strategy is unlikely to reach all—or even most—parents. For example, because local parent organizations are few or nonexistent in some rural areas and small towns, meeting with PTAs is not a solution there.

Regardless of how effectively SROs appear to be working with administrators, teachers, students, and parents, for several reasons it is important to evaluate just how successful the program is—the focus of the following section.

SECTION 8: EVALUATING THE PROGRAM

SECTION SUMMARY

Despite the importance of evaluation, very few of the 19 programs included in the study conducted useful and valid assessments of their programs. However, *program evaluation is essential* for two reasons:

- to learn whether and how the program needs improvement and
- to provide evidence to funding sources of the importance of continuing the program (assuming the evaluation is positive).

To be most effective, evaluation needs to be a significant focus of the design and planning of the program so that baseline data can be collected with which to compare future data after the program has been running. However, evaluations conducted after the fact can also be useful.

The first step in any evaluation is to review the program's objectives and then *decide what questions to ask about each objective*. For example, if a program's objectives include reducing truancy and improving kids' image of the police, the evaluation can ask:

- By how much have truancy rates changed since the program began?
- How have students' opinions of the police changed since the program began?

The second step is to *identify the information to collect* that will answer the questions (e.g., truancy rates for the past seven years; student responses to opinion surveys). The third step is to *determine how to collect the information* (e.g., school district records; focus groups with students).

The law enforcement agency and school system should collaborate on the assessment. Several programs have involved their schools in evaluating program effectiveness, typically by interviewing or obtaining written assessments from principals and assistant principals. One school district conducts annual focus groups at each grade level at each of the five junior high schools that have an SRO asking about:

- student trust in the SRO and police in general,
- student perceptions of whether the SROs have reduced crime, and
- problems (e.g., bullying) that are still going on that the SROs need to address.

Program supervisors distribute the findings to the school board to bolster their case for continued funding and to each school to identify problem areas that need addressing.

Administrators of any program are often understandably reluctant to evaluate their efforts because they lack time or expertise, or have concerns about violating confidentiality.

They may also be apprehensive that the evaluation results will not show that they are doing a good job. However, *program evaluation is essential*:

1. Without a formal assessment, it is very difficult to know *whether the program needs improvement* and, if so, what specific changes are needed.
2. Agency heads need the results of evaluations *to provide evidence to funding sources of the need to continue the program*—and program staff need the results to convince their agency heads to continue to request funding for the program.

Despite the importance of evaluation, only one program included in this study conducted a useful and valid assessment of its programs.

Basics of Program Evaluation

To be most effective, *evaluation needs to be a significant focus of the design and planning of the program*. Without collecting baseline measures (e.g., assessing students' current level of fear), it is difficult to determine with certainty whether the program has achieved certain desired goals. In addition, program evaluation done as an afterthought typically is given short shrift and rushed because staff have decided to conduct an assessment quickly in response to a sudden outside demand—for example, from the agency head or a funding source—for evidence that the program is working.

The law enforcement agency and school system need to collaborate on the assessment.

- Typically, the law enforcement agency conducts a broad but formal evaluation of the SROs—for example, are they following department rules?
- School administrators evaluate the SROs informally but based on their day-to-day work in the school—for example, does the SRO act appropriately in breaking up a fight? Set a good example for purposes of mentoring? Arrive on time?

Examples of Program Evaluation

Evaluations should be designed to determine whether the program's goals were achieved. Therefore, the first step in any evaluation is to review the program's goals and then *decide what questions to ask about each goal*. For example, if a program's goals include reducing truancy and improving kids' image of the police, the evaluation can ask:

- By how much have truancy rates changed since the program began?
- How have students' opinions of the police changed since the program began?

The second step is to *identify the information to collect* that will answer the questions (e.g., truancy rates for the past seven years; student opinions of the SRO). The third step is to *determine how to collect the information* (e.g., school records; focus groups).

The National Assessment's mail survey of 322 programs found that there is little consistency among programs in terms of the data they collect. This proved to be true among the 19 programs studied for this report. This inconsistency in part may reflect differences in the programs' goals, but even programs with similar goals collected different data. The box "Sample SRO Program Evaluation Data that Programs Can Consider Collecting" lists the types of information an SRO program can think about collecting depending on the program's goals (and, of course, availability of the data).

Research conducted for this cross-site report illustrates four examples of the types of data that can be collected that can help assess whether a program's goals were achieved. For example, if reducing *student misbehavior* is a program goal, the program can compare the number of disciplinary actions by school by year, starting with a few years before the SRO program began. The bar chart below shows that disciplinary actions in one large new site declined in 6 of 10 schools after the SRO program began.

SAMPLE SRO PROGRAM EVALUATION DATA THAT PROGRAMS CAN CONSIDER COLLECTING

Qualitative Data
Meeting agendas, notes
Memorandums of Agreement/contracts
Training or technical assistance provided to SROs
SRO activity logs or reports of activities

Quantitative Data
Number of students SRO advised
Number of students SRO taught
Police calls for service
Arrests and citations
Weapons and drugs seized
Number and types of safety or disorder problems solved
Crime incidents in school by type of incident (e.g., fights, bullying)
Crime incidents in vicinity of school
Noncriminal disorder incidents in school
Noncriminal disorder incidents in vicinity of school
Victimization in school and in vicinity of school
Truancy
Suspensions (in-school and out-of-school) and expulsions
Student tardiness
Student levels of fear
Student satisfaction with the SRO

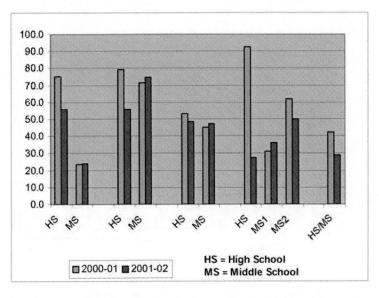

Disciplinary Actions per 100 Students at 10 Middle and Senior High Schools before and after the SRO Program Began.

If a program goal is to *reduce truancy*, supervisors can compare graduation rates before and after the program began. The table below shows the graduation rates before and after program implementation at a large new site.

Several SRO programs were developed in part *to reduce the burden on beat officers who have to respond to repeated calls at the schools*. Programs can assess whether they have freed up these officers to perform other vital patrol functions by examining the number of calls for service at each school before and after program implementation. The figure below shows how calls for service from one school district's high school and its surrounding areas declined steadily after the program began in 2000.

Finally, as partial evidence of program effectiveness a police chief kept records showing that the number of *incidents involving firearms* at one school had declined from 18 to 1 over the program's three-year life to date.

Graduation Rates for Five School Districts before and after Implementation

Year		School District				
		#1	#2	#3	#4	#5
Pre-SRO	1996	70.4	74.8	74.2	74.1	82.8
	1997	86.0	85.4	83.5	82.6	81.4
	1998	90.3	88.5	88.7	76.2	87.2
	1999	81.8	81.4	87.9	88.5	86.4
4 year average		*82.1*	*82.5*	*83.6*	*80.4*	*84.5*
Post-SRO	2000	90.6	78.5	85.8	90	90.1
	2001	92.0	87.5	91.1	87.3	86.7
	2002	90.5	91.6	94.5	89	92.7
	2003	92.0	90.8	96.6	89.1	94.5
4 year average		*91.3*	*87.1*	*92*	*88.9*	*91*

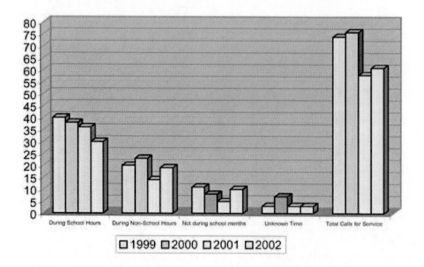

Trends in Calls for Service within a Six-Block Radius of the High School.

Of course, programs may have to limit the data they collect in light of feasibility, need to preserve confidentiality, time, and cost. In addition, some data may be readily available but not useful. For example, because two schools in a small new site did not need SROs for purposes of preventing crime since they already had such low rates of disorder, the programs' success could not be measured in terms of reductions in crime—the level was already extremely low. An alternative in such a community might be to measure the reduction of student and parent concern about school security and safety. The program could also measure program effectiveness in terms of teacher, student, and administrator satisfaction with the program.

Programs need to interpret their data carefully.

- The data may initially show increases in the number of incidents as SROs detect and report misbehavior that previously went unnoticed or unreported. For example, in one small new site reported incidents rose significantly with the introduction of the SROs. However, both the police and the schools interpreted the increase as the result of the additional surveillance provided by the SROs— evidence that the program was in fact working.
- There are frequently other events taking place around the time the SRO program is begun or after it has become established that could also account for any positive evaluation findings that are identified. For example, student smoking in a school in a small new site almost completely ceased due in part to the SRO but probably more importantly due to security cameras installed outside restrooms and smoke detectors installed inside. Other events that could be responsible for part or all of any positive evaluation results range from a new and stricter principal to the introduction of student uniforms.
- In assessing changes in student and parent perceptions of danger in the schools, programs need to distinguish between student and parent fear of *crime*, on the one hand, and concern about *security and safety*, on the other hand. Programs should also distinguish between student and parent fear of *"normal"* crime (e.g., vandalism, fighting, theft) versus their fear of *exceptional events* along the lines of the Columbine tragedy.
- As with all program evaluations, simple comparisons of aggregated data may not reveal or may even mask program effects. Issues such as timing of the program, levels of student involvement, and unanticipated outcomes may influence overall program effects.

Involving the Schools in the Evaluation

Several programs have found that *it is valuable to involve the schools in evaluating the program's effectiveness*, typically by interviewing principals and assistant principals or by asking them to provide written comments on the SROs' performance. A summary of some performance reviews from one site illustrates the types of information a program can obtain when it involves school administrators in the evaluation.

- One high school principal reported that "the program works better than I thought it would, and it works *differently* than how I thought it would work." While he originally conceived of the program in terms of providing increased security and a sense of safety at the school, he now understands the proactive role the SRO plays, as well. He had not anticipated the level of trust that the SRO would foster among the students. He sees now that, because the deputy has formed positive relationships with many students, the kids get to know him "as more than just a cop." This particular principal also appreciated the close relationship that the SRO has with many of the high school's teachers and staff. He believes that they have confidence in his judgment and handling of sensitive matters. The administrator summarizes that the SRO is "a member of our team."

- A high school assistant principal reported that the SRO has helped him and other staff members respond to potentially dangerous situations as they arise. He specifically mentioned a bomb scare and an incident in which a student brought a knife to campus and threatened suicide. In the latter incident, the SRO's crisis intervention skills helped diffuse the danger until the school secured professional psychiatric care for the child.

- Another high school principal observed that students had begun to see police officers in a more positive light because of the SRO's regular presence in their lives. The principal feels that young people have begun to accept the SRO as more than "just another institutional employee"; the SRO acts as an intermediary with delinquent students, helping them to think through their decisions and accept responsibility for their actions

- A school superintendent said she had observed a behavior change in students because of the SRO's presence. Although police and incident reports may have increased in her schools during the program's early history due to greater responsiveness and awareness on the part of the SRO, she noted that truancy had become less of a problem for administrators. She suggested that students were more likely to come to school on their own now because they knew that truancy violations were enforced.

- The principal in a large new site reported that the SRO's arrest powers had dramatically affected student behavior for the better. He is certain that there have been fewer fights at his school.

One must, of course, be cautious in evaluating "testimonials" from individuals who have a stake in the program. Some school administrators (as well as law enforcement participants), because they believe in and support the program, may report more benefits than problems. However, programs can obtain more objective information. For example, one school district in a large established site has conducted annual focus groups at each grade level at each of the five junior high schools that participate in the program. The groups include a random sample of 10 seventh graders, a random sample of 10 eighth graders, and a group selected by the principal, assistant principal, and SRO of about 10 combined seventh and eighth graders who have dealt with the SRO personally. School guidance counselors moderate the groups, which include a significant focus on the SRO program. A review of the results for the school years 1999-2000 and 2000-2001 suggests that the focus group participants generally found the program helpful. The students participating in the 2000-2001 focus groups said that they—

and their parents— overwhelmingly liked have an SRO in school and felt safer because of the officer's presence.

As explained above, the purposes of conducting an evaluation are both to identify how the program needs to be improved and to help convince funding sources to continue to support the program. This site was unusual in using evaluation findings successfully for both purposes.

- The school district gives the focus group results to each school for purposes of improving the program's operation. For example, when the early focus groups showed that students saw the SROs as law enforcers, the program coordinator reminded the SROs of the need to spend more time building relationships with students. Because the focus groups also indicated a need to address bullying and sexual harassment, the SROs added these topics to their classroom offerings.
- Program administrators submit the focus group findings to the school board every year to bolster their case for continued funding.

The focus groups were discontinued after the 2001-2002 school year because they had served their purposes of pointing out weaknesses in the program to the SROs when they were new at the job and convincing the board of the program's value. In addition, the process and logistics for conducting the focus groups are arduous. However, the school district may resume them for the 2004-2005 school year because there will be two new SROs.

Precisely because good evaluations can be costly and time consuming, programs can reach out to local universities for help in designing and implementing a program assessment. Professors in departments of criminal justice, political science, government, psychology, sociology, and other disciplines are often only too happy to supervise graduate students in conducting an evaluation—and giving them a publishable article— with little or no cost to the program.

End Notes

[1] Hickman, Matthew J., and Brian A Reaves. *Local Police Departments 1999*, Washington, D.C.: Bureau of Justice Statistics, U.S. Department of Justice, May 2001.

[2] Goldberg, Andrew L., and Brian A. Reeves. *Sheriffs' Departments 1977*, Washington, D.C.: Bureau of Justice Statistics, U.S. Department of Justice, February 2000.

[3] The National Assessment expected to include five large new programs. However, because one of the large new sites selected for inclusion rejected its COPS in Schools grant, it had to be excluded from the study. By the time the site turned down the grant, it was too late to substitute another site.

[4] Other studies have identified many of the issues this report identifies as problematical for SRO programs. However, existing materials that raise these issues either are not based on much empirical evidence or do not treat the topics with the depth that this report does.

[5] The Office of Community Oriented Policing Services will be making a report available that discusses in greater detail how programs have successfully gone about screening and recruiting SROs.

[6] The same report will also address issues of SRO training and supervision.

[7] Office of Community Oriented Policing Services, U.S. Department of Justice. COPS in Schools: Keeping Our Kids Safe, p. 16.

[8] Office of Community Oriented Policing Services, U.S. Department of Justice. COPS in Schools: Keeping Our Kids Safe, p. 16.

[9] This assumes, of course, that the program was not established with the express and permanent goal of exclusively providing law enforcement services.

[10] Thomas A Gavin, "A Partnership Clearly Defined." *School Safety*, Fall 1995, pages 9–11.

In: School Resource Officers
Editor: Andrew O'Murphy

ISBN: 978-1-62808-850-2
© 2013 Nova Science Publishers, Inc.

Chapter 4

SCHOOL AND CAMPUS SAFETY PROGRAMS AND REQUIREMENTS IN THE ELEMENTARY AND SECONDARY EDUCATION ACT AND HIGHER EDUCATION ACT[*]

Gail McCallion and Rebecca R. Skinner

SUMMARY

In the United States, more than 75 million students are enrolled in elementary and secondary schools and institutions of higher education (IHEs). Safeguarding their security while they pursue an education is a paramount concern of federal, state, and local governments, as well as the school districts, schools, and institutions that enroll these students. The December 14, 2012, shooting deaths of 20 children and 6 adults at Sandy Hook Elementary School in Newtown, CT, have heightened congressional concerns about school security.

Both the Elementary and Secondary Education Act of 1965 (ESEA), as amended by the No Child Left Behind Act of 2001 (NCLBA; P.L. 107-110), and the Higher Education Act of 1965 (HEA) contain requirements regarding crime and student safety. The ESEA also includes specific grant programs that support efforts to prevent school violence.

The ESEA authorizes the federal government's major programs to assist disadvantaged students, address teacher quality issues, provide support to limited English proficient and immigrant students, prevent school violence and drug abuse, and provide support for public school choice in elementary and secondary schools. While the prevention of school violence is not the primary focus of the ESEA, several ESEA programs could potentially contribute to this effort, most notably ESEA Title IV, Part A, the Safe and Drug-Free Schools and Communities Act (SDFSCA). In addition, the ESEA contains specific provisions related to students attending unsafe schools— the Unsafe School Choice Option.

---

[*] This is an edited, reformatted and augmented version of a Congressional Research Service publication, CRS Report for Congress RL33980, prepared for Members and Committees of Congress, from www.crs.gov, dated December 19, 2012.

The HEA authorizes the federal government's major student aid programs that support postsecondary education attendance, as well as other significant programs such as those providing aid to special groups of IHEs and support services to enable disadvantaged students to complete secondary school and enter and complete college. While the HEA does not authorize specific programs to address campus crime and security issues, Section 485(f) of Title IV of the HEA contains statutory requirements related to campus crime and security, known collectively as the Jeanne Clery Disclosure of Campus Security Policy and Campus Crime Statistics Act (the Clery Act). Institutions must comply with these requirements to participate in the federal student aid programs and other programs authorized by Title IV (e.g., Pell Grants).

This report discusses these provisions and programs as they apply to elementary and secondary schools and IHEs. It begins with a description of programs and requirements included in the ESEA, which is followed by a discussion of relevant requirements included in the HEA.

OVERVIEW

In the United States, more than 75 million students are enrolled in elementary and secondary schools and institutions of higher education (IHEs).[1] During the 2009-2010 school year (most recent data available), there were 33 school-associated violent deaths in elementary and secondary schools.[2] In 2010, students aged 12-18 were victims of approximately 828,400 nonfatal crimes at school, including thefts, simple assault, rape, sexual assault, robbery, and aggravated assault. At IHEs in 2011, about 31,823 criminal incidents were reported as having occurred on campus, including 16 incidents of murder, 3,396 forcible sex offenses, 2,440 aggravated assaults, and 20,072 burglaries.[3]

The December 14, 2012, shooting deaths of 20 children and 6 adults at Sandy Hook Elementary School in Newtown, CT, have heightened concerns about school security. Safeguarding the security of students as they pursue an education is a paramount concern of federal, state, and local governments, as well as the school districts, schools, and institutions that enroll these students. Both the Elementary and Secondary Education Act of 1965 (ESEA), as amended by the No Child Left Behind Act of 2001 (NCLBA; P.L. 107-110), and the Higher Education Act of 1965 (HEA) contain requirements regarding crime and student safety. The ESEA also includes specific programs that support efforts to prevent school violence. While the HEA does not authorize specific programs to address campus crime and security issues, Section 485(f) of Title IV of the HEA contains statutory requirements related to campus crime and security, known collectively as the Jeanne Clery Disclosure of Campus Security Policy and Campus Crime Statistics Act (Clery Act). Institutions must comply with these requirements to participate in the federal student aid programs and other programs authorized by HEA Title IV (e.g., Pell Grants).

This report discusses these provisions and programs as they apply to elementary and secondary schools and IHEs. It begins with a description of programs and requirements included in the ESEA, which is followed by a discussion of relevant requirements included in the HEA. Where available, the most recent funding level for each program is provided.[4]

RECENT DEVELOPMENTS

On December 14, 2012, the Sandy Hook Elementary School in Newtown, CT, was attacked by a 20-year-old armed man. He shot and killed 20 6- and 7-year-old children and 6 adults at the school, in addition to his mother at her home and himself.

This tragedy has focused congressional attention on what can be done to avoid future attacks, and what federal programs are currently available to address school violence. This report discusses U.S. Department of Education (ED) programs that address school safety.

ELEMENTARY AND SECONDARY EDUCATION ACT (ESEA)

The ESEA, whose programs are administered primarily by ED, includes the federal government's major programs to assist disadvantaged students, address teacher quality issues, provide support to limited English proficient and immigrant students, prevent school violence and drug abuse, and provide support for public school choice.[5] While the prevention of school violence is not the primary focus of the ESEA, there are several ESEA programs that could potentially contribute to this effort, most notably ESEA Title IV, Part A, the Safe and Drug-Free Schools and Communities Act (SDFSCA). In addition, the ESEA contains specific provisions related to students attending unsafe schools.

This section of this report first discusses the SDFSCA program and the activities it authorizes. It then provides a summary of additional ESEA programs that could support mental health programs for students. The section concludes with an examination of the Unsafe Schools Choice Option, with which all elementary and secondary schools receiving funds under the ESEA are required to comply.

SDFSCA[6]

Brief History

As previously mentioned, the SDFSCA is the federal government's major initiative to prevent drug abuse and violence in and around elementary and secondary schools. The SDFSCA was initially enacted in 1994 (P.L. 103-382) in response to concerns about increased school violence and drug use among school-aged youth.[7] The 1994 legislation extended, amended, and renamed the Drug-Free Schools and Communities Act of 1988 (DFSCA; P.L. 100-297). Violence prevention was added to DFSCA's original drug abuse-prevention purpose by incorporating the Safe Schools Act. The Safe Schools Act was originally created by Title VII of the Goals 2000:

Educate America Act of 1994 (P.L. 103-227). Funding was authorized for federal, state, and local programs to assist schools in providing a disciplined learning environment free of violence and drug use, including alcohol and tobacco.

The SDFSCA was subsequently reauthorized as part of the ESEA in P.L. 107-110, the No Child Left Behind Act of 2001. The SDFSCA program as authorized supports two major grant programs—one for State Formula Grants and one for National Programs. Like all No

Child Left Behind Act (NCLBA) programs, the authorization of appropriations for the SDFSCA expired at the end of FY2008; funding has continued to be provided for National Programs through appropriations legislation. Reauthorization of the SDFSCA as part of a comprehensive reauthorization of the ESEA may be considered by the 113th Congress.

Current Program Operation

FY2009 was the last year that funding was provided for the State Formula Grant Program. Since FY2010, funding has only been provided for National Programs. The State Formula Grant Program distributed grants to all LEAs, as required by law. Critics argued that this resulted in funding being spread too broadly to support quality interventions. The Obama Administration proposed significant changes to the SDFSCA as part of its proposal to reauthorize the ESEA. The proposal would have consolidated several smaller programs into a new broader program titled "Successful, Safe, and Health Students."[8] Presently, the SDFSCA program funds several National Programs (see discussion on National Programs). In addition, the SDFSCA includes a provision requiring all states receiving ESEA funds to have a law requiring not less than a one-year expulsion for any student who brings a firearm to school.[9]

Total funding for SDFSCA was considerably lower in FY2012 than it was in years when the State Formula Grant Program also received funding. The SDFSCA program received a total of $65 million in funding in FY2012. In contrast, for FY2009, the last year in which State Formula Grants received funding, the total funding for SDFSCA equaled $435 million: $295 million for State Formula Grants, and $140 million for National Programs.

Overview of the SDSCA State Formula Grant Program as Authorized

Grants to States

To receive an allotment under the SDFSCA State Formula Grant program under the provisions included when it was last authorized through NCLBA, a state is required to submit an application, providing extensive information to ED that includes, among other things, a comprehensive plan to provide safe, orderly, and drug-free schools and communities through activities that meet the "principles of effectiveness" under Section 4115(a) of the SDFSCA.[10] Funded activities are required to foster a safe and drug-free learning environment supporting academic achievement. States are required to develop their applications in coordination with all appropriate state officials, and to coordinate all funded activities with other relevant programs, including the governor's drug and violence prevention programs.11 The application must include the results of a needs assessment for drug and violence prevention activities in the state based on the state's evaluation of relevant data, including detailed information on illegal drug use and violence among youth. The state must indicate how the needs assessment will be used to establish state performance measures, in consultation with LEAs, for funded programs; and how the state will provide technical assistance as needed, and how it will monitor, assess, and report on progress toward meeting performance goals.

Grants to LEAs

States are required to distribute at least 93% of their grant after reservations via formula to LEAs. To receive a SDFSCA grant, LEAs are required to submit an application to the state education agency (SEA). The application must include, among other things, a detailed explanation of the LEAs' comprehensive plan for drug and violence prevention and an assurance that funded activities meet the SDFSCA "principles of effectiveness" contained in Section 4115(a). The application must describe how the plan will be coordinated with other agencies and what performance measures will be put in place and evaluated. The application must be developed in consultation with experts, state and local officials, and representatives from the schools to be served. The LEA is required to provide assurances that it has, or the schools to be served have, appropriate policies in place prohibiting, among other things, the illegal possession of weapons, and that the school has implemented prevention activities designed to create and maintain a safe, disciplined, and drug-free environment. The LEA is required to provide an assurance that it will implement security procedures both at school and while students are on their way to and from school. It must also provide an assurance that the LEA has, or schools to be served have, a crisis management plan for responding to violent or traumatic events on school grounds.[12]

The programs and activities provided by the LEA are required to be designed to prevent or reduce violence. They also must create a well-disciplined environment that includes consultation among school personnel to identify the early warning signs of violence. While some authorized activities might be more directly relevant to the prevention of school violence, many if not all of the allowable activities could potentially contribute to these efforts. Below is a list of the authorized activities that are most closely related to prevention or amelioration of school violence:

- Acquiring and installing metal detectors and related devices;
- Reporting criminal offenses committed on school property;
- Developing and implementing comprehensive school security plans or obtaining technical assistance on such plans;
- Supporting safe zones of passage for students to and from school;
- Violence prevention and education activities to reduce victimization due to prejudice and intolerance;
- Alternative education programs for violent or drug-abusing students, particularly students who have been or are at risk of being suspended or expelled;
- Developing and implementing character education programs as part of drug and violence prevention that takes into account the views of students' parents;
- Expanded and improved school-based mental health services, including early identification of violence and illegal drug use, assessment, and counseling services for students, parents, families, or school personnel by qualified providers;
- Conflict resolution programs, including peer mediation programs and youth anti-crime and anti-drug councils and activities;
- Counseling, mentoring, referral services, and other student assistance practices and programs, including assistance from qualified mental health service providers;
- Programs that encourage students to confide in and seek advice from trusted adults regarding violence and illegal drug use;
- Establishing and maintaining a school safety hotline;
- Programs that respond to the needs of students who are faced with domestic violence or child abuse;

- Professional development and training in prevention education, early identification and intervention, mentoring, or rehabilitation referral, for school personnel, parents, and interested community members;
- Hiring and mandatory training of school security personnel;
- Conducting nationwide background checks on all school personnel and prospective employees to see whether they have been convicted of a crime that bears upon the employee's fitness to be employed by the LEA and to work with children;
- Creating an action plan and providing training to school personnel to prevent youth suicide.

National Programs

The SDFSCA provides general authority to the Secretary to award grants for a wide variety of National Programs to prevent substance abuse and support violence prevention. Authorized National Programs that may be of help in ameliorating the impact of a crisis or traumatic event include the following:

- *Readiness and Emergency Management for Schools:* This competitive grant program provides funds to LEAs to strengthen and improve their emergency response and crisis plans at the district and school levels. LEAs are required to form partnerships and collaborate with community organizations, local law enforcement agencies, heads of local government, and offices of public safety, health, and mental health as they review and revise these plans. Plans are required to be coordinated with state or local homeland security plans and must support the implementation of the National Incident Management System (NIMS).[13] Grants may be used for training school safety teams and students, conducting facility audits, informing families about emergency response policies, implementing an Incident Command System (ICS),[14] conducting drills and tabletop simulation exercises, preparing and distributing copies of crisis plans, and, to a limited extent, for purchasing school safety equipment. Grantees under this program may receive support in managing and implementing their projects and sustaining their efforts over time from the Readiness and Emergency Management for Schools Technical Assistance Center.[15]
- *Project SERV (School Emergency Response to Violence):* This program provides education-related services to schools that have been disrupted by a violent or traumatic crisis. LEAs and IHEs are eligible to apply for these grants. Project SERV provides grants of up $50,000 for short term needs (up to 6 months); and grants of up to $250,000 for extended services (for a period of up to 18 months). LEAs and IHEs may apply for both Immediate Services funding and Extended Services funding; however, a separate application must be submitted for each. Project SERV funds may be used for a wide variety of activities, including mental health assessments, referrals, and services for victims and witnesses of violence; enhanced school security; technical assistance in developing a response to the crisis; and training for teachers and staff in implementing the response. Appropriations for this program are requested on a no-year basis, to remain available for obligation at the federal level until expended. Thus, funds can be carried over from year to year in the event that there are no school-related crises in a given year.[16]

- *Safe Schools/Healthy Students (SS/HS) grant program:* The SS/HS initiative is funded jointly by ED and the U.S. Department of Health and Human Services (HHS), Substance Abuse and Mental Health Services Administration (SAMHSA). The program is administered by ED, SAMHSA, and the U.S. Department of Justice (DOJ). The SS/HS initiative is a discretionary grant program that provides schools and communities with federal funding, via LEAs, to implement an enhanced, coordinated, comprehensive plan of activities, programs, and services that focus on healthy childhood development and the prevention of violence and alcohol and drug abuse. Grantees are required to establish partnerships with local law enforcement, public mental health, and juvenile justice agencies/entities. Currently the program only receives funding from ED and HHS. The program received $17 million in ED funding for FY2012.[17]

In addition, there are three authorized activities within the National Grant Program that have never received funding—Hate Crimes Prevention, the School Security and Resource Center, and the National Center for School and Youth Safety. Other specifically authorized National Programs that have received funding in the past, but are not currently funded include data collection by the National Center for Education Statistics on the incidence and prevalence of illegal drug use and violence in elementary and secondary schools; the Safe and Drug-Free Schools and Communities Advisory Committee; the National Coordinator Program; the Community Service Grant Program; Grants to Reduce Alcohol Abuse; and mentoring programs.

ESEA Programs Focused on Mental Health

In addition to support that may be available through the SDFSCA program the ESEA includes three programs that address issues related to student mental health: (1) The Elementary and Secondary School Counseling program, (2) Grants for the Integration of Schools and Mental Health Systems, (3) and Promotion of School Readiness through Early Childhood Emotional and Social Development. All three programs are authorized under Title V-D, but only the Elementary and Secondary School Counseling program is currently funded. A brief description of each program follows.

Elementary and Secondary School Counseling Program

The Elementary and Secondary School Counseling Program is authorized under ESEA Title V-D2. The program provides competitive grants to LEAs to establish or expand elementary and secondary school counseling programs. Programs that receive funding under this program must meet several requirements, including having a program that is comprehensive in addressing the counseling and educational needs of all students; increases the range, availability, quality, and quantity of counseling services; expands services through qualified staff; involves public and private entities in collaborative efforts to enhance the program and promote integrated services; and provides appropriate staff training. If program appropriations are less than $40 million, all grants must be used to establish or expand counseling programs in elementary schools. If appropriations equal or exceed $40 million, not less than $40 million must be used to establish or expand counseling programs in elementary schools. The program received funding of $52 million in FY2012.

Grants for the Integration of Schools and Mental Health Systems

The Grants for the Integration of Schools and Mental Health Systems program is authorized under ESEA Title V-D-14, Section 5541. Under this program, the Secretary may award competitive grants or enter in contracts or cooperative agreements with SEAs, LEAs, or Indian tribes for the purpose of increasing student access to quality mental health care by developing innovative programs to link local school systems with the local mental health system. The program last received funding of $6 million in FY2010.

Promotion of School Readiness Through Early Childhood Emotional and Social Development (Foundations for Learning)

The Promotion of School Readiness Through Early Childhood Emotional and Social Development program is authorized under ESEA Title V-D-14, Section 5542. The Secretary, in consultation with the Secretary of Health and Human Services, is permitted to award Foundations for Learning Grants to LEAs, local councils, community-based organizations, and other public or nonprofit private entities to assist eligible children with school readiness. Children eligible for assistance must be under the age of seven and must meet two or more of the following characteristics:

- The child has been abused, maltreated, or neglected;
- The child has been exposed to violence;
- The child has been homeless;
- The child has been removed from child care or an early education program for behavioral reasons or is at risk for removal;
- The child has been exposed to parental depression or other mental illness;
- The child's family income is below 200% of the poverty line;
- The child has been exposed to parental substance abuse;
- The child has had early behavioral and peer relationship problems;
- The child had a low birth weight;
- The child has a cognitive deficit or developmental disability.

Funds may be used for several purposes, including to deliver services to eligible children and their families that foster eligible children's emotional, behavioral, and social development; coordinate and facilitate access by eligible children and their families to relevant community resources; and provide ancillary services (e.g., transportation, child care) to facilitate the delivery of services and activities. The program last received funding of $1 million FY2010.

USCO

The NCLBA established a new Unsafe School Choice Option (USCO) policy under ESEA Title IX-E-2. The USCO policy is administered by the Office of Safe and Drug-Free

Schools at ED. Under the USCO policy, in order to be eligible to receive ESEA funding, states are required to establish statewide policies under which students who attend persistently dangerous public elementary or secondary schools, or who become victims of a violent crime while in or on the grounds of the public elementary or secondary schools they attend, must be offered the opportunity to transfer to another public school within the same LEA. It should be noted that each state is permitted to define what constitutes a "persistently dangerous" school.

Each year, states must certify their compliance with USCO requirements prior to receiving ESEA funding for the next year. States are required to develop their USCO policies in consultation with a representative sample of LEAs within the state. ED has issued non-regulatory guidance outlining the steps that states must take to comply with the USCO policy. These steps include the following:

- Establish a state USCO policy;
- Identify persistently dangerous schools;
- Identify types of offenses that are considered to be violent criminal offenses;
- Provide a safe public school choice option; and
- Certify compliance with USCO.[18]

States were required to implement the USCO beginning with the 2002-2003 school year. Each state's USCO policy is somewhat different. While most states establish some threshold number of violent offenses relative to school enrollment that must be exceeded for either two or three consecutive years in order for a school to be designated as persistently dangerous, the definitions of violent offenses or incidents measured tend to vary considerably across states. Typically, states' USCO policies identify which crimes or types of crimes constitute violent offenses, although these tend to differ from state to state. Some state policies reference primarily felony offenses (e.g., homicide, manslaughter, aggravated assault, or sexual assault).

Others also reference violation of weapon possession laws (e.g., Gun-Free Schools Acts), or drug possession laws. Some state policies also consider student expulsions for offenses such as drug or alcohol possession, or violence.[19]

Limited information is available on schools being determined to be persistently dangerous, and on students transferring to different schools under the USCO policy. The U.S. Department of Education, Office of Safe and Healthy Students reports that for 2003-2004, 47 schools were identified as persistently dangerous (5 states); for 2004-2005, 39 schools were identified as persistently dangerous (4 states); and for 2005-2006, there were 36 schools identified (7 states).[20]

More recently, based on Consolidated State Performance Reports submitted by states for the 2009-2010 school year, a total of 266 schools were identified as being persistently dangerous: 13 schools in Maryland, 113 schools in New York, 124 schools in Pennsylvania, and 16 schools in Puerto Rico.[21]

Since the enactment of the NCLB, federal funds have not generally been provided specifically to address the needs of persistently dangerous schools. However, Section 5502, Title V, Charter 5 of the U.S. Troop Readiness, Veterans' Care, Katrina Recovery, and Iraq Accountability Appropriations Act, 2007 (P.L. 110-28) authorized and appropriated funding for grants to address youth violence and related issues for persistently dangerous schools. The

$8.6 million appropriation was provided for FY2007 only. LEAs in which at least one school was identified as persistently dangerous during the 2006-2007 school year were eligible to apply for funding. Grants were awarded to LEAs in New York, Pennsylvania, South Dakota, and Texas.[22]

HIGHER EDUCATION ACT (HEA)

The HEA, whose programs are administered by ED, includes the federal government's major student aid programs that support postsecondary education attendance, as well as other significant programs such as those providing aid to special groups of IHEs and support services to enable disadvantaged students to complete secondary school and enter and complete college. Although important support from outside of the HEA is provided through multiple federal agencies for activities such as research and development, the federal government's presence in postsecondary education is shaped to a substantial degree by the HEA.

The principal objective of the HEA is to expand postsecondary education opportunity, particularly for low-income individuals, and increase college affordability.[23] Title IV of the HEA authorizes programs that provide student financial aid (e.g., student loans, Pell Grants) to support attendance at a variety of postsecondary education institutions. In order to participate in these programs, IHEs must meet specific institutional eligibility requirements, including requirements related to campus crime and security.

This section of this report begins with an overview of institutional eligibility requirements that institutions must meet to participate in the Title IV programs. That is followed by a detailed discussion of the campus crime and security requirements included in the HEA, including provisions to enforce compliance with these requirements. The section concludes with an examination of funding and related support available for complying with these requirements and addressing campus crime and security issues, as well as a discussion about crime statistics and information made publicly available.

HEA Title IV Institutional Eligibility Requirements

To participate in the Title IV federal student aid programs, institutions must meet specific criteria, including requirements related to program offerings, student enrollment, and operations.[24]

For example, Title IV eligible IHEs must be licensed to operate in the state in which they are located, be accredited by an accrediting agency or association recognized by the Secretary, and meet eligibility and certification requirements established by ED. Institutions that do not meet these requirements are ineligible to participate in the Title IV programs, meaning that students attending these institutions are unable to access federal student aid. While not all postsecondary institutions in the United States are Title IV-eligible institutions, the vast majority are.

Campus Crime and Security Requirements in the HEA

Campus crime and security requirements were first included in the HEA with the enactment of the Student Right to Know and Campus Security Act (P.L. 101-542) in 1990. Title II of this act, the Crime Awareness and Campus Security Act of 1990, amended the HEA. HEA campus crime and security requirements were subsequently amended in 1992, 1998, 2000, and 2008.

Under current law, Section 485(f) contains the statutory requirements related to campus crime and security. These requirements are collectively known as the Jeanne Clery Disclosure of Campus Security Policy and Campus Crime Statistics Act (the Clery Act).[25] Institutions must comply with these requirements to participate in Title IV programs.

As part of these requirements, each institution[26] is required to provide an annual security report to all current students and employees and to any prospective students or employees, upon request, that provides information about campus security policies and campus crime statistics.[27] The report must include, at a minimum, the following items:

- Statement of current campus policies regarding procedures for the reporting of criminal actions or other emergencies occurring on campus and the institution's response to these reports.
- Statement of current policies concerning security and access to campus facilities, including residence halls, and security considerations used in the maintenance of campus facilities.
- Statement of current policies concerning campus law enforcement, including the relationship between campus security personnel and state and local law enforcement agencies, and policies to promote the accurate and prompt reporting of all crimes to campus police and appropriate law enforcement agencies.
- Description of the type and frequency of programs designed to inform students and employees about campus security procedures and practices and to encourage them to be responsible for their own security and the security of others.
- Description of programs designed to inform students and employees about crime prevention.
- Statistics on criminal offenses reported to campus security or local police agencies that occurred on campus, in dormitories or other student residential facilities on campus, in or on noncampus buildings or property, and on public property during the most recent calendar year and two preceding calendar years for which data are available.[28]
- Statement of policy concerning the monitoring and recording through local police agencies of criminal activity of off-campus student organizations that are recognized by the institution, including those organizations with off-campus housing.
- Statement regarding the possession, use, and sale of alcoholic beverages and enforcement of state underage drinking laws, and a statement regarding the possession, use, or sale of illegal drugs and enforcement of federal and state laws and a description of drug and alcohol abuse programs required under the act.[29]
- Statement indicating where information about registered sex offenders may be obtained.

- Statement of current campus policies regarding immediate emergency response and evacuation procedures, including the use of electronic or cellular communication. These policies must include having procedures to "immediately notify the campus community" about a significant emergency or dangerous situation occurring on campus that involves an immediate threat to the health and safety of students or staff, unless such notification would "compromise efforts to contain the situation." The policies must also include procedures to publicize emergency response and evacuation procedures in a manner designed to reach students and staff. There must also be procedures to test emergency response and evacuation procedures on an annual basis.
- Statement of policy regarding the institution's sexual assault prevention programs and procedures that will be followed if a sexual offense has occurred.

Institutions are also required to make timely reports to the campus community on crimes considered to be a threat to students or employees that have been reported to campus police or local law enforcement. Statutory language notes that these reports must be made in a manner that is "timely" and will aid in the prevention of similar occurrences.[30]

Each institution that has a police or security department is also required to maintain a daily crime log that includes the nature, date, time, and general location of each crime, as well as the disposition of the complaint, if known. All entries, unless prohibited by law or where disclosure of the information would jeopardize the confidentiality of the victim, must be made public within two business days of the initial report. Information may also be withheld if there is evidence that releasing such information would jeopardize an ongoing investigation, cause a suspect to flee, or result in the destruction of evidence. The information must be released, however, once these factors are no longer a concern.

HEA, Section 485 includes additional requirements related to campus safety and security that are not part of the Clery Act. Section 485(i) requires each IHE that participates in any Title IV program and maintains on-campus housing to publish an annual fire safety report, to be available to the public and submitted to the Secretary that contains information about fire safety practices and standards at the institution and provides data on fires that occurred in on-campus housing facilities. In addition, Section 485(j) requires each IHE that participates in any Title IV program and maintains on-campus housing to develop missing person procedures for students living on-campus.

Enforcement of Requirements

As previously discussed, institutional compliance with the Clery Act, as well as all safety and security requirements included in Section 485, is required for participation in Title IV programs.[31] All institutions that are eligible to participate in these programs are required to sign a Program Participation Agreement (PPA), which conditions an institution's initial and continued participation in any Title IV program on the institution's compliance with the relevant statutory and regulatory requirements. The PPA also lists specific requirements with which an institution must comply. Included on this list is a requirement that the institution certify that it has established a campus security policy and that it has complied with the disclosure requirements of the Clery Act.[32]

The PPA includes an additional reporting requirement related to safety and security. Upon written request, an IHE is required to disclose to the alleged victim of any violent crime or nonforcible sex offense, the results of any disciplinary proceeding conducted by the IHE against the alleged perpetrator of the crime or offense.[33] If the alleged victim of such crime or offense dies as a result of such crime or offense, the next of kin may request the aforementioned information.

While failure to comply with the requirements of the PPA can result in a loss of Title IV eligibility, if it is determined that an institution has substantially misrepresented the number, location, or nature of crimes, the institution may be subject to civil penalties. For each violation or misrepresentation, the Secretary may impose a fine not to exceed $25,000.[34]

Other Relevant Provisions in the HEA

HEA Title VIII-L authorizes the Secretary to award competitive grants, required to be matched with non-federal funds, to IHEs and consortia of IHEs to develop emergency communications systems, measures to improve campus safety, and mental health service coordination with local agencies.[35] It also authorizes the Secretary, in consultation with the Attorney General and the Secretary of Homeland Security, to advise IHEs on model emergency response policies, procedures, and practices and to disseminate information on these policies, procedures, and practices.[36] The Secretary is also required to coordinate with the Secretary of Homeland Security and other agencies to develop and maintain procedures to address the needs of IHEs in the event of a natural or manmade disaster for which the President has declared a major disaster or emergency.[37] HEA Title VII-L also authorizes the Secretary to establish and promulgate regulations for an Education Disaster and Emergency Relief Loan Program for IHEs impacted by major disasters to help fund recovery and operations.[38] It also requires the Secretary, in consultation with the Secretary of Homeland Security and the Attorney General to undertake the following: (1) disseminate model emergency response policies; (2) develop preparation, response, and recovery procedures for IHEs involved in disasters; and (3) provide guidance for IHEs relating to student mental health issues with a potential to cause harm.[39]

Funding and Related Support

IHEs do not receive specific funding from the federal government to aid in compliance with these requirements. ED has published a resource for IHEs on the requirements of the Clery Act, it is titled the "Handbook for Campus Crime Reporting."[40] It provides procedures, examples, and references for IHEs to use in complying with the Clery Act requirements.

ED provides support for campus-based violence prevention through the SDFSCA.[41] One SDFSCA National Program, *Grants to Prevent High-Risk Drinking and Violent Behavior Among College Students,* provided funds to IHEs to develop, enhance, implement, and evaluate campus-based or community-based prevention strategies designed to reduce high-risk drinking and violent behavior among college students.[42] Grants were made to consortia of IHEs and other public and private nonprofit organizations. SDFSC National Program funds were also used to support the Higher Education Center for Alcohol and Other Drug Abuse and Violence Prevention.[43] The Center served as ED's primary provider of services related to alcohol and drug abuse and violence prevention in higher education. One aspect of the Center's mission was to assist ED in serving IHEs in developing and implementing programs to promote campus and community safety by preventing violence among college students. For example, the Center published a newsletter, *The Catalyst*, which provided information about relevant innovative practices at IHEs. However, the Center was defunded in 2012. Most recently, it had received a four year contract from ED for the period between September 1, 2009, through August 31, 2013. ED funded the first three years of this contract, but on June 25, 2012, it notified the Center that it would not be exercising its option to fund the final year of the contract (September 1, 2012, to August 31, 2013).

Public Information Availability

As previously discussed, the Clery Act requires IHEs to make information about crime public and to submit an annual report on campus security to ED. In addition to the measures taken by individual IHEs to provide this information to current and prospective students and their families, ED makes the data publicly available online. ED maintains a campus crime statistics website known as the Campus Safety and Security Data Analysis Cutting Tool (CSSDACT).[44] For each Title IV eligible IHE, data are reported on the number of criminal offenses, hate crimes, and arrests over the most recent three-year period for which data are available. Information is provided to indicate whether the data include incidents occurring in residence halls and whether data include local statistics. Data are provided on criminal offenses, hate crimes, arrests, disciplinary actions, and five statistics.

End Notes

[1] U.S. Department of Education, National Center for Education Statistics. (2012). Digest of Education Statistics: 2011, Table 2; available at http://nces.ed.gov/programs/digest/d11/tables/dt11_002.asp.

[2] U.S. Department of Education, National Center for Education Statistics. (2012). Indicators of School Crime and Safety: 2011 (NCES 2012-002); available at http://nces.ed.gov/pubs2012/2012002.pdf.

[3] CRS compilation of data available from the U.S. Department of Education, Office of Postsecondary Education, Campus Crime Statistics Online, available at http://ope.ed.gov/security/.

[4] In some instances, where activities can be supported with funds allocated at the discretion of a Secretary, current funding may not be available.

[5] For more information about programs authorized by the ESEA, see CRS Report RL33960, The Elementary and Secondary Education Act, as Amended by the No Child Left Behind Act: A Primer, by Rebecca R. Skinner.

[6] CRS Report RL34496, Safe and Drug-Free Schools and Communities Act: Program Overview and Reauthorization Issues, by Gail McCallion.

[7] On October 20, 1994, President William J. Clinton signed into law the Improving America's School Act (P.L. 103- 382), which reauthorized the ESEA, and created the SDFSCA as Title IV.

[8] For information on reauthorization proposals see CRS Report RL34496, Safe and Drug-Free Schools and Communities Act: Program Overview and Reauthorization Issues, by Gail McCallion.

[9] The chief administering officer of a local educational agency may modify this expulsion requirement on a case-by-case basis. In addition, the LEA may provide the student with educational services in an alternative setting (§4141).

[10] As has been noted, although the NCLBA authorization of appropriations for SDFSCA expired at the end of FY2008, appropriations for State Formula Grants continued to be provided through FY2009. Subsequently, State Formula Grants have not been funded, but appropriations for National Programs have continued to be

provided (most recently through a government-wide continuing resolution that provided funding through March 27,2013 by P.L. 112-175).

[11] State governors are permitted to use up to 20% of their state's grant allocation for comprehensive activities to deter youth from using drugs and committing violent acts in schools. Governors award these funds as discretionary grants to LEAs, community-based organizations (CB)s), other private or public entities, or consortia thereof.

[12] ED maintains a website that provides links to resources of potential use to school leaders developing a crisis management plan. More information is available at http://www.ed.gov/admins/lead/safety/ emergencyplan/ index.html.

[13] For more information about NIMS, see http://www.fema.gov/emergency/nims/index.shtm.

[14] For more information about ICS, see http://training.fema.gov/EMIWeb/IS/is100.asp.

[15] Additional information is available at http://rems.ed.gov/.

[16] Project SERV, administered by ED, was created following the 1999 Columbine shootings.

[17] The Safe Schools/Healthy Students Act was first funded in 1999, following several school shootings in the late 1990s.

[18] U.S. Department of Education, Unsafe School Choice Option: Non-Regulatory Guidance, May 2004, p. 6, available at http://www.ed.gov/policy/elsec/guid/unsafeschoolchoice.pdf.

[19] For a compilation of criteria used by the various states to identify persistently dangerous schools, see Education Commission of the States, Persistently Dangerous School Criteria, compiled by Gloria Zradicka, September 2004, available at http://www.ecs.org/clearinghouse/52/98/5298.pdf.

[20] U.S. Department of Education, Safe and Drug-Free Schools and Communities Advisory Committee, Unsafe School Choice Option Report, 2006, at http://www.ed.gov/about/bdscomm/list/sdfscac/topics.html#Unsafe, and U.S. Department of Education, Safe and Drug-Free Schools and Communities Advisory Committee Meeting, October 23, 2006, Unsafe School Choice Option presentation, http://www.ed.gov/about/ bdscomm/list/sdfscac/kesner10-06.ppt.

[21] For more information on the Consolidated State Performance Reports submitted for the 2009-2010 school year, see http://www2.ed.gov/admins/lead/account/consolidated/sy09-10part1/index.html, Item 1.7.

[22] For more information about the grant awards, see http://www.ed.gov/programs/persistentdanger/awards.html.

[23] For more information about HEA, including federal student aid programs authorized by the HEA, see CRS Report RL34654, The Higher Education Opportunity Act: Reauthorization of the Higher Education Act, by David P. Smole et al.

[24] For more information about institutional eligibility requirements, see CRS Report RL33909, Institutional Eligibility for Participation in Title IV Student Aid Programs Under the Higher Education Act: Background and Reauthorization Issues, by Rebecca R. Skinner.

[25] The campus crime and security requirements were named for Jeanne Clery, a freshman at Lehigh University who was asleep in her residence hall before she was raped and murdered in 1986. The 1998 HEA amendments formally named the law in memory of Ms. Clery.

[26] An institution must comply with these requirements for each separate campus (34 CFR 668.46).

[27] Regulatory requirements for the annual security report and reporting and disclosure of information are included in 34 CFR 668.41 and 34 CFR 668.46.

[28] Criminal offenses must be reported in the following categories: murder; sex offenses, forcible or nonforcible; robbery; aggravated assault; burglary; motor vehicle theft; manslaughter; arson; and arrests or persons referred for disciplinary action for liquor law violations, drug-related violations, and weapons possession. For each of these criminal offenses, except for those in the last category, and for larceny-theft; simple assault; intimidation; destruction, damage or vandalism of property; or other crimes involving bodily injury to any person, if the victim in any of these types of crimes was deliberately selected due to the individual's actual or perceived race, gender, religion, sexual orientation, ethnicity, or disability, the crime must be reported as a hate crime. The statistics must be compiled according to the definitions used in the uniform crime reporting system of the Department of Justice, Federal Bureau of Investigation, and the modifications of these definitions included in the Hate Crimes Statistics Act. These statistics must be submitted annually to ED. (See 34 CFR 668.46 for related regulatory requirements.)

[29] See HEA, §120 for more information about the required drug and alcohol abuse programs.

[30] See 34 CFR 668.46 for related regulatory requirements.

[31] §§487(a)(7) and (12).

[32] §487(a)(12).

[33] §487(a)(26).

[34] §487(c)(3)(B).

[35] §821.

[36] §822.

[37] §823.

[38] §824.

[39] §825.

[40] The handbook is available at http://www2.ed.gov/admins/lead/safety/handbook.pdf.

[41] U.S. Department of Education. Justifications of Appropriation Estimates to the Congress: Fiscal Year 2008, Volume I, p. F-31.

[42] Additional information about this program is available at http://www.ed.gov/programs/dvphighrisk/index.html.

[43] Additional information about the Center is available at http://www.ed.gov/about/offices/list/osdfs/resources.

[44] The CSSDACT can be accessed at http://ope.ed.gov/security/.

INDEX

D

Q

R

S

T